Voices and Echoes
Tales from Colonial Women

Voices and Echoes
Tales from Colonial Women

Joan Alexander

Quartet Books
London Melbourne New York

First published by Quartet Books Limited 1983
A member of the Namara Group
27/29 Goodge Street, London W1P 1FD

British Library Cataloguing in Publication Data

Voices and echoes: tales from colonial women
   1. Colonial administrators
   I. Alexander, Joan
   325'.31'41   DA16

   ISBN 0-7043-2366-4

Typeset by MC Typeset, Chatham, Kent
Printed in Great Britain by Mackays of Chatham Ltd, Kent

For Diana, Araminta, Helen
and Rufus

ACKNOWLEDGEMENTS

The main source material for this book has been the interviews and conversations I have had with over 100 colonial women, whether in education, nursing, missionaries, doctors, or District Officers' and Governors' wives. Without their cooperation my task would have been impossible, and their kindness in entertaining me throughout has been overwhelming. I cannot thank them enough. Not all the 'ladies' listed below appear in this book, which swiftly took on the proportions of a vast tome. But whether they are mentioned or not, their influence is there and each person contributed something to this author, and nothing ultimately will be wasted. I have been literally carried along by the enthusiasm, warmth and help I've been given, while the Royal Commonwealth Society library has been unstinting with help and advice.

I am indebted to Lt. Commander Thomas Hornyold-Strickland for the use of his mother's diaries, and other papers which helped me piece together Mabel Strickland's eventful life. I am also grateful to Viscountess Monckton of Brenchley for the use of her book on the Stricklands of Sizergh Castle, and to Mabel herself who gave me the fragments of her own writings intended for her own autobiography. I have also been lent papers by Mrs Suzanne Wainwright; Mrs Joan Day and Mrs C.R.V. Bell MBE; Miss M. Aguis, who was secretary to Mabel Strickland for twenty years; Lady Kirby; Miss Mary Northcote and Mrs Diana Dawkins.

I am grateful, for the time and hospitality given to me during personal interviews, to the following, all of whom proved invaluable:

Miss M. Aguis; R. Aguis, (Editor of the *Sunday Times* of

Acknowledgements

Malta); Lady Arrowsmith, (Clondagh); Mrs Nell Baines; The Hon. Mrs Barnes; Mrs Jane Bell MBE; Mrs Rachel Bleackley; Mrs Nancy Burden; Mrs Anthea Bush; Mrs Peggy Campbell; Lady Caradon, (Sylvia); Mrs Anne Carver; Miss Nina Caulfield; Mrs Margaret Chamberlain; Mrs Diana Dawkins; Mrs Joan Day; Lady Deverell, (Margaret); Mrs Ann Dowson; Mrs Pauline Drayson; Dr Rex and Joan Cheverton; the late Mrs Aileen Chubb; The Hon. Betty Clay; Mrs Hilary Clarke; Mrs Barbara Corrie; Mrs Jean Crosland; Sir Hugh and Lady Elliot, (Elizabeth); Lady Fenner, (Joan); Mrs Rosemary Greenwood; Mrs Mollie Grinsted; Miss Freda Gwilliam CBE; Mrs Betty Hall; Mrs Morwenna Hartnoll; Lady Haskard, (Phillada); Mrs Shirley Heriz-Smith; Mrs Henriette Grenfell Hicks; Mrs Pat Hodgson; Mrs Rosemary Hollis; Lt. Cdr. Thomas Hornyold-Strickland; Lady Howick, (Mary); Mrs Monica Hunter; The Dowager Countess of Iddesleigh; Mrs Joan Jenkins; Mrs E.J. Kendall; Lady Kirby, (Winifred); June Knox-Mawer; Dr & Mrs J.M. Liston, (Isobel); the late Lady Lloyd, (Cathy); Mrs Kathleen McCall; Mrs Mary McEntee; Lady Maddocks, (Patricia); Mrs Mary Marshall Smith; Mr Jack Masefield; Mrs Betty Matthews; Mrs Nona Meek; Viscountess Monckton of Brenchley; The Hon. Mrs Doreen Norman; Miss Mary Northcote; Mrs Jean Norton; Lady Peel, (Rosemary); Stewart Henry Perowne OBE; Mrs Lloyd Philips; the late Sir Hannibel Publius; Mrs Elizabeth Purdy; Lady Reece, (Alys); Mrs Jeanne Renshaw; Lady Robertson, (Nancy); Mrs Joan Russell; Mrs Diana Shirtcliffe; Mrs Veronica Short; Mrs Eleanor Stephenson; Mrs Joan Stevens; Mrs Kitty Stevens; Mrs Mavis Stone; Mrs Gerald Strickland; The Hon. Mabel Strickland; Lady Templer, (Peggie); Mrs Dorothia Temple-Richards; Miss Mary Thomas; Mrs Joan Thorne; Lady Thorp, (Doreen); Lady Turnbull, (Beatrice); Mrs Bridget Wainwright; Mrs Suzanne Wainwright; Miss Helen Wallis MBE; Mrs Felicia Wand-Tetley; Mrs Jill Weston; Mrs Patrick Wolridge Gordon.

CONTENTS

Voices and Echoes
Tales from Colonial Women

INTRODUCTION

Enter the Ladies

When, in May 1953, Queen Elizabeth II was proclaimed Queen of England, the words used by the Archbishop of Canterbury were as follows, 'By the Grace of God of the United Kingdom of Great Britain and Northern Ireland and of her other Realms and Territories, Queen, Head of the Commonwealth, Defender of the Faith', which was as grand a title he could bestow on a Queen who was no longer Empress of India.

Her father, George VI, in May 1937 had still been crowned with a Victorian ring to his titles, 'By the Grace of God of the United Kingdom of Great Britain and Northern Ireland and of the British Dominions beyond the Seas, King, Defender of the Faith, Emperor of India'. But slowly, what had appeared to Queen Victoria as a beautifully red-marked map of the world, was being drained of its transfusion of British blood. This slow blood-letting would continue until the tiny corpuscles, like pink dots, would leave the great British Empire with a few scattered islands, rocks and Northern Ireland. On her Diamond Jubilee Queen Victoria sent out this message, 'From my heart I thank my people. May God bless them,' and these words 'my people' encompassed a quarter of the land-mass, and a quarter of the world's population. Her words rang out to Canada, the colonies of West Africa, the rocky ports of the Mediterranean, the Cape, the sugar islands of the Caribbean, Australia, the China seas, Egypt, Central and Southern Africa, New Zealand, to areas in the Atlantic, and places like British Guiana. But most of all she prided herself on being 'Empress of India'. This was the pearl beyond price, the pearl which could no longer be included by the Archbishop when he crowned the young Queen Elizabeth II.

In 1947, the Raj rule ended in India, and the world – and

Britain, in particular – moved into a new era. After 250 years on Indian soil, beginning with the East India Company, on 15 August 1947, the Union Jack was lowered all over the country, and the flags of the two newly created Dominions flew out proudly in their place. So ended the largest British-owned land-mass, and from then until now, it has been a long history of withdrawal – a withdrawal from responsibility, opportunity, strangely fumbling friendships, and often from danger, adventure and excitement.

In 1876 a Bill had been passed creating Victoria Empress of India. By 1897 the Colonial Office List consisted of 506 pages and was steadily growing. By 1947, Africa was Britain's major responsibility and the Colonial Development Corporation was formed, publicly financed, and charged with the building of communications, irrigation, town planning and any other activity which might help an underdeveloped country. Young men were still being recruited into the Colonial Service well into the fifties, and all imagined that they were setting forth on a dedicated and interesting life's career.

Nevertheless, the writing was on the wall if anybody cared to decipher it. It was there quite clearly when Mountbatten handed over his Viceroyalty, and it was there when another earlier Viceroy, Lord Curzon, had said these valedictory words, 'As long as we rule India we are the greatest power in the world. If we lost it, we shall drop straight away to a third-rate power.'

The writing became indelible when Harold Macmillan made his famous 'Wind of Change' journey around Africa.

The whole world was stirring. Already there was Enosis in Cyprus, whose Greek citizens vehemently desired union with Greece. By 1953, the Mau Mau troubles were in full swing in Kenya. The fiasco of Suez in 1956 which so fatally discredited us, opened Pandora's box. The time had come for Great Britain – with as much good grace as it could muster – to withdraw from its Empire.

The Commonwealth Relations Office replaced the India Office and Dominions. In 1962, South Africa was refused membership in this Commonwealth because of apartheid. In 1960, this writer was present at the ceremony of Independence in Kaduna, Northern Nigeria. This, out of all such ceremonies in other countries, must surely have been one of the most moving.

The Premier of the North, Alhaji the Hon. Sir Ahmadu Bello KBE, Sardauna of Sokoto, decreed that the British flag was not to be lowered as was usual when the new national flag was raised, 'for the British are our friends', he said, 'so let our flags fly side by side to cement it'. There was scarcely a dry eye in the grandstand. Surely this was an act without parallel? In the south, Princess Alexandra graced every public function with her presence, a pattern to be followed by other members of the Royal Family in other countries.

As one colony after another became independent, so the hopeful Residents, District Officers and young Assistants became redundant. Some were absorbed into the Commonwealth Relations Office to discover the régime as strange as a can-can girl learning ballet. Africans were no longer their children but their equals – if not their superiors. It was all very odd and difficult to absorb unless one had studied the words of Gladstone who had predicted it, in the case of India, long ago. Others young enough found jobs at home, and regretted the authority of their colonial careers. There was still the Development Corporation but it was unable to absorb 6,500 or more colonial servants. There were too many men for too few jobs, and it was fortunate if one had been about to retire anyway.

Sadly the colonial servant – idealistic, fatherly – watched as the British withdrew their generally benevolent rule, and the blood baths began. It had happened in India, in Palestine, Iraq, Aden, the Sudan, Ghana, Uganda, Cyprus. Only Nigeria seemed the exception. But somehow, in this great country, the different tribes were puzzled by the lack of bloodshed. It had all gone too smoothly, too easily – there must be more to Independence than this! Only the colonials patted themselves on the back. They had taught their 'boys' how to behave – they *were* the exception. Alas, the jealousy set in with the Muslim north and the Christian south and soon they had their blood bath in the Biafran war.

There are still outposts of the Empire where the Governor dons his smart official uniform to greet official guests. The flag is raised at sunrise and lowered at sunset as the trumpet blows.

It may be anachronistic, but it is still rather splendid. In Muscat a British Consul-General guides the Sultan. British Honduras (now Belize), with its terrible climate, is thankful to be guarded from the threat of Guatemala by the Governor in his beautiful house. In Hong Kong, the flag still flies over the square grey Government House – dwarfed now by a positive web of roads and skyscrapers. The Falkland Islands sought British protection against being annexed by the Argentine and the British Task Force sailed, while Northern Ireland sadly remains a military headache. Gibraltar still stands a British rock, and one can pick out other pink dots on the map: – St Lucia, St Helena, Tristan da Cunha, the Cayman Islands, the Bahamas. A tiny portion of what was once that vast Colonial Service.

According to a Major Africanus Horton who retired to a house in Freetown, this was the advice he gave to anyone about to live in Sierra Leone, 'The society of *real* ladies will be found preferable to any other.' Undoubtedly, this was very true, but how difficult it was for the colonial to find such company. 'The Ladies! God bless them!' Ladies, relegated for years to faded sepia photographs, scorched by the heat, warped by humidity, or nibbled away by termites. Reunions were moments of apprehension and the lady found to be as faded and old as the photograph, bearing no relation to the girl by the bogus pampas grass in the small snapshot carried in a wallet against some manly chest. Separations, particularly before steamships, were heart-rending and appalling. Little wonder that, like so many of Somerset Maugham's characters, husbands or any man for that matter, took native concubines. Who was to blame them, and surely the higher authorities – probably guilty themselves – turned a blind eye?

In the eighteenth century, when the journey to India took months, there were very few wives – and on the whole, those who did travel were unique, in search of adventure, of change, both interested and intelligent. With the steamships, there arrived the more traditional wife, with her sewing-machine, her chintzes, her carefully chosen wardrobe from the Army and Navy Stores all packed in vast wardrobe trunks with drawers and hanging space. Wherever her husband chose to take her she would create – whether it was in a bungalow, a two-storeyed colonial house or some modest hut – her own little England. Along with her worldly goods, as likely as not she brought her prejudices, and possibly a preconceived intolerance for the 'natives'. In the homely atmosphere of her pseudo-England she could prove a blessing or a curse. In the damp humid climates or the dry dusty wastes, she would age prematurely, her skin becoming wrinkled like crêpe – air-conditioning would take at least another hundred years to bring that blessed relief. With servants to wait on her she was often idle and bored. Imbibing too much liquid, she grew either grossly fat or appallingly thin. It was too hot for her to do the cooking, but she often hated the local food. She gossiped if there was anyone to gossip with, she flirted, she lived for retirement.

When at last retirement came it was bitterly disappointing. No one showed the slightest interest in her adventures; the snake which nearly bit her, the river which flooded, the awful earthquake, the streak of lightning which flung her across the length of the room. It was discouraging and disillusioning.

'Andaman Islands? What did you say, dear? Why, I've never even heard of them.'

Nor did the recipient wish to know where they were, or, for that matter, any more about them. So it had all been a dreadful waste of life except that it probably kept dear Freddie or Jimmie on the rails, or from picking up some unmentionable disease.

Of course they were not all like this. There were the fantastic women like Emily Eden who went with her sister, Frances, and her brother, Lord Auckland, to India where she remained during his term of office as Governor-General from 1835 to 1842. Her books *Portraits of the People and Princes of India* and *Up the Country* (the latter being letters to her sister) portray not only the liveliness of her mind, but also her enlightenment. There was Lady Sale who followed her soldier husband to Kabul from which the small British force retreated in disarray in January 1842. As it says in the *Dictionary of National Biography*, 'She did what she could to alleviate the sufferings of the women and children and the wounded. Her clothes were riddled with bullets and she was twice wounded and had a bullet in her wrist.' Her diary, which was all she saved of her belongings by tying it to her wrist, was published in 1841. Another diarist was Frances Simpson who at eighteen married her cousin and went by canoe from Montreal to Hudson Bay. Then, of course Mary Slessor of Calabar, Nigeria, who worked among the up-river tribes for thirty-eight years to correct notions about EXPE and witchcraft, to improve the status of women and children, and to dispel fear and to fight diseases. And many others.

All these women have either had their biographers or have left their published diaries and letters. This book is to be about those who from 1900 have not yet been recorded, but who, from the very nature of their colonial lives, are becoming a unique part of history.

But why did young men join the Colonial Service at the beginning of the century? Other than the fact that it was fairly easy to get in, I believe that it was because it offered adventure, individualism, and the ideal life for a loner, or a man who wanted to make a niche for himself outside the nine-to-five job. He was able to shoulder responsibility at an early age and form remarkable and original friendships. He was seeing a part of the world – often very limited – at someone else's expense. He was magistrate, doctor, priest, treasurer, tax-collector all rolled into one at an age when he scarcely needed to shave.

But why did the women go? Why did they choose this life of loneliness and isolation, far away from home? First, of course, if married, a wife had chosen the man, and she had little idea of the life she was embracing – except from what he told her. At home in England when a colonial servant wished to marry, he could hardly be blamed for embroidering the truth a little. Did the small bungalow with the wilting garden become a palace? Did the arduous journeys into the bush become comfortable safaris? Very likely. Obviously it was better to know the country a woman was travelling to beforehand as did Flora Shaw and Olive MacLeod, whom we shall meet later in Nigeria. They knew what they were taking on. By accepting the life willingly one could be enriched by it. The greatest sacrifice of all was the long separation from one's children, but they were in the future, and not to be imagined. Husbands and the challenge came first.

The men have had their share of publicity and undoubtedly will continue to do so. The women who accompanied them have only been recognized by a word here, a short chapter there. The part they played in our diminished colonies was not unimportant. So! 'Enter the Ladies! God bless them!'

PART ONE

East and Central Africa

1

Betty

I hope she will forgive me if I say she is still very pretty. After the life she has led one would expect a grey exhaustion to have settled permanently on her features. Even her hair is the colour beloved by Titian, and certainly not the hair or skin for the rigours of the African climate. One is struck immediately by her gentleness, her kindness. Certainly she is a woman who should have someone to lean on, someone with a strong right arm, an air of reassurance. Her frailty goes with big hats, fingers trailing in the Cam, feet up on *chaises-longues,* long dresses with the morning dew on their hems. Yet there is nothing about her life which encourages this vision. Her story happens to encompass every aspect of colonial life: its joys, fears, friendships and enmities, the bitter-sweetness of it all.

In marrying into the service a woman married a job, a way of life, a privilege, and a deprivation. Betty embraced all these and took them in her stride. She told me her story as if she were describing the intricacies of a tapestry, and stitch by stitch, it was woven, and I know that her story was the story of almost every colonial woman in Africa. But there was one difference.

Betty had been brought up in Egypt, and had a preconceived idea that the rest of Africa would be like that – dusty, sandy and dry. She was helped throughout her life, I imagine, by having had left-wing liberal views. This was not uncommon among the young people who went to school during the Spanish Civil War, and most of her friends were in sympathy with the government in Spain. She went on to university to read history, where one of her lecturers was Louis MacNeice, the poet, so that her left-wing views were encouraged by the atmosphere he created, especially when she appeared in one of the plays he produced.

At university she met Bernard, the man she was to marry. During the war he went to Africa to serve with the KAR, while Betty worked with Lord Walton for five years. They married in 1947 and went out to Nyasaland (now Malawi) where her husband had joined the Colonial Service. They travelled out on an old BI ship to Beira, which in those days took approximately three weeks. The scars of war were apparent everywhere, and to a young woman from an urban flat, even with her childhood memories of Egypt, it must have made a deep impression. Betty takes up her story:

We took a very ancient train which crossed the Zambezi bridge to Blantyre. We stayed in the capital, Zomba, which was just recovering from a flood; the mountain had collapsed and the town was full of large rocks and boulders. There was a round of parties to welcome us, and then we went down to the lower river district. My husband hadn't known where we were going but he was a bit shocked when he was told because it was a very unpleasant place for someone straight out from England. It was only 123 feet above sea-level, and, of course, swarming with mosquitoes. I had one of these big double-storeyed houses, covered in mosquito gauze, with four large rooms and little rooms off with arches upstairs and huge verandas. The water was brought in petrol tins, and the kitchen was outside, beyond a small square, so that in the rainy season food got pretty cold by the time it had all the rain falling in it.

After about a year, during Bernard's absence, I took the staff and moved them, with all the furniture, to another house four miles away. It was about 400 feet above sea-level on a tiny platform in the hills, and although it wasn't very much higher, it gave you an impression of height with its view over the valley to Mozambique. It was dilapidated but I liked it because I had a view and could see enormous storms starting over the mountains.

It was a very lonely life. The European population consisted of myself and my husband, one customs officer who drank terribly and used to sit at night and shoot holes through his mosquito gauze, a Catholic priest and a Dutchman who didn't speak English at all. About thirty miles away at the top of the hill, 3,000 feet up, there were some South African missionaries, and thirty miles up the river two old men with African wives. One was a very powerful man in the area called Bobi, who terrified all the Africans. He had lived there for a long, long time. He had been a remittance man, but he had made a lot of money and owned huge estates.

We had no luxuries. Our loo downstairs was a huge room, and it was the place where all the spiders and creepy things lived, so that when you went in there at night with a hurricane lamp you used to see the shadows of enormous spiders and other creatures on the walls. There were bird-eating spiders which are like the tarantula – large, brown and hairy. There were puff adders, large mambas and tree snakes. Then we had a lot of storks, horrible storks that used to come once a year and live in the palm trees round the house, and left a deposit of what looked like whitewash everywhere.

We had a large staff as everybody did in those days. The cook's wife was detailed to teach me the local language because my husband wouldn't let me have any staff who spoke English. So I spent my time having language lessons, or going round the country studying anthropology, though I didn't get very far with that!

About three months after we got there, I discovered that Bernard had African wives. It was a terrible shock. He couldn't understand why I objected to them, and he actually asked my permission to import an African wife into the house. I didn't take him seriously at first; I was too astonished.

When we first arrived, I used to go on safaris with him. I walked with the carriers and when we reached a village, they would make a little house inside a stockade, with my own loo and a place to wash. Then all the people would gather round and there would be a meeting, at which my husband would tell them of the various new laws and listen to all their complaints. In the evening there would be a great dance. In many of the villages they had never seen a European woman – the children certainly hadn't – and they didn't know whether I was a man or a woman because I wore trousers.

Once Bernard had told me about his African wives, he left me very much to myself and I used to go on my own safaris. I got to know an old African who used to carry the kind of litter the DC used to travel in. He was a kind of witch-doctor; he didn't speak any English but he did have names for flowers and trees – the only African I ever found who did – and he would tell me what medicine they were used for. He showed me one plant from which they made snake-bite inoculations. It was rather like deadly nightshade. They used to pound up the roots and take the fangs out of a dead mamba mixing this with other things and then make cuts on their ankles and wrists, and rub it in. This worked and would last for two or three years. It was quite extraordinary how they could deal with someone who had been bitten by a snake – far better than the hospital could. In fact, my husband always sent someone who had been bitten to a witch-doctor and not to hospital.

Our social life was rather limited, though we did have visits from the Governor occasionally, and other VIPs. Of course, meals were never on time, because my husband drank quite a lot and we never used to get through drinking at lunchtime until three o'clock, while dinner was never before midnight. The poor old cook had to keep everything hot, and it was amazing how he could produce perfectly good meals hours and hours after he had thought it would be needed. His stove was very primitive. To begin with, he cooked on two piles of bricks with corrugated-iron over the top. Then I had a thing made which looked a bit like a copper. It was filled with brushwood through a hole at the back and then set alight. We had a beautiful porcelain bath – the only one in the country outside Government House – but there was no water to put in it, so the boys used to carry water on their heads, a mile and a half from the stream, and pour it into the bath.

We were eventually sent a refrigerator – again one of the first, but it was a paraffin one and smoked to high heaven! The woman who lived in our house while we were on leave was actually found by the Provincial Commissioner with her feet in it – it was so hot.

The government offices were very old and consisted of a

double-storeyed building which hung out over the river on stilts with a terrible old Union Jack. I remember one evening Bernard went back to the office for something and found the guard asleep on the floor with all his family wrapped up in the flag.

There were no African shops, and the stores were all run by Indians who had come across at the time of Sir Harry Johnson, or with the KAR, to do all kinds of labour and cook. The African Lakes Corporation had what had been quite a big store at the beginning of the century when the steamers used to come up the Zambezi from Beira. They were no longer there, but there was still a huge emporium – with very little in it – run by an extraordinarily fat Indian. When I went round to the back I found boxes of *papier poudré* that ladies used to put on their faces in Edwardian days. I saw some of the letters of direction sent to members of the University Mission to Central Africa – they were still giving people these instructions in the 1950s, warning the ladies to take out plenty of whalebone for their corsets because it couldn't be obtained.

I found I was unable to buy a brassière, so I thought maybe the local African tailors would be able to copy one if I gave them some thin cotton. They did, and then a few months later I saw that all the lovely African girls, who usually wore nothing above the waist or a cloth tucked in, were all wearing very clumsy bras made out of thick calico with wide straps. Obviously, they thought this was the latest fashion. Some Indian had had them run up in hundreds and made a fortune that way.

My husband was away more and more, three months out of four, on safari or seeing his African friends, but even if we went to a dance in the capital he would disappear during the dance and I wouldn't see him until the following morning. I used to wait and wait, and then give up and go home. It was a terribly difficult time.

When I was away, his wives used to come to my house. He used to have them for a year or so then marry them off to someone and have a new one. The first one was very young and he married her off to the station master at one of the stops up the line. Once, I came back to find they had been writing in some of my books – trying to learn to write. They did, more or less, keep out of my way, but they had a curious system. They would send their younger brother as a kind of token – I suppose to keep a foot in the door, and my husband would insist on employing these small boys to run errands, so that meant there was always one of them around the house.

I went away in 1948, ostensibly for good, to work in Blantyre for the Provincial Commissioner, but he eventually asked me to go back to my husband. There were rumours going round about his wild parties, and the PC said if I went back it would put an end to the rumours. They didn't want to have a public scandal, because in those days they were fairly strict, and they would have to ask him to resign, which was the last thing they wanted to do.

When I got back, it was obviously quite hopeless. I had only been there about two weeks when my husband went off to one of his African wives. I decided that once again I'd better lead my own life. I knew a rather nice old man in the Public Works Department who had gone down to build roads on famine relief. Unfortunately he was a dreadful drunk. He was all right at the end of the month when all his money had run out, but at the beginning he was hopeless. He was a remittance man, and he always tried to preserve certain standards because he drank his gin at teatime out of a tea-pot. Maybe that was because he had married an African woman, the daughter of quite a famous Chief, and she used to try and keep him clean and look after him. She had antimacassars everywhere – perhaps she put the gin in the tea-pot as she probably thought it was the thing to do. She had a pretty little girl called Margaret, and so, with our cook's wife, we went up to the hills – 2,000 feet – where there was a very old rest house made of mosquito gauze, and we lived up there.

I decided at one stage that if my husband liked African women, perhaps it would be better if I learned to do the things they did, so I used to hoe the gardens – or rather, tried to. Unfortunately, a messenger would then appear from somewhere – we had to take one up with us in case we needed to send down for anything – and he would rush and take the hoe out of my hand. I learned to pound yams, and I discovered why, no matter how old an African woman is, she has such a wonderful straight stomach. In the evening we used to sit round the fire and I ate their food, while they told me legends. I tried to live more or less as they did. We used to bathe in the spring down in one of the little valleys. But it really didn't have the slightest effect on my husband. He said that I couldn't compete because of the colour of my skin.

I don't think he should have married anyone, but it was rather sad and an awful waste. The Africans call all the Europeans by nicknames after you've been there a time. My first husband was called 'the Bwana who doesn't care about anything'. It was a good description of his attitude to life.

But he was a good DO because, basically, he loved the Africans – they amused him, he liked them, he was interested in them. He was scrupulously fair and just, and he made them laugh. He had a lot of money and he spent a great deal of money on entertaining. He didn't like money being spent on the house, improving furniture or curtains or even on clothes, his own or mine, but when it came to entertaining or lending people money, he was terribly generous. He was brilliantly clever, too.

I decided finally it wasn't any good staying. We were due back on leave in 1950, so we kept up appearances until we returned to England, and then I divorced him.

In 1951 I returned to Nyasaland to marry my second husband, Derek. He had had rather an unhappy first marriage and let his wife divorce him and I had been looking after his two children in England. Anyway, I took the children out to Nyasaland and we married among all the dusty files in the government office, right out in the bush. We were then sent to another hot station, Salima, which was on the lakeshore about ten miles in from the lake. It was a new station which Derek more or less built from scratch. There were quite a few hotels there, and life was interesting because we had a life with the Africans and some very strange eccentric Europeans in Salima itself. At weekends we would go out to the lakeshore hotels where they used to have weekend package tours from Rhodesia. Then we would have a completely different life, wining and dining with the friends we made who used to come year after year.

I had the same staff, which was my only bit of malice when I left my first husband! When we married he said that if it was ever a question of me or his cook going, it would be me, so when I went I took his cook with me. It left me in rather a position because the cook knew this. If I ever sacked him, he would, of course, go straight back to my husband. He was a dear old man – but a dreadful cook. He had come to me just after I had left Bernard to say that it was very bad for me to be alone, that the staff were my family and he had come to tell me that I should find another husband and he gave me a list. The man I did marry was the first on the list!

Our house was exactly like a hotel because we were on the main road between the capital of the province and the lake, and everyone used to come in on their way through.

We were always terribly hard up, and we never had new clothes except when we went on leave. When I first went out to join Derek, a DC of an enormous area, his salary was £600 a year. With two children, we really lived on the edge of bankruptcy, but we managed somehow.

Then I began to have children of my own, but it was a dreadfully unhealthy place to have children. I remember the water was analysed just before we left there, and every kind of germ you could imagine was found in it. Of course we used to boil and filter all the water. We did have a bath but water was still brought in the petrol tins. The children were frequently unwell and it was a constant worry. It was in Salima that my first daughter died. It was the result of being too far from a hospital where she should have gone to have her vaccination, but the local untrained African health assistant did it. My husband and my stepson both had septic arms, but she died thirty-six hours after the vaccination. They said it could have been cerebral malaria when we got her to hospital, though they never decided what it was. And during all this period, my husband was away on safari two weeks out of every four.

After that, I got blackwater fever. When I had more or less recovered, I was sent away to a cool station to stay with some missionaries, but there wasn't a doctor there. I was very ill and I was very lucky; there was so much blackwater in the old days. I remember going round the graveyard in Port Herald, and the average age on the graves was twenty-three. The early missionaries died in their thousands, not knowing how to deal with malaria; if they took huge quantities of quinine, it brought on blackwater fever by affecting the kidneys.

At the end of 1953 we left Salima and went to a lovely place in the Kirk range, 5,000 feet above sea-level. We had a beautiful old house with a garden already laid out, and we were there until 1960. While I was there, I had two more children. It was a very feudal way of living. We had a marvellous nanny, Jean, who had been brought up in the Belgian Congo where her father was a Seventh Day Adventist parson – she had had a partial training there as a nurse and spoke French. I spent a lot of time with Jean; the goings-on of the African community and her private life were sources of constant amusement. I had sewing classes, amateur dramatics and quite a big baby clinic. In 1954 we were sent the first African doctor in the country – he was half Indian and excellent at his job. We had a hospital at the place but he said he couldn't run the whole thing with all the babies as well. There were so many sick babies, so, although untrained, I started the clinic and with a midwife to help me we had eighty babies a day. While we were there, the mortality rate in the country dropped so amazingly because of the introduction of modern medicines.

I was rather disheartened because just before I left, the man who was the Director of Agriculture came to lunch and said, 'What on earth do you think people like you are doing, keeping more and more people alive to live on less and less land?'

We were not allowed to preach birth control, certainly not after Dr Banda came back and the Nationalists started to take over.

Even though it was cool and pleasant, there were many things I didn't like. I remember once there was a man-eating leopard at large, and I had a dreadful experience. I had had a row with my husband. Some people had come to dinner and I thought he had been rather severe and unkind to a new young police officer and he was angry with me. In a huff, I went out into the garden about midnight, and suddenly remembered there was the leopard at large. I was caught between staying out and risking the man-eating leopard or going in and eating humble pie, so I decided to climb through the bathroom window, only to meet my husband who was cleaning his teeth.

We also had those big spiders that lived all over the place in holes in the ground which had little strands of spider's web across the top. I met one in the bathroom. That wasn't at all nice. They were huge, covered with long, dark brown hair. I threw something at it and it ran at me and I jumped on a chair; it actually attacked me! It had a big red mouth which it opened wide; I hit at it with a hairbrush and finally killed it.

When we were just about to go on leave and, for a change, were flying, Theresa developed cerebral spinal meningitis –

spotted fever – the epidemic kind, which was very common in that part of Africa. It developed on arrival in England and we got her into Bart's. They treated her with antibiotics which were quite new then and within twenty-four hours she was much better. It was like a miracle.

There were always these health hazards. Timothy got hookworm through walking barefoot; my stepson got dreadful veruccas on his feet. We still had no water laid on, no electricity, but we did have a telephone – for the first time, but only during office hours.

When we were in Salima the children had to go away to boarding-school because of the heat. You felt it was awfully hard on them going away so young. When they were at home most of their friends were Africans. They learned to eat the most extraordinary things. Duncan brought me a grasshopper once as a great delicacy. He thought I might like to bake it. Then there was a Professor of African Music called Hugh Tracy, who came from Rhodes University, making recordings of African music. When Theresa was three years old, she went up to the Professor on our veranda and he asked her what she had in her clenched hand. She showed him. Her hand was full of chickens' intestines which again is a great delicacy among Africans. She had collected them and was taking them to the cook.

The children's health always troubled me. At one point my relations in England got very indignant because I took my son to the vet when he had ringworm. The hospitals and doctors had nothing to treat it with, but the vet had some new fungicidal tablets from England. Timothy had to stand in a row with all the cats and dogs waiting to be treated. And when one of the others had skin trouble in Zomba, I took him to the local leprosarium because they had a skin specialist there, so it was the best place.

In 1960 we moved to Kota Kota which again was a very hot station beside the lake where many of the Arab slavers had had encampments. There were a number of Arab doors on the houses and you could see the Arab influence. It was also the headquarters of the University Mission to Central Africa and of the Rice Company of Nyasaland. Now it's run by the Chinese. Everything was different at the time because we were working up to Independence and there was a lot of antagonism. When lorry-loads of Congress Party supporters went by, they used to shout insults, and I'm ashamed to say that my children, who spoke the local language, used to shout things back.

Some odd things happened at Kota Kota. A madman picked Timothy up when he was only three and ran away with him, which was quite frightening. They called me and I ran after him and when we caught up with him he was standing with Timothy over a large tank of water, and I had to talk and talk to him, eventually persuading him to give Timothy back to me.

Some of our staff used to frighten the children with their stories. I remember when Theresa had to have an X-ray. I couldn't understand why she was screaming until I learned that one of the staff had told her they were taking her to hospital to cut her head off, and when she saw this machine, she thought it was a guillotine.

I learned judo at this time because things were so unpleasant. We had a policeman out from England and he taught a few of us. At Christmas, there was a great amnesty and all the people who had been shouting rude things at me when I did my shopping or walked down to the town, which was a long and rather lonely road to the Indian stores, came round with a collecting-box, singing carols, expecting me to give them money. I said, 'This is ridiculous! You were shouting rude things at me last week.'

'Oh, no, now this is Christmas! It's different!'

I once had a sea voyage that was a nightmare. My father-in-law had a friend on the board of P & O or BI, so I was put in care of the Captain, which meant that I was at the Captain's table. As we were broke, we were going back in two very cheap cabins in the bowels of the ship. Timothy was six months old, Theresa was three and had just come out of Bart's after her meningitis, Duncan was eleven and Sue a bit older. The ship was the first to go through Suez after the Suez crisis. The children were dreadfully sea-sick. When we embarked, I discovered that there was measles on board. Naturally I did not want Theresa, who had had a gamma globulin injection some months before against measles, to come into contact with it. A friend of mine who had worked in the East End of London had told me that a very good thing for getting rid of infection in those frightful tenements there, was to hang raw onions up. So I got some from the galley and had them hanging from the ceiling of the cabins, and with the children being sick, I can't tell you what it was like!

I was with the children all day, and at night all the grand people – there was the managing director of ICI – would come down in their evening-dress to collect me from my cabin, where I would be in this kind of Hogarthian scene of onions and chamber pots, to take me up to dine with the Captain.

Unfortunately, when we got near Aden, Theresa became desperately ill. They would have put her ashore at Aden but I begged them not to. They put her into the ship's hospital and let me nurse her. They also radioed to Mombasa to a children's specialist to meet the ship. One met the ship and we were told that Theresa's measles was not coming out in the right way. Measles can be bad if it is complicated. Then, on top of everything, we got a new Goanese crew at Dar es Salaam and they brought Asian 'flu on board, which the children then developed. We were the first cases of Asian 'flu to arrive in central Africa.

We stayed in Kota Kota for two years, and in 1962 we went to Zomba which, once more, was a completely different life. We had a house with all modern conveniences, schools for the children, private nursery schools, government schools for older children, hospitals, running water and electricity. There was sport for my husband, sport for the children and in the holidays it was one long party; they were terribly spoilt.

After Independence, there came a time when some of the ministers revolted against Banda, and there was a lot of fighting. Derek was away and his secretary – who very nearly married one of Banda's ministers until he was told that if he married her it would ruin his career – and I went to a party, where I think a lot of this was being plotted.

Two or three weeks afterwards, I was at dinner when someone came and called my husband and me to what was then the African hospital because Jean, our old nanny, was there and she had been shot. She and some of her stepchildren and grandchildren were at supper in their little house in the African township – she had married a man who had the same name as one of Banda's opponents. Some of Banda's bodyguard had gone down there and had just shot at random through the window, shooting Jean and one of the children. I'll never forget it. It was dreadful. They had no lights – they had failed – they had lamps and there was sawdust and blood all over the place. I took the children, who were terrified and covered with sweat, and they stayed with us for several weeks. Finally, a marvellous African doctor, who is now a consultant at Worthing, operated on Jean and she recovered, although she had bullets through her lungs, but I don't think she will ever be quite the same again.

He was an amazing doctor. When he was with us in the bush, he had an agreement with the witch-doctor, that he would send the patients he couldn't cure – the ones suffering from psychiatric disorders – a thing called African madness – to the witch-doctor, and the witch-doctor would send his surgical patients and tropical ulcers to Dr Sam.

It was time to go. We had moved to Blantyre, but my husband's job was purely administrative, and it was time he went if he was to start again. He resigned, and in 1967, left. He took a job in London for a month which he didn't like. He also took the examination for the Diplomatic Service, and they decided that he wasn't quite good enough but then someone dropped out, so they wrote and asked if he'd like to join the Foreign Office, and so he did.

We shall see them again in Montserrat, a very different scene from the one Betty has just recounted.

Out of the very fascinating and interesting lives I have been told, there are many I could have chosen. I chose Betty because it seemed to me that nearly everything that happened to her was not as concentrated in the other colonial lives – or, if it had been, then they didn't tell me so. My impression was that she took the rough with the smooth, enjoying the moments of pleasure with intensity, the beauty of the mountains, of her children, the sudden change from the primitive life to one of luxury. As for the comparative luxury, she described it in a perfect throw-away line which perhaps many colonial women have felt, 'You felt you were rather killing time.'

2

'I Direct Your Attention to Africa'

Sir Evelyn Baring became High Commissioner in South Africa in 1944, replacing Lord Harlech, and Colonial Governor of the three High Commission territories, Bechuanaland, Swaziland and Basutoland. His wife, Lady Howick, said: 'Quite a bit of the time we spent touring the three territories, which were very primitive, very interesting. The King – Sobhuza II – had a hundred wives. Evelyn was always anxious to get medicine pushed out into districts. He was very keen on that. Of course, when we first went to Rhodesia, the Prime Minister was Sir Godfrey Huggins who was a doctor, so that got us off to a good medical start. I shouldn't think the hospitals have changed very much since Independence. Evelyn became very knowledgeable about farming. He was interested in administration and African welfare, natural history and land reform – anything that was really going to benefit the peasant on the land.'

Mrs Hall's husband was in Basutoland for seven years. Though she felt it was 'a wonderful privilege' to be there she had mixed feelings after being in the WRNS during the war: 'It was so totally different, and I was terribly homesick. I found it incredibly uncivilized. I thought it would be lovely to undo my wedding presents and have a super house, but for nine months we lived in the annexe of an hotel. My husband's salary was half what it had been in the war as a major, so he couldn't live on it. I think it was £450 per annum. Leaving the services to go to Basutoland was like going back into Victorian England. All the District Commissioners and their wives had been there all through the war, so they didn't know what it was like to be bombed or machine-gunned. They were terribly patronizing I thought. It was like going into a completely different world and you had to get used to it or go home. But I didn't know what real heat was until I got to Botswana.'

Mrs Hall returned to Botswana again in 1965 for three years and felt a great admiration for Seretse Khama and his English wife, Ruth: 'They had been married fifteen or sixteen years before we got there and they absolutely adored each other. When they gave parties at Government House, every now and again Seretse would look round to see where Ruth was. He couldn't bear her to be out of his sight for long.'

There was always a shortage of money and with three children to educate it was not easy. In spite of her reluctance to let him go, their son John was sent home at the age of eight. His father believed that unless they went at that early age they never caught up: 'He went back in the plane by himself but with another girl, whom we put in charge of him. My mother got him off the plane and she said he didn't speak for two days, it was such a terrible shock to him.'

According to Cathy Loyd, Swaziland is a lovely country. It is, in many ways, like a miniature version of Kenya. Like Kenya it has immense variety; the highest part is over 6,000 feet, going down to about 200 feet in the Low Veldt. The low hot country is very productive, pioneered by the Commonwealth Development Corporation, with great fields of sugar and citrus; higher up are the large new soft-wood plantations. One of the most important things about Swaziland is that it is almost entirely populated by Swazis. There are a few people from Mozambique and a certain number of Zulus, but that is all.

Frank Loyd, who was High Commissioner from 1964 to 1968 found it a very unsophisticated country: 'The economic developments, the railway and the iron mine, and the planting of pine-apples and sugar, were bringing them into the modern world at high speed. This produced all the usual problems that it does if you try to do these things at high speed.'

In 1857, Livingstone said to the undergraduates of Cambridge: 'I direct your attention to Africa. I know that in a few years I shall be cut off in that country which is now open. I go back to try to open up a path to commerce and Christianity. Do you carry on the work that I have done. I leave it to you.' His great ambition was to rid Africa of the slave trade, but what he did not foresee was that Christianity would be followed by trade and the partition of Africa among commercially minded Europeans. After Livingstone came a whole generation of explorers, all seeking their 'spheres of influence'.

Largely through the drive of Cecil Rhodes, British influence extended northwards to Northern and Southern Rhodesia – now Zambia and Zimbabwe. In 1951, it was suggested that to preserve Southern Rhodesia, a Federation should be formed between Northern Rhodesia, Southern Rhodesia and Nyasaland, now Malawi. Robin Short, who was a cadet in the Colonial Office in 1950, says about that idea: 'If we did not, Southern Rhodesia would be swallowed up by the Afrikaner Government of South Africa. The idea of Federation was the brief a man named Ronald Bush brought to Northern Rhodesia. He had to go round trying to persuade unwilling African Chiefs through unwilling District Commissioners. He was such a nice man, and he was not the sort of man who would say, "Well, the Federation is going to be and if you don't like it, you can do the other thing." He tried to persuade everybody, but he could not succeed because he was not really persuaded himself. So it was imposed. In my view, the idea was impossible, ridiculous, and I think that most of the DCs thought that the circulars which they received were very foolish and they put them in the wastepaper basket. That is what we all felt about the Federation.'

In England at this time, a Conservative government was more preoccupied with advancing Britain's position in Europe than in the so-called Empire. Nyasaland achieved independence as Malawi in 1964, and Northern Rhodesia became Zambia a few months later.

I asked Robin whether, by this time, they had enough lawyers, doctors or even artisans.

'Artisans, yes. They had plenty of good artisans, but not many people who knew how to run things. They had some doctors – very few – two or three, they had some qualified lawyers – four or five, that was the sum total. I think we should blame ourselves for not bringing these people on.'

Then in 1978 the white settlers in Southern Rhodesia conceded the inevitability of black rule, and new maps were drafted.

Tanganyika was mandated to Britain from Germany by the League of Nations in 1918. The difference between the two forms of government will be shown through the eyes of some of the colonial women later in this book. The Arab sultanate of Zanzibar was deposed by a black majority two weeks after Independence, and the new government offered to unite with Tanganyika. The two became known as Tanzania.

When Tanganyika became independent in 1962, Charles Meek became Julius Nyerere's Permanent Secretary, which has resulted in a loyal and lasting friendship. Nona Meek has an intense admiration for Nyerere. Certainly he began very well. Corruption, which is so pervasive on the west coast of Africa, was not so prevalent, thanks to village self-sufficiency and to the unostentatious way of life which Nyerere chose. He wears the simplest of garments designed like a Chinese robe; does not drive round in a large car or cover his wife with jewels as did many other African leaders. He admonished his ministers for their extravagance and cut their salaries.

Nyerere learned his form of socialism in England. One of his first actions was to throw out the Indian traders, replacing them with bureaucratically controlled cooperatives.

Nona said: 'He used to come into our house in Park Road, Dar es Salaam, at the end of the day – his house was dead opposite ours, just beside Government House – and he would come in and sit down and just chat about things and we'd probably say, "Oh, wouldn't you like something to eat?" and he'd reply, "Yes, I'd like – I'd like scrambled eggs." So we'd sit there and have scrambled eggs on our knees while we talked. There was the time he came back from America when he'd seen Kennedy – it was the year of the Bay of Pigs. He said what a brilliant vat of brightness and intelligence Kennedy was. It struck me as rather funny that he was one day with him and the next sitting quietly with me. His wife, Maria, was also a great friend of mine, but she was not quite so sophisticated and didn't speak good English.'

In 1901, the British, using Indian labour, completed the railway which was to run from Mombasa to Lake Victoria, the head-waters of the Nile. The Kenya–Uganda Protectorate was formed and settlers appeared to be the only method of making the two countries pay for themselves. By 1915, 4.5 million acres of land in Kenya had been taken from the African inhabitants by about 1,000 farmers and 7.3 million acres by the 1950s.

Kenya is a beautiful and immensely varied country. The Highlands rise to 10,000 feet, Mount Kenya to 17,000 feet and the Aberdare range to 12,000. This is the roof of Africa and from it water flows to the Nile, the Mediterranean, the Congo and the Atlantic.

The settlers appeared to have the best of all worlds. Labour for their farms, a wealth of wildlife to hunt, and what, for a time, appeared to be rich farms to hand on to their children. However, in 1952 the Mau Mau disturbances began. The Kikuyu were by far the strongest and most intelligent tribe and the Mau Mau was entirely their business. When Sir Evelyn Baring arrived, in September 1952, it was to a thoroughly troubled country.

The Administration of the country was, according to Robin Wainwright, over-worked and under-staffed. At the time he was District Commissioner in Embu with 250,000 population in an area of 8,000 square miles. He had one DO and a police force of thirty-two men. He had no time, or very little, to collect intelligence, or to indulge in the slow touring which in the early days was the hallmark of a good DC allowing him to make contact with the man in the *shamba* (garden).

In 1963, Kenya achieved its independence, though Robin Wainwright doubts that the Mau Mau as such had much to do with it. He points out: 'If the Mau Mau's aim was independence, why didn't other tribes join in? It was much more likely that its objective was land.'

Until 1884 British Somaliland was under Egyptian rule. Then it became a British Protectorate. In 1898 it was considered a dependency of India and was governed by a Resident from Aden. It was then transferred to the Foreign Office and in 1905 it came under the Colonial Office. Between 1901 and 1920 there was a spasmodic war between the British and the 'Mad Mullah' – Mohammed ben Abdullah Hassan. During the Second World War it was invaded by the Italians. In 1948, Sir Gerald Reece became Military Governor and, until 1953, C-in-C of the Somaliland Protectorate. The peaceful uncluttered life of the NFP which suited Alys Reece was to change drastically: 'It wasn't until I got to Somaliland that entertaining became a nightmare. Wireless messages at seven o'clock in the morning that an aircraft with twelve people or whatever was coming down from the Middle East for a quick conference and would be staying to lunch and possibly overnight.'

Life changed drastically for the children, too. Kenya is a paradise for children, and there are suitable schools. But in Somaliland things were very different: 'There was no school at the time that took girls. Eventually there was one school but that was towards the end of our time when they'd settled in at Aberdeen at the Albyn school there. It was an awful feeling, seeing your young going off in an aeroplane by themselves – it was terrible. Sarah was nine, when I left her at the Albyn on her first visit. It was all rather sudden because we didn't know we were going to Somaliland and it was rather rushed, so she wasn't conditioned for it as much as one would have liked. She was marvellously good. Anyway, when I took her there she was very quiet but very stoic, and just as I was saying goodbye to her, she said, "But Mummy, I don't even know the language!"

'I loved Somalia. I didn't like the set-up there, though. I mean, those sort of gatherings round the polo field, mid-morning coffee parties and things like that. I tried to avoid them until I discovered I was giving offence and complaints that somebody had got the wrong place at dinner – because her husband was Acting Treasurer now, and didn't I realize that, because I should have! I wrote back – and it was truthful – that I'd put her where I did because I thought she'd enjoy herself more as I had put her next to someone who was very entertaining and charming – but, no – it mattered much more to her to be seen to be a temporary Acting Treasurer's wife! Otherwise, things were fairly unsophisticated, thank God! I remember when we were having a huge party and the electricity failed the day before and all the refreshments were bubbling like mulled wine. Of course, there were no hotels I could fall back on, and no shops, except that you could get some chapatis from Indian places. Sometimes we would have some Ethiopians visiting us and would discover – having asked heads of departments in to meet them – that it was their fast day and they couldn't have any fat, meat, or eggs! Try and run a dinner party on strictly vegetables – it was a bit difficult. I got rather inventive. There were celebrations when the first rains came. The river ran just at the edge of our garden and it used to thunder down when they came at the beginning of the year. I remember the first time that happened. It was in the middle of a dinner party and we all trooped out, the sound was too exciting. We all rushed out and there was the river in spate – tree trunks hurling around in all directions, the servants all out dancing and whooping, and all the stately guests in their long frocks and everything else, more or less dancing too! It was a lovely feeling. It was a good land.'

In 1862, the explorer, Speke, arrived with his companion, Grant, in Buganda and met the famous Kabaka Muteesa on his journey to discover the source of the Nile. Ten years later, Samuel Baker with his beautiful Hungarian wife, whom he had bought at a slave market in Budapest, moved south from Equatoria and advanced to Masindi, the headquarters of the King of Bunyoro which he captured in May 1872. In 1884 Muteesa died, and in 1890 the Germans and British formed an agreement establishing Uganda and Kenya as being in the British sphere of influence.

In 1890, Frederick Lugard went out, not only to map the route from the coast to Uganda, but to establish the Imperial British East African Company. In December of that year he made his first contact with the region (which was to become the Protectorate of Uganda) by entering Busoga, occupied by a Bantu people. On 13 December, he crossed the Nile. Lugard contacted Sultan Wakoli, whom he flattered by telling him that he was a 'a big and powerful sultan, second only to Mwanga' who favoured French occupation. Wakoli was in great fear of Mwanga, but in a whisper promised to fight with the English against him. Lugard then formed a blood brotherhood with Wakoli. He had to eat a berry, dipped in Wakoli's blood from a cut in his stomach, off the palm of his right hand without chewing, and then Wakoli had to do the same. In 1893, Sir Gerald Portal, on behalf of the British government, took over the responsibilities of the Imperial British East African Company and in 1896 the Protectorate was extended to most of the regions within Uganda. In 1962, less than seventy years later, Uganda got its independence.

Jane Bell spent many useful and creative years in Uganda: 'I feel, looking back, that my life in Africa, which lasted over twenty-five years, was a progress from being a spectator of a colourful, strange, exciting panorama of totally different cultures, to the time when I became completely absorbed into the frustrations, problems, hopes and ambitions, joys and sorrows of the people whom at first I'd just been watching. It was this gradual change from spectator to participant that gave the whole of that period its central significance, though I didn't realize or understand it at the time.

'Because of my husband's job as Deputy Director of Education we had been posted to Kampala, the commercial capital of the country, where the headquarters of the Education Department were situated. It was a busy, prosperous town, expanding fast with booming trade and plenty of money around. The residential area was largely European with a few large enclaves occupied by the Indian community.

'Most of the Africans lived in the countryside round about on their own small plantations, but under the enlightened Governorship of Sir Andrew Cohen African housing estates were being built on the outskirts and every morning you could see hundreds of Africans bicycling into Kampala to jobs of all kinds and at night returning to their homes, leaving the town once again to the Indians and Europeans. Consequently, unless you made a deliberate effort, you could easily find yourself completely insulated from the life of the country. After Somaliland, where I'd been so happy in daily, effortless contact with our Somali neighbours, I felt chilled and wondered how I was going to live in this artificial community.

'There were, as well, divisions within European society: between the missions, the government officials and the people working in commerce and the professions. All three mingled and were on friendly terms, but seemed to be a little bit suspicious of each other.

'Before long I was fortunate enough to meet with three very remarkable European women who were sensitively aware of the need to draw all these elements closer together. Mary Suart, the wife of the Anglican bishop; Helen Neatby, the senior woman Education Officer; and Barbara Saben, whose husband was influential in the commercial world, were the moving spirits behind the formation of the Uganda Council of Women, which was fully inter-racial from its inception. Membership was open to any woman, irrespective of creed, caste or race, who shared a

27

desire to improve relationships between women whatever their background.

'The founders had in mind that the time was soon coming when the women of Uganda would need a voice in international forums of discussion, and they took steps to affiliate to the International Council of Women and to the Associated Country-women of the World, so that in time delegates would travel to speak for themselves and their people at international conferences – an opportunity which they eagerly welcomed and performed with growing confidence and success.

'At UCW meetings I found a gateway through which I could slip to meet African and Indian women as friends. One day, perhaps nearly a year later, one of them, Catherine Kasule approached me and said, "I have heard you are a teacher. I belong to a group of women who meet every week and we are very anxious to find someone who will teach us English. Will you come?" I was delighted, really delighted, at this first overture and agreed at once.

'This was the beginning of weekly visits to her home among the banana plantations. She and most of her friends could speak a little English; they had received such limited education as their fathers had permitted them to have. They were keen to learn more English, because their own children, now at school, were learning to speak it. Their children and their husbands had the chance of getting scholarships or bursaries, given by the government, British Council and a variety of charitable institutions to go overseas to the UK or the United States, Europe or India and the women felt that they were being very much disadvantaged by not speaking English.

'So we started the classes. I enjoyed them immensely and established the happiest of friendships. I had the great pleasure of seeing their leader go off to England on a British Council bursary to study nursery schools to help her to improve her own private pre-school group which she ran in the garden of her home. I feel doubtful if the older women learned very much because it was too late for most of them, but it was a very interesting and valuable experience for me because I realized that there was a growing number of women who were looking for further education of a different kind from the excellent programmes of basic education in health, hygiene, child care and nutrition provided in the rural women's clubs. I saw it particularly in regard to the wives of prominent Africans who were beginning to take public positions, such as the Mayor of Kampala.'

From then on, until she left, Jane Bell's hands were full. She helped establish nursery schools, having discovered that they existed only in a private capacity. She became President of the Council of Women, ran the Council of Voluntary Services and taught English: 'I was so busy that I didn't really have time to think. But when I got back to Uganda from home leave for the last time in 1961, it seemed to me that it was high time for all the women of Uganda to meet together to look at what faced them when Independence came in the following year. It was an enormous undertaking and was only made possible by the enthusiastic cooperation of all the many women's clubs and societies. With the advice and help of Africans and Indians a pre-conference study booklet was produced covering such subjects as women's position in marriage and the home, in public and political life, and the need for more and better education for girls.

'Finally in August 1961 the conference "Uganda Women Look Ahead" was held under the auspices of the UCW. Representatives came from all parts of the country. They queued up at the microphone to speak with courage, honesty and modesty to the very large gathering. They exhorted and encouraged each other to grasp and use their opportunities and appealed to men to accept the contribution they could make. It was a marvellous and moving occasion. There was a great spirit of optimism and determination to take their full share when their country became independent.

'I really felt tremendously hopeful for the future at the time. It hasn't, sadly, worked out as we hoped. Some of the people I worked with are still living there, waiting and hoping for better times. Some have died in the disasters that have overtaken the country. Others have sought refuge in other countries.

'I grew to have a tremendous respect for the Ugandan women and to admire their dignity, humour, kindliness and patience. They have a great contribution to make if and when they get the opportunity.'

3

Nell Baines

Nell Baines! She was born in 1884 but the bride of twenty-seven still looks at me as she relives her past. There is great intelligence, humour and many a remembered sadness. How was it possible in 1912 for a girl to face the choice of being forced to leave either a child or a husband, let alone to anticipate the physical discomforts of Africa with its variety of heat, humidity, termites, dirt and dust, and the constant battle against a low standard of living?

Dick Baines had already made a name for himself as a District Commissioner before he married Nell. It was necessary to have a degree before joining the Colonial Service and Dick was educated at Wellington and then at Christ's College, Cambridge. In 1904, at the tender age of twenty-two, he was appointed Assistant Collector in Uganda, an appointment made through the Foreign Office. He went to Jinga, near the source of the White Nile, under a District Commissioner named Borfu. Then he was sent to Musaka for two and a half years and then on to Nimule in what was then the Nile Province. Here, Kitchener came up from Khartoum to pay a brief visit and Dick spent the entire time with his hand on his revolver like a modern security guard. He spent two years helping the King's African Rifles mop up Abyssinian gun-running before returning home. It was during this vacation in England that he married Nell.

It wasn't long before Nell was on her way to Musaka with her husband. She set off for Marseilles, where they were to pick up their ship for Mombasa, with no sense of foreboding. Indeed, she was in a high state of excitement. This was real adventure! She was leaving behind the carefully nurtured and sheltered life she had always known. Like Isabel Burton, she had found the man who would widen her horizons and take her from an

England still held in thrall by Victorianism so far as women were concerned to an independence which she could only imagine but had never tasted.

She had shopped for this journey with great care. Her trousseau consisted of beautiful gowns, long skirts and blouses for day wear and pretty, elegant shoes. The necks of her dresses were high, the skirts full, and she might even have worn button boots. To please her husband, she had added mosquito boots, a double-*terai* (a double-layered felt hat, eventually dispensed with for the solar topi) and pyjamas for safaris. They had also bought an enormous amount of stores from the Army and Navy which, in spite of their foresight, they found they had to renew at the end of a year.

Trustingly, they had ordered *The Times* and the *Daily Times* which had the habit of arriving in Musaka, not separately, but at least forty at a time. Once they had read the news they were reduced to reading advertisements – in Dick's case, for cars, while Nell read advertisements for horses, especially in the spring when all the hunters were being sold off.

Throughout their journey they were accompanied by the Governor of Uganda and his wife, Sir Frederick and Lady Jackson, and Sir Frederick's two maiden sisters. Little did Nell realize when they stopped off at Naples and she visited Pompeii that she was seeing the last of civilization as she knew it for many days to come. Perhaps the change began at Port Said, which was a sad disappointment, especially the famous Simon Arzt's shop where everybody bought their topis en route for India. She said scornfully: 'It might have been in the Brompton Road. I was expecting something Eastern-looking.'

At last, Africa was sighted in the gloaming. Since there is no twilight in tropical Africa, it was dark by the time they docked at Kilindini, the port for Mombasa, and Nell had to judge this dark continent by those familiar smells of wood smoke, sweet decay, urine and sweat. They spent their first night at Trolleys Hotel, which, by Nell's standards, was 'not bad'.

The next morning she was full of anticipation for the journey by train to Nairobi, for Dick had thrilled her with his stories of the animals she would see from the windows.

'But I've nothing to read!' wailed the young wife of a customs officer.

'You won't *want* to read on this journey,' rebuked an older woman, long accustomed to Africa. It was true, for though they were unpleasantly hot and sticky, Nell was quite carried away by the various wild animals she saw from her ring-side view as they trundled at a respectable speed along the track.

When they crossed Lake Victoria to Entebbe, Nell found that the presence of the official party made the small boat on which they were travelling overcrowded and oppressive. On arrival, however, she was gratified to see the smart phalanx of officials in their white uniforms and helmets, lined up to greet their Governor. It was all splendid and impressive and augured well for the future. For ten happy days they stayed in a pleasant hotel above the lake near the botanical gardens. They were asked out to dinner every night and Lady Jackson commented on the charm and beauty of Nell's glamorous dresses. This was indeed the life she had anticipated when she shopped at Harrods or at Jay's in Regent Street.

Alas, poor Nell! It was not to last.

After ten glorious days in Entebbe, they set sail for Bakaka. On board, Nell was offered Worcester sauce with her lunch. When she refused, a man sitting close to her said sardonically: 'You had better get a taste for that or you'll never be able to eat anything out here.'

Worcester sauce was a minor irritation at this point. Anchored outside Bakaka, the lake flies were so dense that at meals the cutlery disappeared under a thick black pulsing cloak. There was no way, Nell discovered, to get rid of them. They clouded her eyes, her mouth, found crevices under her long skirt and got into her mosquito boots. A steward lit a large lamp to distract them but still they found this juicy morsel from England more delectable. The hippos, wallowing in the lake all round them, failed to distract the wretchedly uncomfortable Nell.

The next morning they left the launch for the last stage of their twenty-five-mile journey. The porters carried their luggage while Nell and Dick took to their bicycles. Half-way to Musaka they were to camp, so at the base of a bare red hill Nell and Dick stopped to wait for the porters. For the first time Nell heard the African drumming, which she thought meant the arrival of the luggage.

'Oh, no,' her husband told her, 'there is always drumming in

Buganda.' Worcester sauce and interminable drumming! A tired and weary Nell hoped she would grow used to it.

At last the porters arrived and, after a time, lunch was served. Nell described it to me: 'Never had I eaten such awful food! The memory of dinner on the train, which was bad enough, was wiped out by the meal that was put before us. Lumps of boiled meat were followed by lumps of boiled fish. What annoyed me most was that my husband was always talking about the good cook he had had on the preceding tour and I could only wish he had kept him on. Everything was drowned in marrow fat from the Army and Navy Stores. The food was uneatable except to the strongest stomach. Then we had either custard pudding or a thing they called market pudding, which was Swiss roll with custard.'

Early on the following day they started on the last part of their journey. On arrival they pushed their bicycles up to the station which was attractively built on a high hill with avenues of pine and grass as short and as green as a golf course. The DC's house by comparison was a sad disappointment. It had been designed by Sir Hesketh Bell when he was Governor of the Protectorate. It had a very small veranda along the front which was too narrow to give protection from the sun, while inside the match-boarded ceiling lined with calico was so full of cracks that it supplied the perfect resting place for bats which had the habit of falling on the floor below at unexpected moments.

The former DC's wife was ill and unable to leave the house, so for a month Dick and Nell had to live in a camp which had been put up for the Governor's last visit. Though the buildings were pretty, the grass which was spread on the floor was alive with fleas and jiggers and poor Nell was eaten alive. Each evening she suffered the indignity of having jiggers removed from her toes by one of the boys.

When Nell was at last able to take up residence in her new home, she found it very poorly furnished. The Public Works furniture was quite inadequate; the water was carried to the house from a well by the prisoners each day, and the only sanitation was a bucket and disinfectant in a small hut in the grounds. Nell soon learned to avoid the kitchen if she was to eat anything at all. Cleanliness was not one of the cook's assets. To add to her discomfort, she found that she was pregnant. In 1912 few women had much practical knowledge of birth control but, nevertheless, Nell in her innocence had hoped for at least a year of peace without this added complication. The local doctor, a strange man, was not for her. Reputedly his house was so filthy that Dick Baines refused to enter the door. There was no alternative – Nell would have to go to Kampala to have her baby.

To while away her days and to improve her health and appetite, she bought an oil-stove and cooked delectable meals for herself and the visitors who, after hearing of her scones, cakes, chicken pie and chocolate pudding, made a point of visiting her. But in her delicate state she found it all very tiring.

Before going off to have her baby, she had a chance to tackle her home. The Director of Public Works came to stay and with wisdom and guile she put him to sleep in 'a very hot room with a very bad ceiling and so we got a second veranda built, that is the sort of way you had to do things in those days!'

There were, of course, compensations for the poor housing. The *shamba* was beautiful and full of oranges and pineapples. The view over the lake was breathtaking. The aromatic tang of warm grass and fruit, mixed with bougainvillaea, thorn trees and pines, was compensation for physical discomfort. Then there is nothing to compare with the African skies at night, even if, at land level, everything is hideous and sordid. To sit on a roof or a veranda and look skywards is beyond description. It is as if there were no room among those diamond-bright stars to place a finger.

Of course, Nell had to combat the great curse of colonial life – loneliness. She must have longed for female company, to speak of domestic problems, of the expected birth of her baby. In my day in Africa, one made friends with emancipated African women. In Nell's day, they did not exist. As she said to me, in wonder: 'How they've come on!' However, she did have the pleasure of Esterhazy's arrival. One day a vision in a spotless white dress with a basket of vegetables on her head arrived in front of Nell's veranda. She had grown the vegetables with the aid of the Catholic Fathers (frequent visitors of the Baines's where they demanded 'cold tea', a polite name for whisky) and begged to be taken on as the Baines's gardener. Nell was delighted. She not only employed her but began to teach her English, finding her both intelligent and receptive.

From the day of the birth of her baby life was full of problems. The baby was born with a slightly narrow food channel, and for the early years of his life she never knew whether he would get through a meal or vomit. Today he would have had a small operation within three days of birth and all would have been well. To add to her difficulties, four days after the birth Nell caught malaria. The Mission hospital supplied nets for the beds but not for the windows and Nell knew that, as usual, she had fallen victim to a vicious attack from mosquitoes. She was be-friended by the archdeacon's wife who had a chair on one wheel, with two very immaculate servants pushing and pulling it, and Nell was sent out in this to take the air. Nell found her 'a very charming woman, but rather malicious about the other lady missionaries. She said the lady missionaries put on their best clothes to drive across from one station to another.'

Ill and weak, Nell found kindness everywhere. For a few days before returning to Musaka, she and Dick, who had arrived to take her back, stayed with the DC. They lunched with the Bishop, where the chaplain apologized because there were 'two pink sweets'! Such niceties were taken seriously, even in Kampala, in 1912.

The Jacksons sent Nell and Dick down to Entebbe in their second car, to catch the launch. Nell told me: 'It was the most awful car, and an awful road. I was half dead, having had malaria half-way through, which wasn't much preparation for life.' Certainly, from then on, life was no sinecure. War in Europe was looming, though some people in Africa seemed strangely mis-informed. Musaka was fifty miles from the Tanganyikan border which from 1885 had been a German Protectorate, so it could scarcely be rated as a healthy spot at this juncture.

Nell heard the news of the declaration of war on 4 August 1914, from a young man who appeared on her veranda and said breathlessly: 'Mrs Baines, your husband has sent me across from the office to tell you that we are at war with Germany.'

Nell said nothing. What was there to say?

'I came down to tell your husband that I had accidentally shot a female elephant,' her informer told her. It was strictly against the law to shoot more than two elephants by licence in a year. 'Your husband called me a damned liar – but now this changes everything!' And he went off, apparently thoroughly pleased with the turn of events.

Baines had meanwhile sent off the code he had received to the nearest station, one hundred miles away. The DC was out on safari and a not-too-bright ADO cabled back to Baines: 'No code here. What the hell does Gemmyman Gypsyfield mean?'

On his return, the DC could scarcely believe his eyes, for he did know what the cable meant, and he had been on the verge of asking the Germans to help him against the troublesome Belgians on whose border he was stationed.

In those days, very few DCs were allowed to join the forces. They were considered of more value if they continued to live in the countries they knew so well. In 1915 the Baineses came home to England on leave. It was the year the *Lusitania* was sunk, and they docked in Madeira for a week, sitting on deck with their bags all around them, ready to take to the boats. For the next two years, Nell made hazardous journeys to and from England, dividing her time between her husband and delicate son.

In 1917, Tanganyika was mandated by the League of Nations to British administration, and Baines was posted to Bukoba, an old German port. Nell became essential to Dick since she spoke fluent German and he persuaded her to join him for longer than usual. She had to translate German documents and help him to communicate with the Africans who could speak no English. Nevertheless, it was essentially a lonely time for Nell. Though she loved the country, which she likened to the Yorkshire moors or parts of North Devon, and enjoyed going on safari in a country where she could see a view, she was again thrown back on her own resources. She was the only woman among seven men. Her only recreation was sailing in an old German boat until the men infuriated her by declaring it unseaworthy. She was no games-woman, and when she tried her hand at tennis on a cracked asphalt court she found that the tennis ball behaved like a small gas balloon.

Like millions of other women, the highlight of her day, for which she so anxiously waited, was the return of her husband from work. Here again, in Bukoba, she was to be disappointed, for Dick – unlike his wife – was no linguist and used frequently to ask two Chiefs in to talk the local 'lingo'. Nell looked at me, and I could see the remembered frustration in her eyes: 'He was a man who learned that way, you see! I had been alone with the "boys" all day, and when the Chiefs kept coming, I found it rather tiring. I had had such a very female existence before.'

The Africans must have found the British administration very different from that of the Germans. The Germans had governed by direct rule and had been harsh task-masters. The British, on the other hand, began trying to develop native political institutions, hoping gradually to transfer financial and executive responsibilities. At one time, they created two provinces with inter-racial provincial councils of Asians, Africans, Arabs and Europeans. Whatever criticism may be hurled at British heads, it was a very real effort to hand over responsibility slowly to a still underdeveloped country – but, of course, the operative word is 'slowly' and that was not appreciated.

Though Nell had been comparatively healthy up-country, she caught amoebic dysentery on the coast and could not recover from it. She was forced to return to England and to stay here. Her last words to me were these: 'I had to stay at home – it is a mistake, but it's awfully difficult, with one precious child making it even more difficult. It is so difficult, but it is a mistake.' She looked sad, and then for a flash, her eyes brightened. 'In Musaka the KAR bugle sounded Reveille and Lights Out! That was nice.'

4

'Women and Children Last'

The title of this chapter is what a Colonial District Officer said to his young wife, and it sums up the absolute dedication which most of the colonial servants brought to their job. They gave it priority over all other considerations, for they believed the Africans who said to them again and again, 'You are our father and our mother.' It was enough that at an early age, often under thirty, a man was caring for an area as large as Wales. There he would be magistrate, doctor, agriculturist, teacher and friend. That those words were actually spoken by a DO does show some awareness of the reality. Of course, not all the colonial women experienced the same situation. Some were lucky in the countries they were sent to, in the men their husbands served under, in enjoying good health, and, possibly the most important point of all, in having private means to pave the way and enhance the life.

In travelling round Britain and speaking to many colonial women, I have found poverty their greatest enemy, especially when there were children. I cannot count how many have said, 'That year we couldn't pay the *duka* [Indian store] bill,' or 'We had so many visitors we couldn't make ends meet.' Then, the saddest cry of all, 'I didn't see my son/daughter for *x* number of years; we just couldn't afford the fare.' Among all the deprivations, this is the one that counted the most. It was a choice of either an appalling separation from a husband or an appalling separation from children. Not the loneliness, the bad climates, the primitive living conditions or the lack of medical care, counted in comparison.

Asked if they knew the kind of life into which they were

marrying, the answer was generally 'No'. The DO in love might say lamely, 'Well, I'll have to be away quite a bit – a day here or there,' or, 'One has to use one's initiative, it's all very exciting once you get used to it.' If the bride's father had served in the Indian Civil Service, she might conjure up in her mind a house full of obsequious servants attending to her slightest whim. She would perhaps imagine a glorified Kiplingesque world of pomp and ceremony. Or some lucky girl might have been brought up in Kenya which would prepare her slightly for the life ahead, but not completely, for Kenya is a paradise compared with Liwale in Tanganyika, or Benin in Nigeria.

However, though time and time again I heard the words 'Little did I know what I was letting myself in for,' I seldom heard criticism or regret. After the first shock of the hut instead of the palace, the thunder-box instead of plumbing, the humidity or dust, instead of cool fans and insulation, the wind of the Falkland Islands, the endless packing and unpacking, one can almost hear the gasp as the young woman changes course, practically in mid-air, and philosophically plunges down to land in whatever terrain has been offered her. Then, on landing, she has no choice but to get on with life, to contribute, and to make the best of things. And, in the main, that's exactly what they all did.

One last vision of langorous young women being fanned by small black boys as they fling their long gloves and fans away before we step into the real colonial world. It has been suggested that these women should have been ashamed of exploiting the native, ashamed of their husbands' jobs, and most certainly mortified by the word 'Empire'. Except in the rare case, the truth has been just the opposite. The wives or career women gave of their best often under the most difficult conditions. They knew Independence must come to any country which was still a colony; they never doubted it, but (like their husbands) it was not 'if' it should come, but 'when'. I have beside me a card from Pat Hodgson which sums it up: 'We were ashamed only to be leaving them to fend for themselves long before they were ready – as time has shown. When saying goodbye to my well-educated house-girl, who was also my friend, she wept and put her arms round me and asked, "What is going to become of us when you have all gone?" What indeed?'

Before the days when flying was taken for granted, it was a question of compromise and heart-searching before seeing the children. The Corries, when posted to Nyasaland, were there early enough for their terms to be three first-class sea passages per tour, and a tour was anything from two-and-a-half to three years.

Barbara Corrie said: 'The first-class fare was terribly expensive, and we were allowed to travel as cheaply as possible and put the saving towards flying the children out. We could just make this stretch to two air fares for two children twice in three years. We couldn't afford to have them out every summer, but the third year we were due to go home on leave, so there was about eighteen months. We saw them either every twelve months or twelve to fifteen or eighteen months for the third year. It didn't come as a shock and I was braced for it. But we had our daughter and we clung to her when it would have been better for her if we hadn't. Yes, it was a terrible deprivation, and of course we were all worried that we were damaging them psychologically, and worried that they would grow away from us – and none of that happened.'

Nona Meek married Charles in 1947, and with some difficulty managed to get a boat out to Tanganyika, where she arrived pregnant to begin her strange new life. Within nine years they had a son of eight at school in England, a daughter at school in Tanganyika and a small one at home with them. Poverty stared them in the face and when they were sent from up-country to Dar es Salaam, they had to make the hard decision that they could not afford the passage for the son at prep school in England to join them. Even though Nona sacked the cook and took over the cooking in the heat of Dar es Salaam, still their finances wouldn't run to it. After eighteen months they went to the airport for the reunion and had the greatest difficulty in recognizing him amongst all the other small boys. He was extraordinarily shy himself, which was not helped by the fact that Nona went down with hepatitis and the doctor wanted her to stay in hospital.

'Listen,' she said. 'I haven't seen my son for eighteen months, and I'm not going to be separated now.'

Of course, before the problems of education and separations, there was the actual birth – always a hazard unless one was in a capital like Kampala, Dar es Salaam or Nairobi. Pregnancies frequently ended in miscarriages and Rachel Bleackley suffered in this way.

Parts of Tanganyika were extremely unhealthy and more than a third of it was infested by tsetse fly, the carrier of the trypanosome, parasites which cause sleeping sickness in humans and cattle sickness in livestock. The British government cleared a huge area of this pest for their famous (or infamous) groundnut scheme between 1947 and 1951 which lost the country some £30–40m. and became a talking point for the officials and politicians as well as the Administrators. The narrow coastal plain rises to a beautiful plateau with Kilimanjaro in the north and the Livingstone Mountains in the south west.

Peter Bleackley was posted to the Liwale District as a DO during the Second World War. Like most of the Administration, he had tried to join the forces but had been refused permission. Liwale District was the size of Wales, very sparsely populated, with no Europeans but plenty of elephant. Rachel Bleackley accompanied her husband there.

'It was even too unhealthy for the missionaries, and, of course, the population was too small and remote. There was one Somali trader who sold kerosene and bought beeswax and honey – that was about all. We had been allowed to take one case of tinned butter, one tin of tea and one of coffee. We were not to be there for more than three months because the rains were due and someone was to be sent to relieve us. I became pregnant with Robert who in fact walked 500 miles *in utero* before I was to have him! I had already had a miscarriage – with the Red Cross manual in one hand and myself in the other – there were no medical people anywhere near.'

Rachel was sensitive to the oppressive atmosphere in the Liwale neighbourhood. No wonder! In 1905 the local warrior tribes rose against the Germans in the Maji–Maji rebellion. Their witch-doctors told them that if they bathed in a certain spring, this would turn the enemy bullets into water. Believing this, they massacred the German garrison in Liwale.

The Germans waited until they could get together a sizeable punitive force, then marched on Liwale and hanged one in four of their prisoners on a great tree still standing near the Boma.

Even in 1943 this violence and fear cast a sombre shadow over the place. There were still many people who remembered this time but nobody would talk about it.

The distinction between the Germans and British was still very marked, as Rachel discovered: 'When we were in Liwale we had an open rondavel [a round hut with a grass roof] sitting-room with no windows or mosquito wire. We used to listen to Swahili news on the radio every evening, and the local people would gather round and lean on the window-sills and listen too. It was just at that time when the war was at its height in the Western Desert. First of all, Tobruk held out, then when it fell there was lamentation, and when it was retaken there was great rejoicing. That very night there was a tremendous gale and the big tree on which the Germans had hanged so many of the local people was blown down. This was taken as a marvellous sign. They all came the next day and celebrated with dancing and the beating of drums. Alas, only two days later there was a nasty thud in the night and our flag-pole fell to the ground. It had been eaten right through by white ants; somehow we laughed that one off.'

Sleeping sickness, which was rife in that area, was one of the District Officer's major concerns. It was government policy to persuade the people to concentrate in larger settlements which could be provided with a dispensary in each. But they were naturally reluctant to move, preferring to live in their small family groups, often many miles apart. Visiting them and organizing the move to the settlements meant many months walking on safari. While Peter would hold a *baraza*, explaining to the Chief and elders and dealing with local problems, Rachel operated a modest dispensary for women and children. Little wonder that Robert travelled so far before he was born!

The time for Robert's birth now became the major problem. There was no question of her having him at Liwale where there were no facilities, and it meant a journey to Nairobi. Again, that wretched question of money arose. Wives were not included on the pay-roll and the cost of the journey, not to mention the hospital, was more than they could afford. Peter did the only thing open to him, and something which many another District Officer had had to resort to, both before and after. He took out an elephant licence, shot two elephants, and sent Rachel off with four ivory tusks in lieu of currency. It seems in character to think of the indomitable Rachel setting off with tusks and an empty handbag.

All this time, food had been a major problem. The expected relief had not materialized and the original three months had stretched into a year. First of all, the rains came early and those bridges which had not been picked up were swept away, cutting off road communications for six months. Rachel had some packets of seeds which she planted in suitable ground. Three times she planted them and three times locusts demolished the lot. Running out of seeds, she tried her hand with limes and lemons in a bend of the Liwale river; these flourished so long as she was there to tend them.

Walking on safari, sometimes eighteen to twenty miles a day, visions of roast duckling and green peas used to haunt her. All she had to look forward to was a skinny cuckoo or occasionally buck, which the boys would make into *biltong*, sun-dried lean meat. Some measure of their hunger for meat can be gauged by her words: 'We used to eat the liver almost raw.'

When it is a question of survival, almost any food becomes acceptable: 'We ate rubber leaves; they were not very tasty, but one had to have greenery. Then we would make our own flour out of rice and used soda bicarbonate as a raising agent – it was lucky I had this because it was also good for bathing children's eyes. I had a Kenyan cookery book which also told me that I could use baobab seed as a raising agent. We took the baobab pods, extracted the brownish powder and made rice baps with it, which the boys and ourselves all ate though they always tasted rather musty. I think we all went a little round the bend because I remember both Peter and I wrote books, and I even wrote to the Archbishop of Canterbury, then Doctor William Temple, telling him a thing or two, and, bless his heart, he wrote back.'

Having survived the birth, the next consideration for the young mother was to keep the baby well. How to let a child have the necessary amount of freedom but at the same time watch it relentlessly each minute of its waking day. In most areas of eastern and central Africa, the water had to be boiled and filtered. Every garment had to be ironed on both sides to destroy the mango worm which would burrow into the skin. Mosquitoes were probably the greatest threat. In the early days, quinine was the only preventative and this had side-effects. It is thought that too much quinine gets into the kidneys and brings on the dreaded blackwater fever. Only when prophylactics came on the market could a mother feel any form of safety against the dreaded cerebral malaria, the greatest killer of all. Looking back on Africa, it is as if the air was full of unseen germs, while on the ground there were scorpions and snakes for unwary little feet.

Betty Clay went to the Luangwa Valley with her husband and three children. The Luangwa Valley runs on the eastern side of Northern Rhodesia and Nyasaland beyond which there is beautiful mountainous country. One day her husband left her in charge of a gang making a road, while he did a tour into the mountains. They had made a play-pen for the baby out of pieces of wood cut from the bush – four pegs at the corners and a little fence – and her daughter, aged about five, decided to balance on this fence and try and walk round it. At the corner she slipped and the peg went into her eye. There was blood everywhere and poor Betty could not see what harm had been done. Luckily, there was a dispensary in the village and the medical orderly was summoned and between them they cleared away the blood and the orderly stitched up the wound which, mercifully, was beside the eye and not in it.

A year later the baby was ill with a tummy upset. It became desperately ill, growing weaker and weaker and Betty thought it was going to die. She remembers sitting there and crying, and saying, 'Don't die! Don't die!' And by some miracle the baby recovered. She said: 'I was lucky, because some people's babies did die just because you were too far from medical help and you didn't know what to give it for the best and so I was just terribly lucky.'

Jean Norton had three children born at intervals in Tanganyika. She was thoroughly preoccupied with their health and education. However, once when she went off on safari with her husband leaving her children with friends, she returned to find her seven-month-old son had twenty-five mango worms in his small body, all of which had to be squeezed out.

There is no doubt that the mother who brought her children

out of Africa in those days full of health and wellbeing had something of which to be very proud.

Nearly everyone in Africa has their snake story or their soldier ant story. If they happen to be hunters, they will have their lion or elephant story which will probably be as exaggerated as a huntin', shootin' or fishin' story in England. Nevertheless, this one told me by Veronica Short who was in Northern Rhodesia, was neither exaggerated nor unusual – simply horrifying.

'I had a friend called Ruth who had a small baby. She had a friend to tea with her baby. While they were having tea it started to cry. Nobody took much notice to begin with but the crying became louder and more agonizing. It was only a few weeks old. Eventually, Ruth said to the mother, "Don't you think you ought to go and see what is the matter with him?" The mother said, "Oh, no! He isn't going to be spoilt. It's not feeding time yet, he can just get on with it. I am not going to go out there picking him up every time he cries."

'Ruth, who had had two small children of her own and knew the difference between a baby's cry when it was bored and cross as opposed to when it was distressed, said, "Look, I'm sorry, but I can't bear it, there is something wrong with that baby." She rushed out and found the baby covered with red ants. They had gone up its nose, in its ears, down its throat, because as it cried they had crawled into its mouth. They rushed it to hospital and saved it, but it was a very near thing. It very nearly died of shock, with all the bites. After that you can say I spoilt my children if you like, but every time they cried, I went out and looked at them. I didn't necessarily pick them up or do anything, but I did always go and look to see whether there were ants or not.

'I used to go to the Catholic priests for medicines which the local dispenser didn't have. I remember going to one of the American priests one day because one of the twins had been bitten by red ants. I had always brought them up to try and be kind to animals, saying, "When God made them, he put them into the world for a reason, and he loves them so you must not stamp on worms or cut them in half to see what happens," and this rather tearful little twin said, "Well, if God made red ants, why did they bite me?" I thought that was a bit difficult to answer, so I went and saw Father Ansell and put the question to him. He thought for quite a long time, and then said, "Veronica, the only thing I can suggest that you tell Lydia, is that God put ants on the earth to look at but not to touch." It was not a particularly brilliant answer, but it was the only one that anyone was prepared to come up with, there was no one else who was prepared to cope with the question of why red ants bit.'

And so the anxious mothers watched over their children. A flushed face, a crop of spots, a sudden rash, a cry in the night, could all spell disaster. The doctor is 350 miles away, the husband on safari in some remote village, the nearest neighbour cannot be reached because of floods, there is no telephone, and only some small boy with a forked stick to carry the cry of distress. And yet, time and again, that look of longing, of nostalgia, will creep into the tired eyes. Is it the life that they yearn for, or their lost youth?

5

Witchcraft

On the West Coast it is called ju-ju, in Haiti voodoo, but on the East Coast it is witchcraft. You either believe in it or you don't. I believe in it. I have felt the darkness of the bush, the terror of the victim, the power of the witch-doctor. I have seen black satin faces go the colour of dead cinders. I have watched eyes blank with horror. I have heard the drum of the skinned children, I have watched and heard the dance of death. I have seen, but not handled, the symbolic horn of magic. The intestines, the bones, the liver, the tongue, the heart, flesh cut from a still-living being.

Even the missionaries have failed to wipe out dark superstition. From Basutoland to Uganda it flourished like weeds in soft, warm rain. I have seen a Chief lying prostrate before the Christian God in church on Sundays and sacrificing a goat before his own shrine on Mondays. This was not in the dark ages either, but in the sixties. Life goes on but bigotry dies hard.

Taussi was a happy woman. She had a large comfortable bust, big child-bearing hips, a flashing, white-toothed smile, and she kept her wiry hair under control with a spotlessly clean bandeau. It was not enough that she had four children of her own. From 1922 she had nursed white babies. She loved children and they loved her for her whole aura was reassuring. That her husband was serving in the KAR in Nairobi while she was a white woman's ayah in Dar es Salaam, was immaterial. It has always been the black woman's lot to look after the *shamba* while her husband wanders the earth.

Pat Hodgson was a very young mother in 1947. She had given birth to twins in Dar es Salaam. Like some wonderful ministering angel, Taussi came to work for her. It did not bother her that the children were twins, though, had they been black, they might well have been put into a calabash and thrown to die in the bush.

Taussi spent her first night with these little ones, walking first one and then the other, up and down the room. She taught Pat all she need ever know about rearing babies. Their relationship was one of absolute trust and confidence.

In 1948, the time came for the Hodgsons to go on leave. While they were in England Taussi wrote to them. What she had to say was a surprise to them both. 'I have divorced my husband and am now married to a man named Mohammed. He wants a job as a houseboy. Can he come as a houseboy to you?'

It struck Pat as odd that she should have divorced her nice husband by whom she had had four children. Admittedly, the children were all grown up, the sons in jobs and the two daughters safely married. The Hodgsons had been posted to Tabora, right in the middle of Tanganyika, it was Taussi's own district, close to her people. They wrote back and said yes, they would give Mohammed the job.

Mohammed was an excellent servant, very intelligent; though he was black he had the strangest blue eyes. Was there white blood somewhere in a past generation? At first, Pat did not notice any change in her beloved Taussi. She cared for the children, she was gentle and loving. Perhaps she wasn't as flamboyant or as particular in her dress? She no longer sported the beads which she loved, while her bandeau was not changed daily.

One night the Hodgsons were having drinks on their veranda with their friends, the Bateses. They were to go on to the club for a dance. The excellent Mohammed was dilatory with their ice and toasties and Pat chided him in her friendly way.

Before he had appeared, they had been disturbed by awful screams coming from the direction of the bush.

'That sounds like someone catching it!' said Darrell Bates.

But they soon forgot it. There were always such sounds in the African night. Either a husband was beating his wife, or chasing some woman into the bush. Yells and screams, as well as laughter, were part of the Africa they knew.

Three days later, Darrell Bates walked past the Hodgsons' house for his constitutional. He returned more quickly than he went. In some agitation, he said as he passed them, 'I've found the body of a girl in the bush,' and he hurried on to call the police.

Brian and Pat took their bull terrier and they soon found the body. Pat regretted going, for the girl had been dead three days and to this day she cannot stand the sound of buzzing flies. The local police superintendent was in charge of the case, Brian went off on a long safari, and as far as the Hodgsons were concerned, that was an end of the matter.

One day when Pat was still alone, the police superintendent arrived and said, 'I'm sorry, but I've got to arrest your house-boy, Mohammed – all the evidence points to him. The girl, a prostitute, was last seen with him, and that evening he took her out on his bicycle, and I'm afraid that is that.' Pat had a strange feeling that the policeman was delighted that this was happening to such important white people.

They took Mohammed away, and the kitchen *toto* (small boy) and the *dhobi* (washerman) both got up later in Court and agreed that they had seen Mohammed with this girl on many occasions. The case seemed cut and dried, especially when the police raided Mohammed's room and discovered that he was a powerful witch-doctor. He had all the paraphernalia, the rattle of bones, the cornucopia of revolting ingredients. It also transpired that he had used his blue eyes as strong magic against all his relatives and friends.

Taussi was distraught. She wept and then, terribly ashamed, admitted, 'Yes, I knew he was having this girl in his bedroom. He was living on aphrodisiacs, and she wasn't the only one.' Then, pathetically she added, 'As you probably may have noticed, I have had to sell my clothes and my beads, to keep him in money to buy his aphrodisiacs, you see!'

Though the police also put the *toto* and the *dhobi* into prison to question them for a while, they were eventually let out and the Hodgsons settled down to a happy family life again. In Africa, there is no stigma attached to a spell in prison, in fact, it is often a convenient way to get a square meal and a roof over one's head. Even Taussi became lulled into a sense of security when they bought her new clothes, and slowly the beads, too, reappeared.

Some time elapsed and Brian was promoted to District Commissioner. As for Pat, she was pregnant again. Taussi was blissful. Nursing one of the twins, she exclaimed, 'I'm so glad you are having another baby, because now I can stay with you for a very long time yet.'

Then, out of the blue, tragedy struck. Pat was worried about Brian who had gone out on a hunt for a rogue elephant. Rogue elephants are no joke and, though he would be paid for the tusks, Pat feared for his safety. In Tanganyika there was a saying 'You live from tusk to mouth!', which we have seen was the case for the Bleackleys. But it was not Brian who was in immediate danger. Quite suddenly, one of Taussi's children died from what appeared perfectly normal causes. This was bad enough, but in a week or two another, a son, suddenly dropped down dead at his job, running the ferry in Dar es Salaam.

One can imagine Taussi's sorrow, her sense of loss, and the deep sympathy the pregnant Pat would extend to her. Taussi, who had always been radiantly healthy, now developed a hernia. Pat took her to hospital where the doctor, after examining her, said he would have to operate.

Taussi went the colour of a plum with thick bloom all over it. She was terrified and from that moment she began to lose weight. Her comfortable contours, so beloved by children, began to disappear.

While Brian was still away Mohammed's case came before the circuit judge. The police again appeared and once more removed the *dhobi* and *toto*. This time they admitted in Court that they had been lying; that Mohammed had never been seen with this girl. In fact, he had been washing his shirts on that night and he certainly wasn't washing blood away. The result was that they put the two boys and other witnesses in gaol – for perjury at the preliminary hearing – and let Mohammed out.

Once more Pat was left alone with Taussi. That night when she was thinking of going to bed, Taussi came to her, still with that strange-coloured face, only even worse, and told her that a third member of her family had died. Pat was speechless. She had no words left. Besides which, she was very, very frightened. She was eight months pregnant, Brian was away, and they were miles from anyone they knew.

The next morning Taussi brought in her early morning tea for the last time. Then she just disappeared.

Mercifully for Pat's peace of mind, Brian returned that day with some other people, the *toto* and *dhobi* were let out of prison on lack of evidence and life more or less returned to normal.

But nothing would ever be quite the same without Taussi. The atavistic superstitions had proved too much for her. She was certain that Mohammed had put a spell on her. She had lost three children; she was ill and if she went to hospital she had no hope of survival – and if she didn't go to the hospital, there was still no hope. The police, the office messengers, the district officials, all said they had seen her go straight through her village and out the other side. She was never seen again. Like a sick animal she had gone away to die.

When Pat went to her room, she found all the dresses they had given her. She had gone off in her *buibui* (an all-enveloping black garment) as a shroud.

Pat was terrified for her own children, but Brian said, 'Don't worry. You can't cross the barrier between black and white. No witchcraft can affect us!'

Pat did not believe him. She told me, 'He had to say something, whatever he really thought. I had a horrible six months after that, dreaming about Taussi. I saw her as she was the day before she went off, after I had taken her to the hospital, standing at the bottom of the back door steps with tears running down her face, and I kept saying, "It is nothing! You'll just go to sleep and when you wake up you'll be better, and I'll bring you home and look after you." She just stood in her starched blue dress, safety-pins here, and a white bandeau round her head, and all her beads. How she loved those beads! It was a black, dismal, horrible episode in my life, and yet I have only to mention her name and all the warmth and kindness and comfort that she had for us all, comes over me. She was the most marvellous woman. I really loved her. I've loved about three Africans and she was one of them.'

How many people have said to me over the past year, about the African, 'They are so fearful, aren't they?' And it is true. They are even to this day governed by fear, and yet they are not exceptional for in Cyprus and Greece myrtle is hung over doors to keep away the evil eye. Do not try to photograph the Kenyans as I did the other day. I was in a tea plantation and for a moment I thought I had a wonderful picture of tea-picking, but when I looked up from my camera there was not a picker in sight – only a rather belligerent man coming towards me with a long stick. I fled to the car and also disappeared.

In Northern Rhodesia, Joan Stevens had this to say about the witch-doctors: 'They used such mysterious poisons, they used poisons which no laboratory could analyse at all. They got them from vegetables, I suppose; things they knew themselves. But people were very frightened of their influence and I think that was one of the most important things that the administration did and I know Charles used to feel, when we all left the country, "My poor old Africans. They're going to come back under the influence of witchcraft and there's going to be nobody to help them, nobody to support them in resisting".'

'Did it ever come close to you – from your own experience?' I asked.

'I can remember a curious occasion, though a little bit contrary to what we've been saying. It was my old cook. He announced that he was very ill, that his throat was very bad and he grew worse and worse. You know how they get to look mauve instead of brown when they're ill? We sent him to the doctor and I gave him a note each time saying, "My cook says his throat is hurting," and the doctor always wrote back and said, "There's nothing wrong with his throat. I've examined it and his temperature is normal." But in spite of that he got worse and worse. And then one day he came back and said he was completely cured, and there he was, all shiny and brown again, but I said, "But look, good heavens, what's that you've got? You've got cuts!" And it turned out that he'd been to a witch-doctor who'd told him to slash his throat with a razor blade all over to let the evil out and he'd done that and it had cured him. The mystery is that none of these cuts went septic which you would have thought they would, but they didn't.'

Betty Clay experienced one of the worst aspects of witchcraft, again in Rhodesia.

'It was a native habit which we never did solve but which left us a little nervous – the custom of sprinkling blood on grain to bring a good harvest or rain. We heard that somebody was catching children and killing them for the blood and they were using the skins to make drums that they would beat to call for rain. My husband, as District Commissioner, was in charge of law and order, and he had his men out searching for these men, said to be killers, but it was very difficult to find anybody who would give us any information about them – rather naturally, because people were scared of them. This is a terrible story because there is no ending. I remember very clearly going to a Chief's village – he had invited us up for some ceremonial or other – and we were sitting there in his hut while the dancing went on outside with the usual drumming. Then suddenly there was a long silence and a different drum started up in another part of the village, and the Chief said to us, "Oh, that is the special drum – we hope we will get good rains this year." We were told that this was the drum made of the children's skins, and that they had sprinkled the blood as well. Whether the Chief knew this or not, we'll never know. Those were the sort of things that were going on and there were children who disappeared and were never seen again. There were people called the neck-twisters who went about capturing people and it was quite frightening knowing that this was going on among our people and we were quite unable to help them solve it.

'At one time there was a rumour that they were after our children, and it was the only time we ever locked our doors. We used to lock them at night and then unlock them quickly in the morning so that the servants wouldn't know. We didn't want our people to know we were afraid, because they were so lovable, and they were definitely our friends and sometimes they would come in and sit down and say, "You are our father and our mother, we've got this difficulty, will you please help us solve it?" '

PART TWO

West Africa

6

Pain, Partings and Protocol

The Nigeria to which the colonial wives travelled at the beginning of the century was, to all intents and purposes, a British colony. The Royal Niger Company, thanks to Sir George Goldie, was the foundation of the country which later became known as Nigeria. In 1875, Goldie was asked, or alternatively, persuaded, by his elder brother to take over the shaky financial problems of the small family import-export firm of Holland Jaques and Company, which had interests in the Niger region. Goldie therefore decided to travel if possible across Africa from the Niger to the Nile, and at the same time discover why the company was losing money.

For many centuries slave-trading had been flourishing between Europe and West Africa. West African slave-labour supplied the West Indian sugar plantations, increasing the profits of colonial trade and the merchant fleet. The Niger region was the province, mainly, of the merchants of Liverpool, and it was a disaster for them when in 1807 Parliament declared slavery illegal. Fortunately, at the beginning of the nineteenth century, soap-making became a flourishing industry. It was discovered that, although the principal fat used to make soap was tallow, it was necessary to mix it with vegetable oils, the best of which was palm oil. The Liverpool merchants therefore, wisely turned their attention to shipping this valuable product from Nigeria instead of slaves.

By 20 November 1879, Goldie had formed the United African Company which bought all the assets and rights of other British firms on the river. The new company now started on commercial and political expansion, though in 1879 the latter development was still slow, and any idea of establishing a colony or even British administration was a remote dream.

By 1882 the French had expanded their interests with seventeen floating stations on the lower reaches of the Niger river. At the same time there was a formidable threat to Goldie from African traders in Sierra Leone and Lagos.

At first Goldie tried his old tactics: he tried to bring the French into the United African Company, and bribed the Africans not to trade with them. When this failed there was only one solution, and that was to obtain from the British Crown, by Royal Charter, a commercial monopoly in the region. He immediately sent for his company's lawyer and discussed the legal problems of political and commercial power.

In March 1883, France showed further expansionist ambitions in Africa and sent a delegate to make treaties throughout the lower Niger. Neither Goldie nor the British government could afford to ignore this severe threat, and for the next three years Goldie did his utmost to convince the Foreign Office, the Colonial Office, Mr Gladstone and his government of the necessity of granting a charter to the United African Company. In 1886 he succeeded and the Royal Niger Company was founded. The idea of government control under a High Commissioner had been rejected and Goldie now held the reins of civil and commercial administration.

In July 1894 Captain Frederick Lugard made his appearance. His assignment was to lead a treaty-making expedition to all the towns in Borgu, in the north-western part of the region and to protect them from French invasion from the west. In Lugard, Goldie had deliberately chosen a man of iron will. The situation was grave, for the French had just formed the country of Dahomey, making a wedge between Nigeria and the Gold Coast. The French newspapers announced the departure of no less than three 'exploring missions' for the land surrounding Dahomey and, in 1898, with the middle of the Niger undefended against the French, England was brought to the brink of an Anglo–French war.

During this period, Goldie was unjustly blamed for lack of initiative and effective administration, and the Company lost its charter. A Miss Flora Shaw, later to become Lugard's wife, was in the meantime writing as *The Times* correspondent on colonial affairs, and presenting the Company in a favourable light. Another of the Company's greatest champions was the widely read author and intrepid traveller Mary Kingsley, who tried to help Goldie since she believed that the Niger Company had ruled and expanded the territory without bloodshed. Other reporters lauded Goldie for abolishing slave-trading, and the Company appeared to be, once more, enjoying public favour.

However, in spite of this support for Goldie, the Prime Minister, Lord Salisbury, wished to put the Niger in the charge of the Colonial Office under Joseph Chamberlain. Both the French and Germans were spending money on the training of African troops and the Niger Company was hopelessly outnumbered in its struggle to keep the territory. The West African Frontier Force had been founded by Joseph Chamberlain in 1897 and now Lugard was asked to take command.

In April, Lugard's forces marched through Bornu and though flags were defiantly flown both by the French and English, no shot was fired. By June 1898, a convention between the English and the French decided the territorial disputes in both the Gold Coast and Nigeria. The result was a triumph for Chamberlain.

The next step was the transfer of administration from the Niger Company to the Crown. It was taken for granted by the British government that Goldie would become Governor of the new colony, but surprisingly he refused the offer. Lugard was the next choice.

On 1 January 1900, in Lokoja, a ceremony took place of a kind which was to be repeated in later years throughout Africa. Uniformed Africans of the Niger Company's Constabulary and Frontier Force with a few British officers in full-dress uniform, among them Frederick Lugard – the new High Commissioner for Nigeria – watched as the Niger Company's flag was hauled down and the Union Jack rose in its place. Sixty years later the colonial wives accompanying their husbands were to watch a similar ceremony, as the Nigerian flag rose dizzily in the breeze passing the British flag on its way down. Only in the North, the Alhaji the Hon. Sir Ahmadu Bello, KBE Sardauna of Sokoto,

Premier of Northern Nigeria, ordered that the two flags should fly side by side. 'The British,' he announced, 'have always been our friends. Let this be shown.' And so the two flags fluttered side by side bringing many a tear to the colonial women who had devoted their lives and their husbands to this great country.

To make administration possible, Lugard began by dividing the country into three major provinces: the Middle Niger to include the country north and west of the Niger, Ilorin and Bida; the Benue, covering the north and south of the Benue river to include Muri and Buachi; and Kano, which included some of the surrounding country and two military provinces, Bornu and Bergu. Long before this monumental assignment, he had agreed with Goldie that a country of this size and diverse people must be ruled 'indirectly', and that this aim must be slowly but surely to give the Emirs and Chiefs power over their own people but under British suzerainty.

The first colonial wife of any note was Flora Shaw who married Lugard in 1902. She was beautiful, remarkably intelligent, by that time not only being Colonial Editor of *The Times* and a leading authority on the Empire, but also numbering among her great friends Cecil Rhodes, Joseph Chamberlain and many other notable men. To all intents and purposes she was the ideal wife for the man who was to be one of, if not the greatest, administrators of the time. However, after one visit to the Nigeria which she herself had named, her health broke down, and she was unable to return. Those were the days when malaria was treated by quinine and not by drugs. There were no inoculations against yellow fever, or the dreaded blackwater fever. Around Lagos, the lagoons and river were full of floating gin bottles taken as a cure or a preventative by the pale men who had hoped to make their fortunes. The whole coast line was known justifiably as 'White Man's Grave' and it was about this time that young John Holt found himself the only survivor of the import–export business to which he eventually gave his name. No wonder then that Flora, no longer in the first flush of youth and with her blonde hair and fair skin, could not tolerate the taxing climate.

Flora and Lugard were deeply devoted to each other and she studied Nigeria from her home in London. She also wrote an impressive book about its historic past called *A Tropical*

Dependency. Lugard, writing to her every day – even when on a hard tour – turned to her for advice on his work and career. There is no doubt from these letters that their feeling for each other was deep and lasting, and though they were separated for months on end, she can be counted as one of the most valued colonial wives.

Twelve years later another remarkable woman came to live in Nigeria, Olive MacLeod. She had been engaged to the explorer Boyd Alexander who was killed by Furians at Ilarné in April 1910. Boyd had already made an expedition through Nigeria by boat to the Nile in 1904. In 1910 he met and fell in love with Olive. When he proposed to her, she did not accept him straight-away – she needed time to think. How much her hesitation contributed to his determination to return to Africa which had already claimed the lives of his brother Claud and his friend, Ben Gosling, is hard to say. His brother Herbert claims that the fire that had previously driven him was lacking, but when Olive changed her mind at the last moment it was too late to turn back.

It is not difficult, though, to imagine Olive's feelings when the news of Boyd's murder reached her. If she had accepted his proposal it was possible that he would not have gone. Her sister, Dame Flora MacLeod, thought that being the extraordinarily courageous young woman she was she would normally, after hearing the news, have taken a packet of sandwiches and gone for a long walk, from which she would have returned to face the world, completely mistress of herself. She blamed the influence Olive's great friend, Violet Asquith, had over her. Violet had suffered a similar ambivalent relationship with Lord Archie Gordon, who had been killed in a car accident. Violet dressed herself in widow's weeds, and when Olive was in a similar situation she persuaded her that she, too, was widowed. For a time there was a hysterical atmosphere, until Olive developed the idea of taking a cross to Boyd's grave in Maidugari. Her father, who adored her, said that he would make the journey possible, and Amaury Talbot, who had gone with Boyd on the first expedition as far as Maidugari, offered to accompany her with his wife.

Overnight Olive became headline news. She was to travel for six months through 3,700 miles of Africa, in parts of the country never before traversed by a white woman. Though her death was reported constantly by the press, she, in fact, had no trouble with the Africans. She had only to let down her beautiful long hair before the fiercest African for him to be lost in wonder, and once this trick was discovered it was used whenever necessary.

Having delivered the cross and arranged for the grave to be cared for, Olive returned in slow stages. At Zungeru she met and was entertained by the Resident, Charles Lindsay Temple, who had the reputation of being a misogynist. Whether this was true or not, Olive impressed the Resident and he must also have impressed her, for two years later they were married. Socially and intellectually they were ideally suited. Both wrote books on Northern Nigeria, while Charles, a geologist and linguist, was also an artist. One can assume that but for Olive's determination, another promising partnership might have gone astray, but this time there was no indecision, no hesitation. When she heard that he was on leave in 1912, she wrote and asked him to dinner at her home. As he had no intention of allowing a woman into his life, and possibly because he was trying to forget her, he did not answer the letter. Olive liked to believe hers had gone astray and wrote a second letter, repeating her invitation. On receiving it, Charles Temple decided, in the words of Dame Flora MacLeod, that this 'was Kismet', and accepted. A few days after the dinner they were engaged, and in three weeks they married. Olive lived for and through her husband until he died in Granada, whither they had retired in 1929.

Though Olive threw all her considerable energies into her life with Charles Temple in Nigeria, it was not roses all the way. When she died she was crippled with arthritis as a result of the Nigerian climate. She learnt the local dialects, she wrote slim volumes on native laws and customs. No man could have married a more ideal wife.

It is no disrespect to Charles Temple's memory to say that she never forgot Boyd. A bronze head by Kathleen Scott was with her until she died, and when Charles died she rented the Alexander home, Swift's Place, for two or three years during the summer for her holidays.

When I visited Eleanor Stephenson she wept whenever she mentioned the long separations from her children though now they are over and the children grown up. But it was still considered, before the last war, that it was more important to be with one's husband. As Nancy Robertson said: 'I left the children with my mother and their nanny. You see in those days we didn't have all the psychologists saying it was absolutely necessary for the children to be with their mother during the first three or four years of their lives, because the emphasis then, when I was young, was on the fact that your husband was alone and that you should go and be with him – and I felt so, too. We were very lucky, in that my mother was a widow and we had a marvellous nanny and a nursery which was always in the same place. Nowadays I don't know what people do! Perhaps very few people have families because there is probably not the accommodation. Of course, the nannies are not available, or if they are you couldn't afford them.'

In 1955 Sir James Robertson became the last Governor-General of Nigeria. Arriving there from her experiences in the Sudan and Cairo, Nancy found it extraordinary. 'Mainly because one was so detached, not having been in the territory before, as well as being detached from what I call real life. People were always on their best behaviour, and we thought that the high-ups – the British – were very much more pompous than anyone we had had in our part of the world; but that was possibly because we had annual leave from the Sudan which gave one a sense of proportion. In Nigeria, everyone was very conscious of rank, and though everybody was very kind to us and I enjoyed it enormously, I always had the feeling that they were going to put on a hat to come and see me! I made it quite clear, right from the beginning, that I really couldn't go out for a drink or just a cup of coffee with the Rolls and a driver. I did achieve a little car of my own, but even then they wouldn't let me go through the markets without a driver – a police driver. I don't think the British would have noticed if there hadn't been one, but it was difficult. There were some small children we used to take over to the beach on Sundays and I was coming back with two of them one day plus the police guard. At some point he held up the traffic and the little things said to me, "Do you know why they do that?" I said, "Well, I don't really know. I suppose it's to save us from being run over." "Oh, no!" they said. "You see we are the government."

Though Nancy did not feel that she could get close to the

Nigerians, she did find it a great refreshment to be with liberated women. In the south, the women were acquiring jobs of public importance. They were no longer the market traders they had been over the centuries, but were lawyers, doctors and consultants of all kinds.

Of course, there was always the battle against the climate, the exaggerated amount of entertaining, the long hours and the lack of sleep. Nancy found it exhausting.

'You had to do so much that I considered a waste of time, but then, on the other hand, it was an enormous privilege because we had so many people who came and stayed and though they, too, found it pretty exhausting, there was usually a time between tea and getting ready for dinner, when the lights were low, the dusk had come, and we used to sit on the veranda and have a drink. Having a drink used to loosen their tongues and they would talk away, which I found fascinating.

'We were in Lagos during Suez and it was awful because the poor British intelligence officer there was given no guidance whatsoever as to what was happening. I was ticked off because I was heard to say to someone that I was absolutely horrified to think that we had done this without consultation with our American allies. Afterwards, we had the Admiral who had been in the Mediterranean when it happened and he had been extremely friendly, with absolute cooperation with his bit of the American Fleet. When he was going to Suez, he passed the Americans and they signalled "Where are you off to?" and he had to tell his friend a lie. We also had Eden's private secretary to stay and he said he didn't resign because he thought it was unkind. It was moments like that, in the dusk, when they let their hair down – there was nobody about and they just talked. We even had Dag Hammarskjöld. I enjoyed that very much. I wouldn't have missed it for anything. It was made so much easier for us because we'd come from a country where the colour bar was a difficulty, because the Sudanese protected their women, like the Nigerian North. We were very astounded to hear that in the North the administrative British never had an invitation to dinner or tea or anything in the Africans' houses.'

In the days before Independence there was, on the whole, a very special relationship between the mistress of the house and her servants. She was not only dependent on them for her comforts, but she was frequently alone with them as her sole companions. Undoubtedly, if the mistress of the house was kind, the servants reciprocated. Nancy Robertson in Lagos was very impressed with her cook: 'He was much more educated than the rest of our staff though he didn't have any sort of certificate. He was distressed when he was leaving because he was a Bini [from Benin] and most of the servants in Lagos were Ibos. I don't know how I got on to it but I found that a lot of people were getting scholarships to the UK for things like bricklaying, and then I found it was possible to have a scholarship for cookery though a school certificate was necessary. Of course my cook hadn't got one. Then Westminster School for Cookery said they'd take him on because of his practical experience. He came over here, and, nothing daunted, he immediately rang Buckingham Palace and said he would like to see the kitchens. Page, a controller, who had been out with the Queen to Nigeria in 1956 looking after the luggage and everything like that and who drank bottles and bottles of gin and beer took him all over the palace and gave him tea in his room. Several years after, we were having lunch at Holyrood House when a voice said in my ear, "And how is Olu?" It was Page, helping out with the waiting. Olu went right up the ladder, ending up as catering manager of that large hotel in Kano doing enormous cocktail and dinner parties outside the hotel as well as in it.'

Kathleen McCall remembered that she received very good advice when she married Johnnie.

'Before I left for Nigeria, my mother who had lived in India had given me a long lecture on the importance of keeping one's husband's servants, if they were any good at all. Too many wives tried to change everything and certainly the servants themselves resented the addition to the family. Fortunately for me, I kept Campbell, who had come to Johnnie when he was eight, until we left when he was thirty-two. Theophilus, the cook, stayed twelve years, and these two faithful boys kept me from being too lonely at the beginning. I never had children so was not torn by loyalties and in a strange and protective way, Campbell had a way of getting rid of the blues. Eventually, too, there was Campbell's wife. Johnnie bought her for him for sixty pounds but she was Campbell's choice, and was an Ibo like him. She was called

Mabel after my sister-in-law, and they eventually had five children all named after some member of our family. Not only were they company and a source of interest, but one felt responsible for them – and they took some looking after! For instance, we might be on tour when Mabel's hour to deliver a child had come and we might be miles from a hospital or any form of civilization. I remember one time when we were sixty miles from a doctor! We bundled her into a lorry and I kept asking Campbell whether he felt up to delivering a baby, to which he replied with his usual aplomb, "We'll manage, madam!" As it happened, we just made it!'

Serving in the North, Gilbert Stephenson's wife, Eleanor, had Muslim servants whom she kept for many years. She was never robbed though in the years immediately before and after the last war, nothing was kept under lock and key. I once saw a steward run after his master with a silver cigarette case just as he was disappearing out of the front gate on his way to the airport to leave the country finally. The steward was like all his kind – scrupulously honest, and this was even more remarkable in a country where an empty tin is an untold treasure.

Protocol was often a headache for the new wife. It was extraordinary to observe how strictly the British DO stuck to it, even in the 'bush' where one might think he could let his khaki shirt flap a bit at the neck! Kathleen McCall arrived in Nigeria in 1951 where her husband was a Senior District Officer in Benin Province. She says that she was so ignorant that rank meant nothing to her, and she had to learn about it the hard way.

'The Resident's wife was a fearsome woman, and though I was twenty-eight, I felt like a little girl in her presence. In those days life in the Residency was very formal and one always changed for dinner even if there were riots all around one. There was one famous Resident and his wife who had their house set on fire while they were having dinner; before the flames reached the dining-room he had the table taken out onto the lawn and continued with his meal as if nothing was happening.

'With such a record of true British phlegm, I felt that I was walking a tightrope during those first few weeks. I remember two mistakes I made with the Resident's wife. I had been given a small cocker spaniel on arrival and to my horror it jumped up and covered her white dress with red laterite. On the other occasion, I was properly put in my place by this lady when I was asked to play the piano after one of their dinner parties. I had taken my LRAM and had been teaching music at St Leonard's. Rather pleased to be asked to show off, I rose to my feet to oblige, when the Resident's wife hissed in my ear, "The Resident plays first!" I collapsed back into my seat with embarrassment.'

Unlike the English, the African women had not learnt their protocol and Kathleen found that they never knew when to bring a visit to an end.

'I became adept at getting rid of guests who had out-stayed their welcome. I used to spring to my feet and say, "How very kind of you to come and we do hope you will come again, but now we have to go and see so-and-so, but perhaps on such-and-such a date you will come again?" with which they rose easily to their feet, and nobody ever took offence.

'A visit was always a great occasion for dressing-up, and it was wonderful to see the Africans on the veranda with their beautiful head-dresses, their sticks covered with beads of different colours, the Chiefs sitting on chairs while the smaller fry squatted on the ground.'

If one was a woman who enjoyed the outdoor life, had the ability to get to know the people of the country, and was interested in wildlife, then it was the greatest pleasure to accompany one's husband on his frequent excursions into the bush. Though musical and with a skin like magnolia it was one of the things Kathleen McCall enjoyed most of all. 'I felt I was seeing the real Africa. Off we went with our five-ton lorry going ahead, our staff, our hip-bath, our kerosene fridge, our camp beds, and so on. I suppose we usually went about fifty or sixty miles into the bush where there might be riots in progress or there might not! We would arrive at a rest house which had corrugated roofs, mud walls and a thunder-box for a loo which the local prisoners cleared every morning. On arrival, the first things the boys did was to put up an enormously long bamboo pole, at least twenty feet high, stick the aerial on the top, and place the master's wireless on the veranda – Johnnie's wireless was like our life-line to the outside world. We generally tried to arrive about lunchtime after which Johnnie went off to work. In the evening, the local Chief would come with his dancers and drummers and presents and pay a courtesy call. Johnnie would then make a little speech before they returned to their village.

'By this time the boys had put up the campbeds, the mosquito nets, and got my hip-bath ready. We had about two inches of hot water heated in a four-gallon kerosene tin on a charcoal fire, a little cold water was added and I had my bath. Johnnie then had his in the same water, after which, adding plenty of Dettol, I washed my smalls. I wore a long cotton dress, a shirt right up to my neck and mosquito boots.

'After supper there was nothing to do but listen to the wireless, and, of course, by that time we were pretty sleepy, also the mosquitoes seemed able to penetrate every inch of one's clothing so that it was a relief to go to bed early under the net. I used to lie listening to the sounds of the bush which grew so much nearer at night. I was always thankful when the Aladdin lights were extinguished because of the strange life they attracted.

'On the second day we returned the Chief's visit. If he was old-fashioned, the wives were kept apart and I would visit them alone. Then we would give the Chief our gift of gin or whisky.

'If there was nothing special for me to visit such as a hospital or school, there was nothing for it but to wait at the rest house while Johnnie was out listening to cases – or doing one of the innumerable jobs DOs are supposed to do.

'It was this interminable waiting for one's husband which so many of the Colonial Service wives found most trying. Though the climate of Eastern Nigeria is so ennervating that one has no energy at all, it does not dispel the feeling of loneliness. One waited! One listened to the wireless, one read, and if the sweat on one's hands allowed, one sewed. I tried knitting with a tin of talcum powder beside me with which I anointed my hands from time to time, but I soon had to give that up. However, personally, I was never lonely, though I did understand those who were. I loved watching the birds, and though they never sang, they were very beautiful. I'll never forget the little irridescent humming-birds which shimmered in front of the hibiscus, nor the pygmy kingfishers which darted down to sip the dew on the grass. Above all other sounds, there was always the note of some bird high up in the trees, rather like the "fever" bird of India

which went on and on all day. I never saw one, but was told that
it was some type of dove. There were no Europeans in the bush
except the occasional Catholic Father. Sometimes we were near
a convent, and then I would visit the Sisters who were, in my
opinion, an example of some of the finest women in Africa.'

After a dose of glandular fever, Kathleen MacCall remained
comparatively well, though her tours became shorter and
shorter. Towards the end of their service Johnnie would look at
her in the mirror and say, 'It's time you went home,' so that for
several years her tours were no more than eight months.

Eleanor Stephenson in the North was not so lucky: 'At one time
I became too ill to be moved at all. At three o'clock in the
morning, my dog came into the bedroom and put his head up
and just howled, so Gilbert got up and took my temperature. It
was 105°. He called a Sister Benedicta who served as the local
doctor. She examined me and at the same time the tears ran
down her cheeks – there was nothing she could do to save my
life.

'We had a very big compound at this time, running into a
valley. There were masses of monkeys in this compound and
they were always scratching up the earth. All I could think was
that they would have to bury me in this compound, since there
was no cemetery anywhere near, and that the monkeys would
scratch me up again. I didn't want to die but at the same time I
was too ill to care. Well, amazing as it may seem, I recovered.
Soon afterwards, Gilbert was made Resident and sent to
Makurdi on the Benue river. Sister Benedicta wanted me to stay
with her and not go immediately with Gilbert. However, still
very weak, I went and saw the English doctor who took me off all
medicines including injections of vitamin B to help my balding
head. I still felt so ill that when the doctor went on tour, Gilbert
called in a Zulu doctor, married to an English wife. After
examining me he told me that he could not treat me at home and
that I must go to hospital straightaway. There was no hospital
anywhere near, and the only means of getting out of Makurdi
was by plane on the following Tuesday (it was Friday when the
doctor told me I must be hospitalized). Gilbert got the car and
we drove straight to Jos, a lovely place which had the nearest
hospital, but was hundreds of miles from Makurdi. Once I was

installed in the hospital, the doctor took masses of tests, including X-rays. The next day he came into me and said, "When did you have pleurisy?" I replied that I had never had it. He said, "There is a large patch on your left lung and what's more – you've also had typhoid." I said, "No! I've never had typhoid." "Yes, you have," he answered. "There's the remains of typhoid in your blood. What's more, you've had malaria, amoebic dysentery, as well." He looked after me for some weeks and then cut off what remained of my hair, hoping that it would grow stronger – but it's never recovered from that illness. It took me two years to get over all these infections and I suppose I should have gone straight home – but, of course, I couldn't bear to leave Gilbert.'

To keep her mind off her sadness when the children had to go to school in England, Eleanor started a baby clinic. The Chief allowed her to have a room next to the native dispensary. At this time the women were very backward and everything had to be extremely simple. She burnt numbers onto pieces of sticks and handed each mother a number, one to a hundred, and made them sit and await their turn. Even the Chief's wife was made to wait her turn. The first day one hundred and fifty-nine women turned up with their babies. To publicize this venture she had taped a baby crying and sent it round the town and villages. The main trouble was constipation among the young mothers which was easily dealt with. She taught them to wash their babies and to wean them instead of continuing to feed them until they were running around. The response to this clinic was so good that a properly trained nurse was eventually installed and it is running to this day.

Undoubtedly, the colonial wife often longed to be in England. She thought 'Oh, to be just stepping through the swing doors at Harrods, or dining at the Savoy – or gossiping with my old friends on the telephone.' But the chances are that once in England she would long for Nigeria. She would miss the friendliness of its women among whom she had made long and lasting friends. She would remember the exotic blushing hibiscus which she picked early in the morning, put in the fridge until evening and placed in a bowl on the table where she watched it blush slowly from the palest pink until the end of dinner when it would be crimson and dead. She would remember the trees flowering scarlet at their very tops against the sun. She would remember the smell of wood smoke, and the sound of distant drums, the sigh of a scythe, and the bright little cordon bleus flitting down to collect the grass seed.

Kathleen McCall will think nostalgically of Warri, where she had a beautiful Residency and Johnnie was in charge of a thousand square miles. As it was Delta Province, they had a launch with a captain and crew. They did a lot of touring, travelling among mangrove swamps.

'It was fascinating, watching all the canoes on the delta in our beautiful launch. We had a bedroom – a little saloon with a table and a lovely top deck. When one was steaming down the river it was cool because one got the breeze, but when one tied up for the night in some remote headquarters where Johnnie probably had to hear appeals from the DO's court, it was very, very hot. There were the mangroves growing their extraordinary roots in the water, and the ubiquitous mosquito, and the snakes! Oh, the mosquitoes! We had a Flit spray and one never stopped pumping it; the West African mosquito must be the most famous in the world!'

In 1960 British rule came to an end.

'We had two dogs by this time and the dogs used to howl when the bugler blew each evening as the flag came down – this became a kind of ritual. When it finally came down, the Governor had ordered that there should be no ceremony – I think this was the most moving moment of my life, for all the Europeans came and shook hands with us silently and then went away.'

Sitting in their houses in England there is a deep feeling of nostalgia for Africa, and the Nigeria the colonial wives knew. They all say as if in unison:

'Looking back, it was a great life and I miss the African gaiety. Africa took a great deal out of you – but at the same time it gave it back.'

I had a happy day with Aileen Chubb in Dorset, among the photographs of her children and grandchildren. She was a happy person and the day was punctuated with gusts of laughter. When we went to lunch at her golf club everyone stopped at our table to greet her. She must have been much loved and very popular. I felt I had lost a friend when I was told by her son-in-law that she had died suddenly. It is best for her to tell her own story:

'I went out to Nigeria to get married in 1932. On the journey out I was very much teased by the crew, and one day the Captain said to me, "Do you mind if we make your wedding cake for you?" and I was taken down to see the cook who was preparing it all, which I thought was extremely nice of them. We were married in a tiny little place in Port Harcourt. It was frightfully hot, and the man who married us was called Cook and was a woman-hater.

'Now the words of the marriage service were nothing like our service; I think I was married according to native law and custom as far as I can make out. He made my husband say certain words, then still looking down, he said:

' "Now tell her to say it." Of course, my husband said I hadn't a clue what to say, to which he replied, "Then she had better say it after me." And I said these funny words. Then there was a pause and my husband said, "What about the ring?" and Mr Cook said, "Oh! You can put that on now if you like." The best man handed over the ring and it was put on, and I had to literally pinch myself to realize that I was really married. It was all so fantastic. Then there was another long pause, and my husband said, "Is that all?" "That will be five shillings," said Mr Cook, and that was the end of the ceremony.

'After that it became more like a wedding; they had a lovely reception for us at the Residency, and all was well.

'About eight months later I came home and had a very bad miscarriage, followed immediately by appendicitis. And then we finally went back to Calabar. Two or three months after we went there, my husband came in one evening and said, "You'll be interested to hear we were married today!"

'I didn't believe him! Months later! He told me that he had found a file in the office with "removal of doubts" on the cover, and so he opened it and saw to his amazement our marriage. We weren't married at all actually. John Cook had no right to do it. The Governor had put it right with the stroke of a pen! So I don't know to this day whether I was married or not. Are all my little ones bastards? No longer little ones either!

'I expect you'd like to know my impressions on the way out.

My first was of Sierra Leone where, at Freetown, they did diving for pennies. It got to be sixpences later. There was one called Johnnie who wore nothing at all except a collar, tie and bowler hat! He did take his bowler hat off when he dived! Lovely to see when you've never been out of England before.

'Then, of course, we had to wear those double-*terais*. And if you so much as put your head outside into the sun people grabbed you back again. *Must have your hat on!* The men sometimes had fly-whisks. My husband, prior to going out, asked why they had to wear hats. They couldn't give him a proper answer. So he decided he wasn't going to bother and went all over the place without a hat. He got a letter from the government saying that if he became ill from not wearing a hat he'd have to go back and that would be the end of his career.

'We were in Bende, my husband's favourite place. He built a house for me there when it was known I was coming out. It was big, it had very large semi-circular verandas at both ends, a dining-room, big bedroom, spare room – everything. All for the vast sum of £50! I suppose it was prison labour. I was told by somebody who was out there not long ago that the house is still standing, and being used by an African. It was built of bamboo and palm leaves. Always known as the "love nest" by everybody.

'I was the only white woman in Bende and at dinner parties it was very awkward when it came to the time when ladies had to retire and the men drank their port. I used to sit in the bedroom, forgotten by everyone, even my husband, not knowing what to do, whether to go back, stay in the bedroom or what?

'Once we were having a meal with a man in education, and the time came for me to retire. It was one of those houses on stilts, veranda all round – I didn't know where to go and find the loo, and finally I found a bedroom which had a bush lamp on the dressing-table. There was a door leading out of that so I thought I'd try it. Suddenly two chimpanzees came straight at me with chains on their feet. I was so scared I screamed. They were most aggressive and I was terrified. Apparently this was a joke of our host. Any woman that came, he would wait for her scream! Of course, my husband was furious. There's no doubt whatever that if I had been pregnant I might easily have lost my child.

'Of course, one of my first impressions was being waited on at table by an African with bare feet – that impressed me at first!

'I used to get malaria every single tour I went out until they brought in paludrin during the war. There were so many things people got in those days, yellow fever, blackwater fever, all sorts of ghastly things.

'I made friends with an African matron of the prison at Benbe, and she often came to see me. I was wanting to get rid of a lace evening dress, I gave it to her and she was overjoyed. I loved the way if you gave them anything or said anything to please them they would jump up and down and clap their hands in the most charming way. She was so pleased with the dress that a few days later we saw her playing tennis in it. A long black evening dress!

'The other person I came into real contact with was our cook's wife in Enugu at the time when my husband was Secretary of the Eastern Province. Cook was always cheerful, thank goodness, but one day he came for his daily orders with a very long face. In his pidgin English he told me he wanted to get rid of his wife because "she was no fit to have children". His brother – and, as you know, anybody who lived in their own country was their brother, not necessarily blood brother – had arrived and was prepared to take the old wife back and bring him a new one. But he wanted to borrow £3 to buy the new wife. I knew my husband hated me ringing the office but I thought I couldn't give him £3 without asking. So I rang my husband and got the usual "Yes". Then the poor wretched woman, called Virginia, was brought from her country and they sat her on a packing-case in the middle of the compound for me to inspect. Poor soul, she didn't know anybody! She produced however!

'I was sitting by myself one evening when there was the most appalling explosion outside the compound. I called for the steward, and he said it was cook firing his gun. I asked whatever for. "What's he shot?" The steward explained he'd got his first piccan – child. So I sent for cook and said, "When you have your second piccan, will you please come and tell me first and then shoot your gun, because you pretty well shot me out of my chair." '

'I had one terrible fright when my husband had malaria. He was very fond of cats and we had two kittens at this time, and one evening he had them on the bed and I was sitting by him doing needlework. Finally the boy came in and put the mosquito net down, and my husband dropped off, and the boy took the kittens away. I got into bed, and when I was half asleep I thought, "Oh, those wretched kittens are back on the bed!" We had two beds together and one mosquito net over it. The sheet had been pulled off me and I pulled it up – then I woke properly and on my bare thigh was a black hand! I was absolutely terrified. I saw this black man the other side of the net, a black hand on my thigh! I shot right over my husband, but lost my voice. I couldn't speak! I could only grunt! My husband woke up at once and said, "What's the matter, darling?" He looked up, thinking it might be a snake fallen onto the net. At last I managed to say, "There's a man over there." And my husband saw him getting out of the window. He was out of bed like a shot with his revolver, and went and had a shot. Actually there was a very deep gully in front of that particular part of the house, and the man was not seen again. It frightened me so much I had to be sent home in the end. You see, before I was married I had been what is now called "mugged". I had been collared round the neck at home while out in the dark by myself, when I was about twenty. So I was awfully frightened of the dark anyway. We came to the conclusion afterwards that my husband had had to let out a couple of prisoners before there was time for them to catch a wagon into their own country, and they were wandering round, and they had also been building a patio outside our house, and I think they were after the treasury keys which my husband kept under his pillow. He was just fumbling about, but that was no comfort to me I can tell you!

'It always amused me so much when the prisoners came to do one's compound; there they were with their machetes, which they sharpen like razor blades. There were the prisoners cutting the grass with these machetes and the man in charge of them just had a truncheon. That always intrigued me very much! There was one occasion when things went wrong in Lagos. The prisoners were clearing some ditches and two prisoners whose families were against one another, were working together, and got into a furious conversation, and one just swiped the other's head off! Whereupon all the prisoners and the warder legged it back to the prison as fast as they could go. That's the only occasion I ever heard of those machetes being used to kill.'

Miscarriages appear to be so common among the colonial wives that one begins to take them for granted. However, Aileen who went through her statutory number told me this story with her mixture of pathos and humour.

'We were trekking by car and I had started a child. We were in a rest house and one day were having our siesta when the court messenger arrived with the mail from England. I sat up quickly because I heard his bicycle bell as I was longing for news from home, and I started to miscarry on the spot. We were miles away in the bush. It was absolutely ghastly! I know my husband said, "Have you got any sanitary towels?" and I said, "Yes", and he took them out – he was quite marvellous. He then said, "You do realize I've got to go and fetch the doctor, and I've got to leave you." The steward was excellent and kept an eye on me. I felt anything but well, I must say! Anyway, the doctor was in some other part of the division, so my husband left a message with his wife, asking him to come out to us as soon as possible. I don't know what happened but they missed one another and the doctor arrived before my husband. The doctor said I had to go back into the station and he went back to make preparations.

'My husband tried to get me into the car, but every time I put my foot on the floor I fainted. At last he said to me, "Look here, you can faint as much as you like in the car, but for heaven's sake, come to the car." With the aid of the boy I got into the car and eventually got back, and everything was ready for me. By this time I had lost my baby. There were only three white families there, the judge's, the doctor's and us. The doctor had got the bed ready for me and to bed I went. His wife was being as kind as she knew how and asked me what I wanted. The judge's wife was a beautiful woman, but totally inept. She would come in to me and say, "Would you mend this gown for me?" Then she would lie in a long chair while I did the mending. But she was so sweet. However, she was sent in to see the doctor's wife, and she went to the main room where the men were all sitting down. Do you remember those chairs with the hole in, the PWD provided, to put your whisky in? Well, she came back to me nearly hysterical with laughter. And she set us off. Three men were sitting there with their whisky and sodas making sanitary towels! The doctor had brought gauze and lint – that sort of thing. Now where in the world could that happen? And they were being thoroughly solemn, talking about all kinds of things . . .'

Aileen Chubb's husband retired from the administrative service in 1951, spent three years in England and then went back as bursar at the University of Ibadan, where he remained from 1954 to 1963. The Queen's visit in 1956 was one of the great occasions of Aileen's life.

'We formed a committee with the Chancellor, another lecturer, and the catering officer who was an African, and we had to plan lunch. I think I'm right in saying the lunch was for about 180 people. Anyway, I took the notes. Then we had a frightful time because the catering officer actually wept when we said we were not having Worcester or tomato sauce bottles on the table. He actually wept because he thought it was the height of politeness. And the Chancellor sent for me the next day and he said, "Mr So-and-so was very upset at your meeting the other day." "What about?" I asked. "Well, you mustn't upset him, you know," said the Chancellor. I said, "Well, look here, do you really want me to put Worcester and tomato sauce bottles on the table when the Queen comes?" "Oh, no!" he said. "For goodness sake!"

'But it was a wonderful day, and I think because of our service in Nigeria, we were one of the few presented. I found myself completely wrapped up in the preparations. I had two dressing-rooms to do. One where the Queen was actually going to speak, the other in the principal's house, and I had a car given me with a special sticker on it because of security.

'I had to go to the Governor of the West to find out what they were giving for dinner so we didn't repeat anything. Then I learned an awful lot which I was able to take back to the university. The Queen doesn't like arms to her chairs when she is feeding. Did you know that? We had two lovely carved armchairs, which had to be removed. And she likes smaller knives and forks, doesn't like eating with large ones. All kinds of things we learned.

'Anyway, we had salad at one point and we made the mayonnaise. And one of the stewards made the mistake of passing the mayonnaise at the time we were having the sweet, instead of cream. And do you know, that was all over Nigeria in a second! We had given mayonnaise rather than cream! Well, of course we hadn't! Naturally!

'We'd taken two of the best stewards and really trained them, and while we were being presented at the end of the colonnade, I saw two men dressed in white uniforms and I said to my husband, "Who are they?" The Queen had brought her own people to serve her, so ours were taken away, of course.

'And just as she was coming – it was a very long drive to the university from Lagos – just as the car was coming up and my husband was making a signal for the flag to be loosened, some-body shot past him and said, "Where's the Queen's water?" We knew nothing about it, but she had all her water flown out from home.

'The whole thing went awfully well. We gave a certificate to all the stewards and cooks who had taken part, which they very much appreciated. 14 February 1956! It's a long time ago now.

'The Queen looked marvellous. Her complexion! I can't understand why she wasn't like the rest of us, simply pouring with sweat – not a bit of it! She was cool and calm. We had had rather an interesting time practising the curtsey. There was one woman, not in the university but outside, who said she had been presented and would teach us how to do it. Well, the deputy chancellor's wife sprained her ankle practising it! It isn't all that easy!

'Mercifully, Prince Philip decided to speak to my husband. We'd had all the usual instructions – you mustn't argue with them and all that! My husband was wearing a Hampshire Cricket Club tie, and, of course, the Prince knows all the ties. So he said to my husband, "I see you come from Hampshire." Of course, we come from Dorset. That gave me time to rearrange my feet.'

I can still hear her laughter ringing in my ears. A happy person from a happy family.

Mary and Adrian Davies who had married in Ceylon were posted in 1948 to Onitsha, one of the most unhealthy places in the Eastern Region in Nigeria. As they got into the ship at Liverpool with their first baby, Caroline, in a carry-cot, a woman on board turned to her friend and said, 'Oh, what a lovely baby, but fancy taking a baby to West Africa!' Adrian thought, 'Aye! Aye! That's not a very good start for Mary!' but it didn't worry her.

As Adrian said, 'They weren't used to having white children there, and when Caroline arrived she was the only white baby in the whole of the place. It was the provincial headquarters, so there were quite a number of Europeans there. We lived in the rest house until we could get up to our own house on the hill – no electricity, of course, and all water had to be humped in buckets. No fans, but we did manage to get hold of a kerosene fridge. Mary weathered it extremely well. She was *very* resilient – I can't remember her saying, even once "I can't stand it any longer, I must go." It certainly wasn't comfortable! Like any station on the river, like Yola, Makurdi, Onitsha, Port Harcourt, they were absolute steam baths – appalling! The humidity was dreadful. Every day, without exaggeration, you'd wake up and your whole bed was soaking, wet with perspiration. It all had to be hung out on the line to dry.

'We managed to get an African nanny called Mercedes – she was a sweet kid. We were told the Mother Superior at the convent was the person to see and Mercedes had been her personal maid. So we went down to the convent, and the Mother Superior said, "I'll see what I can do for you." Of course, they hadn't seen a white baby for years, and they made a terrific fuss of Caroline. The Mother Superior said of Mercedes, "She's a very good girl, and make sure she behaves herself – and if she doesn't, you just tell me and I'll see to her." We asked what we should pay her.

' "Don't pay her more than £1 a month."

'We said, "What! A £1 a month?"

' "Yes, it's quite enough, quite enough, if you give her any more she'll only go and spend it in the town on things she doesn't need. Her food's costing her nothing, she's fed here at the convent and £1 a month is quite enough." It sounds ridiculous now, doesn't it?'

Social life after Ceylon must have been rather a travesty, but again Mary did not complain.

'On Saturday nights everybody went to the club after the cinema for a wing-ding, and a dance and heaven knows what to a creaky old hand-wound gramophone. But somehow we survived. Of course, there were dinner parties: people went the rounds of dinner parties, they were very bush affairs. We used to do our own entertaining. Adrian had a pretty fair repertoire of

77

songs, both clean and doubtful, and that was always in popular demand. There was no television or radio, so you just entertained yourselves. Drank far too much, of course.

'We were posted to Enugu from Onitsha where we had fans and a push-pull, so life was a great deal more pleasant!'

Adrian was then posted to the Railway Police and his area was from Port Harcourt to Kafanchan in Northern Nigeria. He had his own private coach on the railway and Mary and Caroline used to accompany him.

'I was the only person in the whole of the Nigerian Railway who had a private coach – which was remarkable because the railway personnel themselves – even the senior officers – had to share coaches. But for some reason that nobody ever explained satisfactorily, this old coach, the OP10, they called it, was personal issue to the Deputy Superintendent (which I was by then), Railway Police, Eastern Nigeria. And I could hook it onto any coach I liked, and beetle up and down the line whenever I chose, with Mary along with me. It was always a great relief to get up to Kafanchan, because it was distinctly cool after the low country. In those days I was allowed to load my car onto a low-loader and hook it on behind my coach, so I used to get my car off at any station we stopped at and drive around into the bush. They've stopped that now – they said it was costing too much.'

They put up with so much, the most appalling discomfort and heat, the flies, the mosquitoes, the bats – but they enjoyed it. Was it only because they were young and in love?

Adrian denied this. 'I honestly feel that we felt we were *doing* something, we *were* helping, in a way. We really *were* helping – I know that the popular image of the old colonial is a dead-beat, gin-swilling so-and-so, who's out there just for what he can get out of it. It's not so, it wasn't like that at all. We felt we were making a contribution to the country and helping them in their development.'

7

Mosquitoes, Sweat and Survival

Reading through my interviews with Nina Caulfield is not unlike reading Mary Kingsley's *Travels in West Africa*. There is the same spontaneity, the same spirit of adventure and fearlessness. There is also a great sense of fun, and an eye for the grotesque. Mary Kingsley travelled there in 1893, Nina in 1925, and the thirty-two years appear to have changed West Africa very little, if at all, except in Nina's field which was nursing. That had undoubtedly improved. I went to see Nina in a beautiful Residential Home near Edenbridge and her enthusiasm for her surroundings was still that of the young girl she had once been. I was rushed from plant to plant, from room to room, to the accompaniment of little cries of joy. Life had been one long adventure and it still was, even though she had thrown away so many mementoes to fit into her light, bright, little room.

Nina went first of all to what was then a very small station, Warri which is south-west of Benin, and north-east of Port Harcourt, but has grown out of all recognition in the last few years because of the discovery of oil. She has little to say of Warri or of Port Harcourt which was her next post, but when the administration asked for volunteers to go to Vermenda in the Cameroons, she was off.

'When I was at the end of my first tour, with not a great deal of experience of dealing with natives, they asked for volunteers to go up to Vermenda because of some mysterious illness, as they thought then, which affected the wives and not the husbands. It was a very small station; just a few political officers, a station magistrate, an ADO, a DO and the doctor. Another Sister had been contacted first. She was at Calabar, and she volunteered to go, and then, of course, I, being a very adventurous person and rarely frightened, said, "I'd like to go," so I started out a day after her, which was very unfortunate for me. First of all I went to Abba where the Director of Railways and his wife had a coach and they invited me in. Then, when I got to Abba I was to get a government launch which was to take me to Calabar. The Commissioner of Police came down and met me and took me to his house; his wife gave me coffee, and then he saw me off on a police lorry, just a native policeman and myself – this was the first of my adventures.

'I might have to trek, so I had to borrow pots and pans, a camp bed and various things from the government medical store.

'I was alone with natives all the way to Calabar. There the Sisters came down to meet me and I stayed the night. The next morning the Sisters and most of the Europeans came to see me off because I was to travel on a terrible old coal barge – the *Sir Frederick* – alone with a native crew. Well, this was a dreadful thing. It had a small cabin and I said to the boys, "I can't sit in here. You put all my loads in there." And I asked the old Captain for a deckchair so that I could sit on the bridge. There was no drinking-water on board, no facilities at all, so I sat on the bridge and fell asleep. I heard the Captain and his crew having a good old laugh. I thought they were probably telling bawdy stories but as I couldn't understand, it didn't matter.'

Nina eventually arrived at Victoria. 'That was the beginning of the Cameroons. The DO and the ADO and various officers came down to meet me, and I had been so ill that I must have looked awful. They held a discussion as to whether I should go on to Douala or whether I should stay a night there.

'I said, "If you leave it to me, I want to go on," because I wanted to catch up with the doctor and the Sister who had gone on before me. The DO took me up to his house and his wife gave me a very nice dinner; she intended to give me champagne but her husband had the key of the cupboard and she couldn't get at it. I think it was just as well!

'I went on in a Government launch and again it was very rough, so I said to the boys, "Put my camp bed down," but before I had time to lie down I was terribly sick. Again, there was only the native crew aboard. I fell asleep and at last arrived at Douala.

'From Douala I went to Nksomba where a Dr Nowdi met me. He was Maltese, and was staying with the European agent of a firm while I had to stay at the rest house, which I didn't like at all because I wasn't used to camping or roughing it. However, I had my boys with me, and the steward boy slept outside the door of the rest house. I washed my little tin basin as well as I could and next morning I went for breakfast at the agent's house. Dr Nowdi was in a bush shirt and shorts and hadn't shaved, even though he had every facility there.

'The next day we had to leave for the tiny little village of Bamenda, where there were just a few political officers. Naturally they didn't know whether we could ride or not. I could ride but I don't think Dr Nowdi could.

'First we went on a lorry with a native driver sitting in the middle and with one of us each side of him. I had brought my riding-kit with me in the hope that I would get some riding. It was a marvellous drive but quite terrifying because it was a road made by the Germans during the 1914 war and it was the only way up to Bamenda. I'm not at all a nervous person but on one side there was a sheer drop. The road was very narrow and winding and the lorry could just get round it. I wondered if we met anything how on earth were we going to get past. Luckily we didn't. But the bridges we went over seemed to be loose sticks over something, I didn't know what, and they rattled as the lorry bounced over. I was so light – I was only seven stone seven then – I bounced up and down and the driver had to put his hand on my knee and hold me down!

'I said to him, "Now at the next bridge I want to stop and get out and have a look!" – I thought it would give me more confidence if I knew it was all right. So I got out and had a look and underneath these thin sticks there were big tree trunks, and so I knew we were all right. So we went on and bounced our way – I don't know how many miles.

'That night we stopped at a rest house where a European post and telegraph man was staying. He had one room for his bedroom, one room for his sitting-room, and a little office in between; since those were all the rooms we were going to put him out a bit. Dr Nowdi said, "Well, we'll take this room for ourselves, and give him that!"

'I said, tartly, "No! We won't." The post and telegraph man

offered to move out, and I said, "It's a shame to inconvenience you." However, he gave me his bedroom and he and Dr Nowdi shared the other room.

'The next morning we found they had sent litters with ponies to carry us. I was delighted. So I rode, and Dr Nowdi rode, but he hadn't been on a horse before so I don't know whether he enjoyed it or not! It was glorious in the early morning with the distant hills.

'The next place we arrived at we met the doctor from Bamenda with the ADC, his cook and his steward. They came by lorry and there was an old hen sitting in the lorry and she had laid an egg on the way down – and then we ate her for our lunch! This was all a new experience for me because I had never been on safari. The cook went off the road and he set up a screen, and he had a kerosene tin – everything was cooked in kerosene tins in those days – and he boiled the chicken in the kerosene tin with vegetables. A little table was laid out on the roadside and we had a marvellous lunch.

'That evening we all sat round a blazing fire which was lovely after the heat of Nigeria. There was the DO, the ADO, the two doctors, and during the evening the young ADO turned to me quite innocently and said, "I hope you had an injection of NAB before you came?" NAB being the injection for venereal disease! There was a roar of laughter and he didn't know what he had said because, of course, TAB and NAB are very alike!

'The other Sister and I were given a house. She had brought two native nurses up from Calabar and we each had our own steward boy and small boy. The whole exercise must have cost the government an enormous amount of money because there was also a pathologist and his assistant, and there were only three sick wives and they all had different ailments. The doctor's wife unfortunately had to have an operation and died on Christmas Eve. The one I was looking after had TB, and the other wife . . . I really don't know what she had. I never discovered much about her; she wasn't very ill, and I went home by car with her and her husband. But we were there quite a time until they were better.

'The place was so small. There was a six-hole golf course which the few Europeans had made, and, of course, there were horses up there. We were perched 7,000 feet up and there was a

Hausa town below us. We were right up as if we were on the top
of a cliff.

'The DO lent me his horse which was called Mantis because it
had the habit of going down on its knees, but the boy had
forgotten to give me the note from the DO telling me so I didn't
know this when I got on him. I reached the top of the golf course
and I wanted a bit of a gallop, but I suddenly realized we were
making straight for the cliff. The ADO's house was right on the
edge of the cliff. I don't know how he could bear to live there
because if the cliff had given way, his house would have gone
with it. Anyway, the pony galloped right to the side of it and I
thought that he'd either realize that it was there and jump, or
he'd plant his feet in the ground and I'd go over his head. Well,
of course, he stopped in time.'

Nina nursed on the west coast for fifteen years. She enjoyed it
all until the very end when war broke out and like many other
people she wanted to come home and do war work. There was a
terrible feeling of isolation during those war years on the west
coast. But her experience was invaluable.

'It was very interesting and we gained much more experience
than you ever get in England because you are allowed to do so
much. In my first station I had great experience because the
senior Sister was invalided home, but I knew nothing about
dealing with Africans. The nurses could all speak English, and,
though they were good, they weren't awfully reliable. If you
asked, "Do you know how to give a hypodermic?" they would
say "No" because they wanted you to show them how to do it all
over again. But my senior nurse and charge nurse were pretty
good on the whole.

'And though I had never had a riding lesson in my life, I
became one of the best horsewomen in Nigeria, so they say. I
went everywhere, to Kano, Kaduna, Lagos, Jos and Port
Harcourt.

'An amusing incident happened in Port Harcourt once. I went
on duty in the morning and found the nurses, the ward servants
and everybody tearing round the compound. I couldn't make
out what was the matter – it was the African hospital, so I asked
one of the nurses.

' "Oh," she said, "A patient who came in yesterday has run
away." He was a bush man and he had been put in a little private

room. None of the nurses knew his language because he came from some remote village, and the poor man, who was used to living in the bush, thought he'd got such wonderful food in the hospital and such a lovely room that they must be fattening him up to kill him! He was going to have an operation the next day, and he was terrified, in an absolute panic, and ran away. They found him and the doctor said, "Send to his village for somebody who knows both languages and can translate for us," and so they did and he was quite all right.

'Those were the days of cannibalism. There was head-hunting when I first went out. A boy's body was brought into the hospital with his head cut off. I was told I must never walk down the Zaria road alone. They used to hide in the bushes, and apparently the more heads the Chief had – they used to hang them on their walls – the bigger man he was!'

Nina did not agree with me that some of the women had a hard life. She thought they had a wonderful life. 'They had a great social life – mind you, it was rather boring after a while, because in a small station every dinner party you went to you met the same people and there was no culture, no cinema, no concerts, nothing at all except your wireless set and the conversation was all about who had gone on leave, who had come out from leave, and all that sort of thing – and who was in hospital. They found me extraordinary. At a dinner party, if somebody said, "Is Mr So-and-So in the hospital? What's the matter with him?" I used to say, "I don't know," and another man would say, "It's no good asking Miss Caulfield. She's only the Matron!" Why should one talk about one's work all the time at a dinner party? So I would say, "Look here," if he was a bank manager who asked me, "I don't ask you who's got an overdraft, and who hasn't! And I can talk on other subjects!" However, you got a bit bored with it all! After fifteen years I had had enough.'

Lagos, Nigeria, 1936

Helen Wallis MBE in Sarawak

'Colonial lives...a unique part of history'

Nell Baines

'Wonderful ministering angel' Taussi, Pat Hodgson and the twins, Tanzania, 1948

Johnnie and Kathleen McCall flank Sir John and Lady MacPherson on their visit to the Deji of Akure, Nigeria, 1956

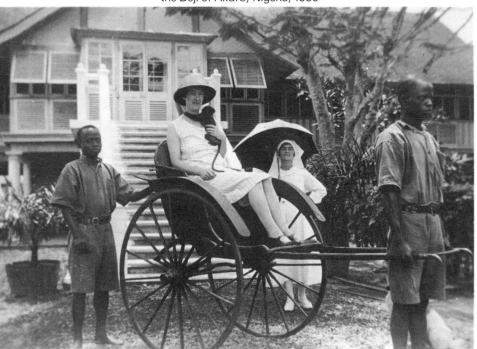

Nina Caulfield posing in a rickshaw outside the European Hospital, Warri, 1927

'Betty' with Derek outside the DC's house, Nyasaland, 1949

'Betty' arriving in Montserrat, 1974

Freda Gwilliam with Margaret Kenyatta, Mayor of Nairobi, at the
Conference on Women in Social Development, Marlborough House, 1965

Lady Templer visiting the WI headquarters, Kuala Lumpur, 1960

Joan and Robin Thorne breakfasting on their veranda, Moshi (Tanganyika), 1946

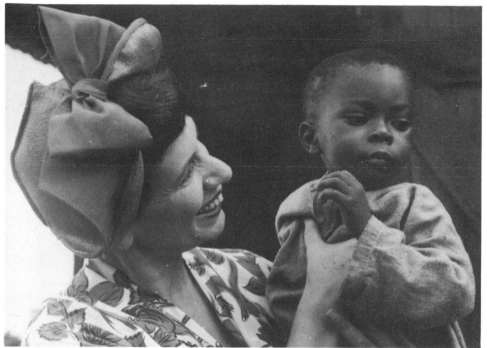

Lady Sylvia Caradon

With Princess Margaret, Jamaica, 1952

A recent photograph of Mabel Strickland

The 'Boadicea of Malta' — official war photograph, Malta, 1939

8

The White Man's Grave

Winifred Kirby went out to the Gold Coast in 1935 where her husband was in railways. This particular part of the West Coast had earned the reputation of being the 'White Man's Grave', possibly more than any other country. It was certainly not thought healthy for children, for as Winifred Kirby says:

'My first tour was of six months' duration because the Colonial Office paid one's fare if the wife stayed at least six months. This meant that one was with one's husband for half a tour without having to make prolonged arrangements for the care of one's children. I seem to remember that some missionaries had children there but no one else would have thought the climate fit for young families.'

Like so many wives she had no idea of the life she was to lead with her husband on the Coast. 'The sum total of my knowledge, before going out, was that it was a hot and humid climate, that food was imported – either in tins, or in the refrigerators of the Elder Dempster Line, whose passenger ships called every fortnight.

'Equipped by a firm of tropical outfitters I was supplied with double-*terais* and thigh-length boots, zipped up the side for wear during the evenings, as well as frocks for every occasion, bathing suits, and masses of intimate things which were then not obtainable on the Coast. Everything was packed into massive cabin trunks.

'After the first trials of sea-sickness, the voyage out proved to be quite a glamorous experience. One remembers with delight the excellent service, the comfort of the cabin, the easy camaraderie of life as a passenger, but also the sadness felt by several women, especially those going out for the first time, because of the separation from their children, sometimes young babies.

'When I arrived at the Gold Coast I was thankful to arrive at Takoradi, because at Accra one had to be swung ashore in a "Mammy Chair" – not a comfortable experience.'

I have experienced this and it is true that it is not comfortable. But it is certainly exciting. The Africans of the Coast are very large muscular men from the exertion of coming in with the waves in their canoes, but though they look strong, their life span is short as a result of the strain which this particular Herculean exercise puts on their hearts.

'Some houses were built on stilts, others were bungalows, furnished with necessities, chairs and beds, but one provided one's own curtains and soft furnishings. When I first went there were no refrigerators, but each establishment had a contraption called an "ice-box", a literal description, for it was like a trunk made of thick wood, into which large blocks of ice were inserted, covered by sacking, and one's meat, butter, drinks, etc., were kept there. The ice gradually melted, and the result was somewhat revolting. The ice blocks were renewed at regular intervals by the ice company in the town. There was a system by which one could give an order to Griffiths Macalister in Liverpool for a regular consignment of food, bacon, joints of beef or lamb, butter and kippers and so on to be sent to one personally every fortnight.'

The primitive conditions were exactly the same as on the East Coast, especially in the out-stations where there was no electricity and no running water. But the Gold Coast African is a happy smiling person, the women being especially friendly and outgoing as Winifred Kirby found:

'Although the clubs were separate for Europeans and Africans there was a good deal of mixing, especially when concerts or dramatic performances were given, and I well remember the enjoyable experience of seeing the *Mikado* well played at the Railway African Club by an all-black cast. There were many well-educated Africans in all kinds of posts, and as there were boarding-schools for girls, the women were also able to hold their own in the world of men, and there was a very pleasant atmosphere.'

To one who has lived on both the East Coast and the West, after experiencing this mixing with the African which is taken for granted on the West Coast (where, as Winifred Kirby says, 'there was a happy community life'), the East Coast comes as a shock. So many of the whites only know their servants to whom they are undoubtedly extremely kind, but the easy camaraderie of the West Coast is lacking.

Winifred found social life was formal in places like Takoradi and Accra.

'Among the Europeans the system of paying calls still existed. When one first arrived, one solemnly left two of one's own and one of one's husband's cards, during the period after office hours, on one's superior officers, and, of course, signed the "Book" at the house of the Provincial or District Commissioner, unless one was stationed at the seat of government, when one presented oneself at Government House. The community was not large, but representative of all departments of government, medical, public works, railways, post and telegraphs, as well as many commercial firms. Shipping and mining companies all had offices at the ports, and their people all played golf or tennis, swam or sailed together, or went out on fishing expeditions.

'One of our enjoyments was to go on board the Elder Dempster ship when it arrived in harbour, have breakfast, and have one's hair done by the hairdresser. Entertainment at the weekend very often took the form of curry lunch preceded by drinking gin.'

Winifred remembers asking an old coaster at one of these parties why he didn't feel the necessity of protecting himself from the mosquitoes.

'They do bite me,' he told her, 'but I've drunk so much gin in my years out here, that they drop off dead!'

Winifred was interested in the lives of the Africans and used to go visiting in the villages with the health visitor, who kept an eye on the children, and 'whipped them into hospital if necessary. There was always opposition on the part of some parents, who preferred to treat the family themselves. I remember how clean the native houses were, and how it added to the interest of life to see the Africans in their own homes.'

Nkrumah, who eventually became Ghana's President, always maintained that if the African had access to water, he would be the cleanest human being on earth. Troubled times were to follow. But, as Winifred said, 'I'm thinking of fifty years ago, about a period when a blessed tranquillity seemed to prevail.

'The natives of the Coast were a cheerful happy people, though one heard stories of dark and fearful happenings, when Chiefs asserted their ancient rights over their own people.

'My admiration for the women who had to travel in the far bush areas is unbounded. But many of them liked the life on trek. I can only speak of this by hearsay, since being with the Gold Coast Railways, our travels were by train, in inspection coaches, equipped with kitchens and sleeping- and living-quarters, the only real trial being the humidity and the heat, and the inevitable mosquitoes.

'Perhaps the main drawback to life in the tropics, to one who had always lived a very active family life in Britain, was having to fill in the long hours of daylight, when the men were at the office from 8 a.m. or earlier to 4 p.m. when outdoor activities had to be crowded into two hours between then and 6 p.m.

'We had no household work; one could not read for ever, and unless one was adept at sewing or other handiwork, time could hang heavily, and boredom creep in. One wrote volumes of letters home, which, unfortunately, one's friends and relatives did not keep, but I do remember trying to find things to do. Many men did not have wives with them, but the clubs provided entertainment, dancing to gramophone music, and there were dinner parties! At the end of our stay there I was very sorry to leave because of the real friendliness of the people of all races.'

The Chevertons, destined to travel more than most people, also found themselves in the Gold Coast. Joan was given permission to join Rex in Cyprus at the end of the Second World War, and ten days before she sailed with her children, Rex was transferred to West Africa. It must have been a blow to Joan who was planning to take her two girls to the beautiful and clement island. She was told that the Gold Coast was no place for children. 'I had two children who spoke better Spanish than English by then because they had been for four years in Guatemala, so I had to stay for a year in England to get them used to the fact that houses had to have chimneys and what snow was – and little things like that.'

Joan and Rex were mainly in Lagos but Joan went to a meeting in Kumasi in the Gold Coast of the women's clubs and women's associations. It was a very different world from the one in Africa before the war when the women were utterly subordinate to their men. I noticed this when I attended the Women's Progressive Society in Benin City in 1962, when the subject which vexed them most was how they were to keep their earnings from their husbands. There was a surge of feeling of independence, and the men resented it as they observed their women slowly flaunting a new standard of life not only for themselves but for their children as well. Women were emerging from their chrysalises and feeling their wings. Joan found that she was one of two white people in a congress of 200 African women in 1950. She also found that there was a clash between the outlook of the town and country women. For instance, the town women would aver that polygamy was a disgraceful thing. 'How could a man set his wife up as a trader properly if he has got to divide his money between four wives? Of course she would not be able to trade properly because there would not be enough money for stock.' Whereas the country woman would say, 'Polygamy! That is the only way of running a country properly. How can I go and till the yam and so on and feed the man when I'm also wheeling the baby?' And so the clash had begun, not between different tribes, or even different countries, but purely between town and country, two absolutely conflicting ways of life.

Since my own proclivity is to leave people to their own tribal norms and customs, I wondered whether Joan thought that the Girl Guides, which she was representing in Kumasi, did help the young girls. She gave me this as an example:

'When I was in Ghana I had to get money from the government through the secretary for social affairs, who happened to be Sir Maurice Dorman, and he, too, said to me, "What use do you really think they are? I mean, does it really help anybody?" and I said, "Will you show me your staff list?" and I think – except for one – every single African woman on his staff list was either working with me at the time or had started as a Guide.

'And another time in Nigeria I went up to Ibadan to a big dinner party and my host suggested that I stayed the night as I was also up for a Guides' meeting as well. [At this time Joan had had a very serious motor accident and her arm was, and still is, in a sling.]

'Because of my sling, my host said, "Don't bother to change," so I went into dinner in my white Guide uniform. They had been having a Council of Ministers so quite a few of them were at the party, and several of the Africans came up to me and said, "What is this?" meaning my uniform, so I told them that it was the Guides. They asked me so many questions that at last I said, "Do you really want to know, or are you just being polite?" and one particular African said, "No, I really want to know." So I explained how I had started the first Guide company in the palace of the Emir of Kano, and how they went to camp, what we were teaching, adapting the badges to suit the Nigerians for things like hairdressing and subjects related to their own traditions. He seemed really interested and asked very intelligent questions. It turned out that he was one of the treasurers visiting from up North! Two months later came the vote for money in the House of Representatives for the whole of Nigeria, and the Guides were given more than they had asked for, while the Scouts were given less.'

Joan and Rex went on to Ghana from Nigeria and they worked closely with the White Fathers for whom they acquired a deep respect. Joan thought that Guiding was more use in Ghana than in England, because in England so much had been done already. 'I had been a Brownie and then a Guide, having started in 1916, and so much in my day which was exclusive to Guiding had become part of ordinary education in England, like going out for hikes and camping and so on. In Africa, they knew more about camping than we did, so we didn't camp outside but would take over a deserted school, and teach them things. I would start them with turning on the lights, turning the taps, because it was a miracle to them, they had never seen anything like it. I had one big camp of 400 children which Lady Baden-Powell was to visit. I asked Rex to drive me down to the camp as my arm was already bad and I couldn't drive myself. The parade was scheduled for seven o'clock and I arrived there at 5.45. Nobody was stirring! Everything should have been bustling; they should have been having their breakfast but there was not a Guide in sight! I nearly fainted. I finally found them huddled in one classroom, solemnly discussing what was the best hair style for greeting the Chief Commissioner for the first time! . . . Anyway, I got them all going and I rushed round and found a police car and I sent a message over the wireless to the castle and said, "My Guides will be a quarter of an hour late because I'm not letting 400 children come unfed, or you will have them fainting all over the floor." The Governor wasn't very pleased but Lady Baden-Powell didn't mind as she had had experiences of girls who had fainted because they had not been fed.'

Though the men put up a fight against the women becoming emancipated, Joan found that the mothers-in-law, the old grannies, objected even more stridently. 'Instead of her word being law she was suddenly told that you should boil the water; you shouldn't *ram* red hot chillies down babies! I have seen them with their thumbs ramming them down the throats of little innocent babies. Who told them? The Guides. So it was the old grannies, the mothers-in-law, who didn't care for them. Though, of course, the men did object to water being laid on in their villages because then the women wouldn't have to go to fetch the water from the rivers and they would have nowhere to meet and gossip!'

PART THREE

The West Indies

9

Islands in the Sun

In 1492 Christopher Columbus went in search of a western route to India and when he discovered one of the islands of the Bahamas he named it San Salvador, and went on to discover Cuba and an island now partitioned between the Republic of Haiti and Santo Domingo. Because of his mistake he named the islands the West Indies, a name which survives until this day. In 1494 he discovered Jamaica, and on his third voyage he went south and discovered Trinidad and Grenada. Cuba, Hispaniola, Jamaica and Puerto Rico have been sometimes spoken of as the Greater Antilles and the other islands, the Lesser Antilles, the latter being further divided into the Leeward and Windward Islands. The sea, of which the Greater and Lesser Antilles form the northern and eastern boundaries, and Central and South America, the western and southern, is the Caribbean.

Still in search of India, Columbus set out on a fourth journey, reached Hispaniola again and found the coast of what is now British Honduras.

Guiana was discovered in 1498, but Columbus did not land there. It is the huge region of South America which lies between the Orinoco and the Amazon, and where the British, Dutch and French all found room to settle. Later these settlers found their way to the West Indies. The Spaniards, almost exclusively seeking gold, were only interested in large countries with rivers, so they settled in Jamaica and Trinidad. If they visited the smaller islands it was only to carry off the inhabitants as slaves. As it was, they almost exterminated the aboriginal population by literally working them to death and then they went to Africa for their slaves. The slave trade was brought to the West Indies, and the Negro population with it.

The British went to trade and began with grants to private proprietors or chartered companies. At the same time, they took with them the political institutions of the mother country. The legislature and local government of Barbados, the Bahamas and Bermuda, to this day bear a strong likeness to the corresponding institutions of England in the reign of the Stuarts.

In 1623, the English and French arrived at St Kitts and agreed to divide it, until 1713 when France ceded her portion to England. Antigua, Nevis, Montserrat and other smaller islands were settled by the English from St Kitts. In 1627, Barbados was settled by the English and has never been under any other flag.

In the Napoleonic wars, France lost all her West Indian possessions to England except for Guadeloupe, Martinique and French Guiana.

The British took Jamaica from Spain in 1655, and Trinidad in 1797. British Honduras had been settled by the British in 1638, and the Dutch ceded British Guiana in 1814.

Though the early English settlers intended to farm the land themselves, they soon found the climate induced indolence and, as they prospered, that manual labour was undignified. And so, like the Spaniards before them, they imported African slaves. When slavery was abolished in 1833, contract labour was imported from China, India and Madeira. Now the islands are inhabited by mixed races living side by side. The Indians run small shops, the Chinese take to commerce, the African and Asiatic races have become doctors, barristers, bankers and politicians.

Though the Chinese and Indians adhere to their own cultures and religions, the African of the West Indies is westernized, there is no colour bar and, with few exceptions, the absence of any nationalistic feeling is conspicuous.

Sugar cane was introduced into Barbados in 1640 and so began the introduction of slaves into British West Indies. By 1688 about 25,000 slaves were imported annually. However, they were not exclusively black. The Spanish and Portuguese had been in the habit of transporting criminals to their colonies, where they were allowed to work out their sentences. They were rewarded with a plot of land and a great many chose to stay either as overseers or to work their own land. Many of today's families in the West Indies are descended from these bondsmen.

Bermuda is a group of very small islands in the North Atlantic, and was Britain's oldest colony. It derives most of its income from its tourist trade, and was uninhabited when the Europeans settled there. Since 1767 it has been the headquarters of a British fleet and its floating repair dock was of vital importance during the Second World War. There is still a Governor, and two Houses of the Legislature.

In 1967 Betty, whom we last met in Nyasaland, was in Montserrat with her husband who was then Governor there. This was an idyllic existence in comparison with the life she had led in Africa. She found the West Indians very much more sophisticated. In Montserrat they were particularly beautiful, perhaps because they were a mixture of Spanish, Irish, Chinese and Indian, though the labouring people are also descended from Negro slaves, or the indentured white people who were there even earlier than the Negroes. Betty found that the people still blame people for enslaving their ancestors. 'They have been emancipated for 150 years,' she said; 'they shouldn't feel that they deserve to be excused and cosseted because they were poor slaves a couple of centuries ago.'

Betty particularly loved the Virgin Islands, and unlike the American Virgin Islands, they were not yet commercialized or had a high rate of crime and drugs. A series of small islands, they depend on their tourist trade. Some are not populated but are beautiful with white beaches and coco palms – 'an absolute haven of paradise'.

At last, Betty had the company of people like herself whatever the colour of their skin.

'There were some extremely cultured people among the people we knew. There was a lawyer with a French wife who had been to a British public school and to Cambridge, and another lawyer was an excellent musician. The people have been in contact with European culture for three to four hundred years.

On the other hand many are violent, and robbery and rape are not infrequent. Where we were, there were many retired Americans and Canadians – they were the ones with the money and the lovely houses, and they weren't very sensible. They had drunken parties with all their windows open, leaving everything open. They would go to the harbour where they chartered a refrigerated ship to come once a month, and they would take away hundreds of dollars' worth of meat, watched by the local working class, mostly black, who couldn't afford meat once a week or once a month unless they were lucky. When there was a crime it was usually directed against them because they had the money and the goods.

'In the same family you would get a man who would be a master criminal – there was one we called Fine Twine – and his brother might be a policeman. The fact that the policemen were black was a very good thing because they managed each other. There were two political murders while we were there, one in St Kitts where the black West Indian Attorney-General opened his door one morning and somebody just killed him. The other in Antigua where a rather demented gardener was paid to slash to death one of the members of the opposition and his wife. Our Attorney-General was absolutely terrified. People would suddenly take out knives and knife each other when they drank a lot of rum. But in spite of all that I liked them, they were so colourful, I loved their music and their carnivals when they danced all day for four days.

'Like so many islands the society was matriarchal, but the women had a tough life. Because of the shadow of slavery, the men will not grow sugar and they depend on tourists for revenue. Even so, they will not serve the tourist since they think it demeans them and they adopt a "take it or leave it" attitude, and naturally the tourist, who has paid a great deal of money to be there, resents it. So the men drift around, neither marrying or establishing families but having children and leaving the women to bring them up. The women would be thankful for birth control, but the men won't have it. One enlightened man from Trinidad who tried to start birth control in Montserrat had his life threatened. It is a sad situation and quite illogical because there are not enough jobs, and yet there are more and more people, and better education. Now that doors have been closed to them in America, Canada and England, what will be the outcome? A work permit is needed to get from island to island, so a man from Grenada is regarded just as much a foreigner in Montserrat, or more so, than a European.'

Betty found women's lib a very strong element in the West Indies.

'Derek said the backbone of his Civil Service was women. I don't exactly adhere to women's lib because I think women can get far more out of life and out of men generally by just being women. The West Indian women criticize men all the time. I went to several meetings where they discussed the problem, saying something should be done about the men and the way they behave. There are some very well-educated women, and if they can get hold of the pill then they take the matter of children into their own hands.'

For a change, the pay in Montserrat seemed adequate, but Derek was told that he must do more entertaining than had been done there in the past, for which he would get an extra allowance. Reassured, he went ahead and spent freely.

'When Derek put in his claim and told the Treasury what he had done, he discovered it was the year they had decided to cut back. Everyone was told they were not to have a huge party on the Queen's birthday. The Queen's birthday was *the* party of the year, and the Chief Minister came and complained and said if it was reduced in any way, he would be blamed. Even the French Consul gave a tremendous party on the 14th of July and the Americans on their Thanksgiving. We found we were digging into our own money. I kept a lot of accounts – it's interesting to see how they went. Of course, in Government House, you always have a flow of people through. We could have sent some of them to hotels, but it is more interesting to have them because that is part of your life, meeting people and being able to talk to them. We didn't have a Royal visit – Princess Anne had just been there for her honeymoon before we went there. That had caused a great stir because the servants were all trade unionists and when she arrived they wouldn't come an hour earlier in the morning to give her tea – her ladies' maid had to get up and do it. But they loved the Royal Family. Neither Montserrat nor the Virgin Islands want to leave Britain.'

In 1953 the Thorps went to St Lucia and found a life not unlike the one they had led in the Seychelles. The indigenous people spoke the same French creole patois, but because it was less cut off, the island was at least fifty years ahead in its standard of living. Doreen Thorp loved the people but she did find that by the time she left, politics, which appear to be as inflammable in the West Indies as they do in France, were beginning to creep in even among her Girl Guides and Red Cross workers.

The Governor lived in Grenada with St Lucia and the four Windward Islands under him. Doreen's husband was the Administrator in St Lucia and he found that he had to do the same sort of work and entertaining as the Governor, without the perks: the same sorry story of a badly paid couple trying to show the flag.

'The one thing I found was that we were always broke in St Lucia,' Doreen said. 'The salaries were small, we didn't get an entertainment allowance; we didn't get duty-free drink or cigarettes. When my first cook left I found it difficult to get another. I really worked hard, and it's all right entertaining if you've plenty of money, but if you do it without spending money, it's extremely difficult. We even had to pay for our own petrol. When the Governor came we used to stay on. On some islands, the Administrator and his family used to move out, depending on whether there was somewhere you could move to. The Governor used to come and I was a sort of glorified house-keeper, while they had their duty-free drink and cigarettes.

'You couldn't say, "Look, this month we're broke, we just won't do anything," because a group of Americans who were on the satellite rocket range at St Lucia always had VIPs coming over. If they came one had to entertain them and give a party for them. It was the same when the Navy came. You couldn't say, "Sorry this is a bad month to have come, we're not doing anything." You just had to do it. And the local people would expect to be invited if there were any VIPs.

'It was a good life, though. I must say I enjoyed it, but it was a struggle. I think the pre-war generation of Colonial Service didn't think of fighting for their rights or complaining. It was part of the service – you just accepted it. Whereas the post-war generation have completely different ideas, and if they were posted somewhere where their wives couldn't go, they just didn't go. They went and complained and said, "No, I can't be separated from my wife." '

Freda Gwilliam – Advisor to Education – did not feel the violence in the West Indies, but she felt that emotions were on the surface and therefore people reacted far more quickly. The English, literally and metaphorically, shut their doors and windows, while the West Indians have no doors or windows to shut, so they react instantaneously from gaiety, fear or misery.

'You'd find yourself in a swimming party in the West Indies with people you were working with during the week. Head of a school, or an education officer, or a Minister or something like that. And you are bobbing up and down in the water, and you suddenly think, "Good heavens! I'm not aware of any difference"; so it's only an accident of colour that blinds judgement. Well, you wouldn't like some people, you wouldn't like to be with them. It doesn't matter about the colour of their skin. I think women are worse than men, perhaps because they're not so good at being objective. Together we are far richer than we are apart, because intuitiveness and illogicality of women can make more out of the rigidity and logicality of men. And we can be disciplined by their logic – and I think the combination is tremendous.'

I have always felt that the Commonwealth Relations Office personnel had a lot to learn from the Colonial Officers. It was quite apparent that this was not a universal sentiment and the CRO were, I think, inclined to ignore the Colonial Office as, on the independence of a colony, they moved in and took over. Though the CRO might have accused the Colonial Office of paternalism, there was absolutely no doubt that they knew the indigenous people as no newcomer could hope to do. Freda obviously felt the same.

'I think the best thing that ever happened to the FCO was when the CRO fulfilled itself and recruited from our Colonial Office. Because it brought an understanding into the CRO which never happened before. When Jamaica became independent, I was going out there because our job continued afterwards, and I was to stay with the High Commissioner and his wife. When I arrived she said to me, "I can't understand it. Ever since it was known you were coming my telephone hasn't stopped ringing." "Oh!" I said, "How lovely – I've got a lot of friends here."

' "But," she said, "they're Jamaicans."

' "But, of course," I replied. "For the last eight years I've been running a seminar in Oxford each Easter for teachers all round the West Indies."

' "Oh," she said. "We've been asked to a party."

'The party came, and "Oh, Freda!" they cried, wrapping me to their splendid bosoms, men and women. And the High Commissioner and his wife just sat there, completely over-whelmed by amazement.'

Freda summed up pertinently what life in the Colonial Service was all about, its advantages and disadvantages.

'If a woman is going to marry a man, she marries the man and his job. She can't separate the man from the job that has made the man she marries. And the success and failure of our service – HM Overseas Service – has been the degree to which the women have accepted that. And how many women have been the mak-ing of the men, and how many have been the breaking. I think history must pay tribute to the one, and say many a good man may well have been caught in mid-career by a not-so-good woman. Or the woman walked out on him.

'The awful dilemma! Do I let my husband go back alone? Do I stay or go with him and leave the children behind? I know many a man in our service who perhaps understandably has gone off with one of my female education officers, or somebody else, because his wife has made, what I think, was the wrong decision. She married him . . . I'm sure where our service has been remarkable, is when the women married the man and the job, and was his right arm, his prop and his stay. With her little groups of women on her veranda, I think she does wonders when there is a gulf between the indigenous people which can't be bridged. Women are awfully good at getting over that bridge and meeting people on equal terms.'

Four hundred and fifty miles north-east of Jamaica are the small islands of Turks and Caicos. Turks is so named becáuse a big cactus grows on the island with a flower which looks like a Turk's fez. The Caicos are so named from the Spanish 'Cayos' meaning islands. The Turks were first colonized in the seventeenth century by the Bermudans who came to supervise their slaves raking salt which was used by ships for salting pork and other commodities. They left some quite substantial stone houses, using the wood they brought down for ballast for their floors, roof timbers and beams. The group of Caicos are separated from the Turks by a channel twenty-two miles wide and were first colonized by refugees from places like Charleston and Georgia, after the American War of Independence.

Both groups are coral, low and infertile. The Americans found that they could not survive on the Caicos and, leaving their slaves behind, soon departed for other lands. The slaves managed to survive on fishing and subsistence crops. For a while, the two groups of islands came under the jurisdiction of the Bahamas, then Jamaica, until Jamaica got her independence in 1962, when they became a Crown Colony of Britain.

Peter Bleackley went out to the Turks and Caicos as its Administrator in 1952. Before his wife, Rachel, joined him he had written to her saying, 'It is ridiculous! Here is Grand Turk which is quite small, and there are twenty-three other islands, mostly inhabited, and many have not been visited for years. We have got a grant for £3,000, so can you find a boat? She must be a sort of cruiser; she must have accommodation for so many people, but she must not draw more than three feet or she will not go through the reefs.'

As Rachel said, she 'whizzed round' until she found one.

'I don't think I would embark on it now, but when you are young, you don't think twice. I eventually found a cabin cruiser which belonged to a Harley Street specialist who was awfully kind and sailed her from the south coast up the Thames to Kingston with me. There the Crown Agent Marine Surveyor looked her over and said, "Yes", she would do but, as she was not copper-sheathed for the tropics, the Crown Agents had that done.

'Then it was a question of getting *Beta Cygni* (she was called after a constellation) out to the West Indies. It was just after the Olympics in Finland and our British Olympic crew – four of them – offered to sail her out, taking small daughter Caroline and me. "We'll gladly do it," they said, "provided we can stay with you for a while once we get there." "Oh, yes," I replied glibly, not knowing then the limitations of our Government House. Sadly it was not to be – for the insurance would have been prohibitive. Lord Hailey had stayed with us in Tanganyika and, meeting him in London, I mentioned this to him. "Oh," he said, "of course you must do it. This is the spirit that built the Empire." However even he could not persuade the Crown Agents. So *Beta Cygni* had to be shipped and, as things turned out, this proved to be just as well.

'Eventually we sailed her the 500 miles from Jamaica to Grand Turk. This was quite enough since we ran into the tail-end of a hurricane, and took shelter behind Tortuga, a pirate haven in times gone by. We weren't worried, but we were terribly sea-sick. We were pinned down there for five days because each time we ventured out of Tortuga Bay, our roll-metre registered forty degrees. This is uncomfortably close to the point of no return – so we quickly put back under the lee of the island! We had no ship-to-shore radio, but an American coastguard plane flew over us quite low, so we thought everyone would know we were all right. However we got back to the Turks to find that they were just about to hold a Memorial Service for us.

'Caroline was six at the time and able to join us in *Beta Cygni* as we set out to visit the Caicos – a voyage of discovery for us and a lovely form of safari. Wherever we anchored, the islanders would sail or row out to bring us in through the breakers. You always got wet, but it was the greatest fun. I used to – because it was expected of me – take my frock, hat and white gloves in a plastic bag. One would land on the beach, usually on a roller, and have to leap out. A very discreet coy grass shelter would have been built to one side. Peter and I would change in there and emerge, rather salty, but dressed as we should be. Then suddenly the population erupted and we would be greeted by "God Save the Queen", played in one case I remember, on combs and lav paper. All the niceties were respected, and wonderful speeches by the elder in biblical English. So one was greeted as the Administrator and the Administrator's "Mistress". A surprise this at first, but there was a lovely elegance about this biblical language.'

Rachel had done jobs for most of her married life to help with the education of her children, but in the Turks Peter's job was all-important. 'There were problems, of course, but in many ways it was a wonderful place. Terribly poor, but the people had such stalwart qualities.

'There was a very high child mortality, mostly because of feeding problems. I was fortunate to have various contacts and was invited to speak at one of the WHO western hemisphere meetings. This resulted in most useful grants for skimmed milk and cod liver oil; and helped us to start children's clinics throughout the islands.

'This was a fascinating and very busy time. Most of the children had deficiency diseases but, after a few months, you could see their skin begin to glow and shine . . . . And their Mums were so grateful. One thing leads to another. Regular visits to the islands gave us the chance to start a number of small libraries. Books were at a premium, but I used to collect magazines. Friends were terribly good sending them in from Jamaica – indeed from all over the place. It was a widening of horizons for people raised on the Bible. But now I wonder whether this increased their happiness? You see, with hindsight, one begins to ask questions.'

There was a very high illegitimacy rate in the Turks and Caicos; at least eighty per cent of the children were born out of wedlock. When the Bleackleys were there, it was almost impossible to sell the islands' only product – salt. So the young men lost their means of livelihood. They went to sea or to the States to find jobs, leaving the islands bereft of men. There were in fact only three weddings during the three years of the Bleackleys' tour. This was also the time when US naval and air force bases were set up in Grand Turk as part of the space programme. If an American serviceman got a girl pregnant, he was immediately shipped back to the States, and would accept no responsibility at all. Rachel took up several cases, but did not get very far.

'It was very difficult. It was American army policy not to accept responsibility. Wretched for these girls, many of whom managed in a remarkable way. We employed girls in Government House and I still write to my cook, Minette, who has three children by various fathers, but she has managed to keep going. She worked very hard and kept them clean and has brought them up well.'

When the Wainwrights were in the same job in 1963, progress

was in full spate. Though, at first, Bridget found it was 'desperately difficult to know what to do with one's life', after a very full life in Kenya, she did find one great joy and interest, in the birds.

'It all began when we had the head of the Florida branch of the Audubon Society to stay with us. I told him that I loved watching the birds that came to the bird-bath in our garden which was the only bit of open water on the island, and which had lots of vegetation round it. He asked me to keep a list of the birds I saw and send it to him regularly. It became a great interest of mine, especially in March and October, when all sorts of fascinating birds went through on their way to or from Canada, the States or South America. It was terribly exciting when a cardinal bird, or a yellow-bellied sap-sucker, went through, and there were lots of buntings and large numbers of different warblers and cuckoos – in fact, I could hardly drag myself from our top veranda, which overlooked the bird-bath, and where I would sit for hours with my field-glasses.'

What she also discovered was that it was a fascinating experience to watch the difference it made to the islanders' lives as the airstrip, the roads and jetties were built. They had got used to landing – as Rachel Bleackley did – on an open beach from a sailing boat, and carrying their belongings on their heads to the villages. One old lady was quite overcome by the wonder of it all!

'I can remember going over to one of the islands and finding an old lady in tears beside the bulldozer putting through the road, and I thought, "We've done something awful! We've knocked down her wall, or something like that." I went up to her and said, "Oh, dear! What's the matter?" and she said, "I never thought I would live to see a road on our island. It's so wonderful!" '

Both Bridget Wainwright and Clondagh Arrowsmith made their own clothes. That did provide them with something to do, and it would seem that in Clondagh's case it was absolutely necessary.

'I had to make all my own clothes, and the children's. One was a baby and the other was about three. Otherwise, we would have had nothing to wear. I took the material and patterns out with me. That was one of the things I liked doing.'

Sir Edwin Arrowsmith was Commissioner of the Turks and Caicos from 1940 to 1946, then he was posted to Dominica. Glamour came to them in the Turks in the form of Madeleine Carroll, but there was reason for indignation when her publicity man tried to pull a fast one on the public.

'She came to the island where Paramount was making a film called *Bahama Passage*. America hadn't come into the war and their publicity man said to me, "Look, I want to put out a story that Madeleine Carroll has been captured by a German sea raider and then released later. I suppose you will pass that?" And I said, "Will I – hell!" Soon after we flew to the States, where Clondagh was due to have her baby. We went up in the train from Miami to New York. When we got there, there was a headline in the *Tribune* – "Madeleine Carroll missing at sea." I think she never left the island.'

Clondagh was still in America for Pearl Harbor in December 1941, but Edwin had had to return to the Turks. One can imagine the pandemonium which broke out in America at this time, and affected Clondagh who was with her daughter aged three and Jennifer, three months old. She felt she must get back to the Turks and went by train from Boston where she had been staying. Arriving in Miami, she went to Nassau and managed to get a lift in a small plane from there to the Turks.

Clondagh had the usual anxiety over her children's education. Our old friend, the PNEU, was not possible during the war, since it depended on frequent posts and these were naturally hazardous, if not downright impossible. She wrote off to a similar form of education in America called the Calvert school, and they sent her down a variety of literature, explaining how she was to teach her children from the word 'go'.

'I had no experience of teaching whatever. And we battled along. The only thing, of course, which was different was the dollars and the pounds and so I had to try and work that out on my own. Susan did learn to read and write, and we had two hours every morning, and took school holidays. When we were transferred to Dominica, she was able to go to the convent there. I thought I would teach Jennifer for a bit, but I couldn't teach her a thing. We just didn't click. I couldn't stand it any longer and sent her to a kindergarten.'

Dominica is exceedingly beautiful. It is scenically the opposite of the Turks, being a volcanic island and mountainous. The Arrowsmiths had a pleasant government house in Roseau and a cottage for weekends in the mountains. They experienced one very bad hurricane in Grand Turk. Susan, who couldn't have been more than three, was asked by Clondagh recently, if she remembered it. She said:

'The only thing I remember is that a crab walked across the floor!'

When I asked Clondagh if she felt that she had missed certain things like theatres, music and exhibitions, she replied as nearly all the colonial women have:

'Not really. Other things made up for it, because we have had such a marvellous life and I think it was worth it – rather than exhibitions and such like.'

Not included among the islands but close enough for our purpose to be included under their heading, is British Honduras (now Belize) on the suffocating coast of Central America. Claimed incessantly by Guatemala, it chose to remain under the protection of the British flag until 1981, when it got its independence, though still with the security of a small British garrison stationed there. To this mangrove, a gaseous, swampy spot, the Chevertons arrived in 1937, blown undoubtedly all the way by the winds of the Falkland Islands. Joan was in mid-ocean between Montevideo and Stanley when she received the news from Rex:

'I had come back with some lovely new Donegal tweeds and things and two days after I left Montevideo, being as sick as a dog, I got a cable from Rex saying we were going to British Honduras. Of course I didn't have any thin things. In the Falklands, 64°F probably meant a heat wave but in British Honduras it was cold. Once, when it was that temperature, the Governor was coming to dinner, and I had a tiny electric stove which I used for airing the nappies, and I switched this on and *all* the men in their tails, including the Governor, *rushed* to the stove and stood around with their hands holding their tails up, and the ladies came with fur capes and goodness knows what.'

The houses, built of wood, were all on stilts, because of the floods. In spite of this water seems to have been a major problem.

'Each house had its own water-tank; by law you were supposed to have so many cubic feet of water for each square foot of floor area; there had been a disastrous hurricane in 1931, and it caused the maximum amount of damage and loss of life. Rex was Director of Medical Services and his tank wasn't the official size for the big house so we really had to watch our water. When my daughter went to Guatemala and someone ran a bath for her, she rushed up to it and turned off the tap, saying "That is waste!" She had got so used to being careful – even at three years old! Water came out of the bath, it washed the wooden floors, then it watered the garden. In the dry season women even used to come and beg for your dirty laundry water so that they could do their laundry.

'Again, food was a problem. Nowadays I gather from a clergyman who has just come back from Belize that it's better, and he talks gaily of vegetables and so on. We only had one little man, a Chinaman, who grew vegetables. We got a lot of native food, so I just sat down and taught myself how to use it. Once in Lagos, I had the Lady Ademola [a Nigerian] to dinner and I gave her breadfruit cooked the West Indian way, and she said, "To think I've had to come to a white house to learn a new way of cooking breadfruit!" But you couldn't get fresh salads, and the eggs were pitiable, so when the war started I went into egg production.'

As in the Seychelles, it was not fashionable to marry. The men went off logging into the country for mahogany and sapodilla for chewing-gum, and it was a matriarchal society. The women worked in the house and Joan only employed maids. One day, one of them was complaining about some boy whose father wouldn't send her any money.

'Why don't you marry him?' Joan asked.

'Marry him! Be tied to him! Oh, no, not me!' for they prided themselves on the number of different men they could collect.

Joan worked in a babies' clinic.

'We had a lovely box file. One day a lady came in with six children. She said the name of one and I looked it up in the index file. When it came to the second child, I naturally looked it up under the same name. Not a bit of it! Six children – six names! My cook was a darling old Jamaican and she had six daughters, and she said, "Mistress, all of them different and all their fathers white!" You would see the most heavenly newspaper articles such as, "The wedding nuptials were celebrated, of Mr and Mrs So-and-so, the bride resplendent in white satin with a train which was held by her six grandchildren."

'It was terribly important what you wore in church; all those old piccaninny ladies, they all had layers and layers of white petticoats, starched and ruffled and beautiful. During the dry season, church attendance dropped because there wasn't enough water to wash the petticoats properly, so you couldn't go to church – it wasn't decent.'

The spirit which has left me with a lasting admiration for colonial women is demonstrated again and again by people like Joan Cheverton. Whatever the problem, or the disadvantages abroad, she tackled them with aplomb. Such as this problem with her own as well as the indigenous babies.

'When war broke out, I was in hospital having my second baby, while Rex painted red crosses all over the place. We couldn't get cod liver oil for the babies, so we laid sharks on one of the hospital roofs and the oil dripped out and we brought up my babies and hens on sharks' liver oil. It was much richer than cod liver oil and when we gave it to the babies at the clinic, they did awfully well on it. The mothers were thrilled. It was wonderful to see those babies getting all shiny-black instead of being all pathetically black. As for my hens, they flourished on the oil, Epsom salts and rice crushings from the mill – the stuff that was thrown away. The Agriculture Department just didn't believe my egg production. I used to bring them round and show them the eggs with proper yolks, not a pale, yellow colour, and I used to say, "Here are my charts, here are the number of eggs I get each day," and they couldn't believe that a tropical hen could produce such eggs.

'When we took our children on a visit to Jamaica – aged one and two – everyone said, "The little darlings will love the nice fresh milk." The little darlings took one taste and spat! They had been brought up on tinned milk and didn't hold with all this funny stuff the Jamaicans provided. People used to like coming to lunch with me on Sundays because I gave them fresh cottage cheese made with tinned milk. Nobody knew you could make it with tinned milk, but I just curdled it and it became a great delicacy. I love cooking, but unfortunately you lost status if you cooked, so I was allowed to make a cake or chutney and, occasionally, a very refined dessert. But in that heat and in that kind of kitchen, you didn't really want to cook.'

Rather naturally, Rex Cheverton was out at night a great deal, either operating at the hospital, or visiting sick patients, leaving Joan very much on her own. The maids left at night to return to their homes and look after their own families which the granny had been tending all day. Joan is not an alarmist, but her house was not built for security. Like all the houses in Honduras, it had verandas, and in this case it had three storeys, so there was a great deal of vulnerable space, and also eleven outside doors which were made of clapboard. One night, when the maids had gone, Joan had what she called a 'scary incident'.

'It was one of those nights when the wind blew and the palm trees scraped on the corrugated roof, and you were certain you heard people. It was very creepy and nasty and I decided that "this was ridiculous" and that I would do the most ordinary thing I could think of, so I sat down firmly and darned white socks, and then – bang . . .. There was a screen door which was locked, but all it needed was a push, and suddenly there was an enormous Negro shouting, "I want my corpse! I want my corpse!" I was petrified. I thought he would wake the children, and once they started screaming I couldn't be sure what he would do. I asked him in, and gradually got his story out of him. He had apparently taken his lady love down to the hospital, dying. She was a very long time dying, so he went off and had several drinks with his friends to console himself. Then he had gone back to the hospital where his lady love had died, so he said to the Sister, "That's all right, I will take her home in a taxi." And the English Sister said, "Over my dead body you will take her home in a taxi." And they went on arguing, and finally she said, "If Dr Cheverton says you can have the woman to take in a taxi, you may." So he had come to ask Dr Cheverton, but the Sister didn't know that my husband was doing an emergency operation at the other end of the hospital. Well, I had to get rid of him, so I showed him an empty bedroom, an empty nursery, an empty sitting-room, an empty dining-room, and empty kitchen, and luckily, he didn't see the little steps going up to the children's bedroom. I told him to go back to the hospital to the operating theatre and ask for Dr Cheverton. As soon as he had gone, I telephoned the hospital and said, "Put me through to the doctor," and was told that he was in the operating theatre. I said, "I don't care a damn. I have got to speak to him. Somebody must come and protect me quickly." '

Joan was also vital to Rex's work among the Mayan Indians. They travelled by mule, canoe, or in the backs of lorries, and wherever they went they had to take their hammocks because the rest houses – if they can be so named – were not organized. Joan has slept in the back of a lorry, in the bush with pumas and other wild animals making nocturnal noises throughout the night. But possibly the worst menace on this coast is the mosquito.

'You have got to have a mosquito net. The net has long sleeves through which the hammock ropes go, and your net is a few inches away from your nose. It is terribly claustrophobic! We would go to one of the villages where they've never seen a white woman before, and we would wake up in the morning and suddenly realize that the *whole* village was peering through the cracks of these shanty houses, all watching to see how the white people lived, how they dressed, how they did things. Rex used to send me ahead sometimes to collect the women and children, because if he had gone all the women and children would have vanished, and he would never see them. Because I was a woman they would come and talk to me. I remember sitting on a log and talking to a Mayan Indian, whose Spanish was just about as bad as mine, trying to explain to him firmly why a person was not dying of worms. *Everybody* had worms. It's true, I always had to worm my children regularly once a month. I never waited to see them, I just gave them the worm medicine in case! Anyway, I was trying to explain that there were worms and worms. The ordinary kind and there is the very bad tapeworm. That's why the man was dying.'

I have known people live in Africa and never see a snake, which may surprise many people. In Honduras, it was impossible not to see snakes. As usual, their favourite place was the outdoor lavatory or BG. Once, while staying in a police station, Joan went off as usual to the bottom of the garden, and, 'Lo and behold, there was a snake! I tell you, I came out of there so fast, holding up my breeches, I didn't wait to see if I had buttoned them up or anything. I just held them up and ran.'

According to Rex, it was a breen snake and very poisonous. There were probably more insects, tarantulas and poisonous snakes there than in the whole of Africa. As Joan put it, 'You literally shook your shoes whenever you changed them.'

Joan used to walk down the town pushing her pram and, in Kenyatta fashion, she carried a fly-whisk. She would wave it at the mosquitoes when the wind came one way, and at the sand flies, when it came the other. Club life, of which there was apparently a great deal, also had its disadvantages.

'As you came into the club, every lady was handed a pillow-case for the mosquitoes. You sat down to bridge with your feet in a pillow-case. You wouldn't have dreamt of sitting uncovered.'

Even the sea offered danger in the form of sharks and barracuda. They used to charter a little schooner and when they got near a village Rex wanted to visit, they would possibly get out the canoes and finish the journey up a river, returning at night to bathe in the bay where the schooner was anchored:

'We would put our watchman on just to make sure that the sharks kept clear of us.'

Judith, their baby, once got pneumonia. They had rented a quarantine station which had to be approached by sea. A storm blew up, there were no windows in the building, and they could not send back for help. Luckily, Joan, who was a shocking sailor, had taken a travelling flask of brandy. They gave Judith little sips of brandy, and rubbed brandy butter on her throat like Vick and saved her life.

It must be difficult to believe but Joan had only one conclusion about her life in British Honduras:

'Oh, we loved it! It was a most interesting place, and we were terribly happy there.' It would not be everyone's choice, but that is the mettle of a genuine colonial woman who works side by side with her husband.

'Belize, Britain's last colony on the American continent, which became independent this morning, is a modest down-at-heel sort of place,' wrote the *Financial Times* on 21 September 1981. 'Guatemalan threat. Belize takes a step into the unknown,' wrote *The Times* on the same day.

Not auspicious notices for the Prime Minister of three decades, Mr George Price, to read, so it was interesting to hear what Mary McEntee, the wife of the one before last British Governor and C-in-C thought about the situation as Belize attained her independence.

'There is still this aftermath of slavedom. The Creoles are reluctant to do anything which has the slightest suggestion of their slave days, so they won't cut cane because it is thought to be like slave labour, so agriculture is not a thing Belizians of African origin like to do. Now that they've got their independence, I think they'll have to let settlers in, which the British tried to persuade them to do, and now I think they'll have to. It's ranching country, really; much of it is totally under-used and people, like Jamaicans, who used to come over couldn't believe that a place was so empty.'

Life, however, was not stimulating for Mary as it had been for Joan Cheverton forty years before. In Joan's case, there was always too much to do, too many obstacles to overcome, the constant experiment, each day bringing its new resolution. Mary found it was entirely different.

'Speaking personally, it was very, very dull, but, of course, in the Diplomatic Service, you always have a job to do, but in Belize as the Governor's wife in a country responsible for its own internal affairs, you don't have a job to do! Naturally the Belize government didn't encourage one to inspect schools or open bazaars, because they liked their own ministers to do this, very understandably, so I was very bored because there wasn't enough to do. Our daughters didn't come out because it was too expensive. One is not on the tourist route in Belize, so when you got to Miami it was over £100 each way to get over the next stage, so we eventually decided none of us could afford it.'

Unlike the diplomats and high officials, the McEntees were almost the only people left with servants; the others had to make do with a cleaning woman if they were lucky, so, in a way, even that necessity was taken out of Mary's hands.

'We were the only people left who had any servants at all. I had a major-domo, a cook, a laundress, a housemaid and a driver, but that was unique. The major-domo had been serving Governors for twenty years but he was the only one. But one wants something to do other than just giving dinner parties; that's not sufficient. We did have our own personal friends coming out to stay for a couple of months in the winter to look at the birds which are quite something. The butterflies, too, were lovely, but it's difficult to do butterflies unless you catch them. So I never got down to that because I didn't want to catch them. I went home twice a year to see the family, which helped, but it was the lack of a job – the lack of a role. In the colonial life you are so used to doing a job. I remember our first FCO senior officer's wife said, "Now, don't get bitter about it. In the FO they get two for the price of one, so you might just as well lump it." Which, of course, one had already realized because it's the same in the Colonial Office, and one wouldn't have it otherwise.'

If Mary had been living in the old Government House the whole tenor of her existence might have taken on brighter colours, for it was a beautiful Caribbean four-square Regency house with pillars in the bustle and activity of Belize City. But when the new capital – Belmopan – was built, the Governor was moved into a modern bungalow there, which appears to have been put together without imagination or artistry of any kind.

Feeling her desolation, I wondered whether she had ever tried writing or painting to while away those long hours?

'No! One reason why I didn't paint there was we had no private garden. There was absolutely nowhere to do something in privacy. Even to get one's hair washed, which, of course, one had to do oneself, nobody had organized a private garden in this new house, so you could not get out of sight. So you either had to sit in your bedroom to dry your hair or wait until the weekend when, ten to one, someone would come and stay. The office was part of the house, built at the far side of it, so that everybody who came to the office passed the house part. I got quite desperate about it, especially as it had louvred windows. There was no privacy at all. So that's one reason I couldn't see myself sitting out with a sketching-block. The house was British-built I may say, I'm not blaming the Belizians for it. We had no facilities for our junior staff. I don't know how our junior staff kept sane, because there was nothing to do. There were no tennis courts, no swimming-pools, and nowhere to go and nothing to do unless you drove fifty-five miles down to Belize City. It was really a very hard place for the young ones.'

It would appear that this little capital, which was meant to be another Brasilia, has no heart to it, and the days of the ground in front of the club in the thirties and forties where they did everything from polo to landing small aeroplanes, was preferable to this comfortable life with deep-freezes, indoor lavatories and baths with taps. One consolation was the sense of humour Mary discovered among Belizians, and the lack of any colour bar. Of the humour, she told me this story:

'We toured the whole of Belize in the real old-fashioned colonial way. The further north you get there are more Creoles and more Spanish–Indian mix. There was one post office I remember I went to where the postmaster didn't come from the north of Belize but from the south and he was very entertaining about this, because he said, "We've just had a new counter made." And I said, "Oh, dear, why? If it was a new post office, why didn't they get it right the first time?" and he said, "Well, everybody had forgotten that most Indians are not more than four feet eleven, and so they built it at the proper height and none of the local population could reach up to buy stamps!"

'But the nice thing about Belize is that he thought that was just as funny as I did – he told it to me as a funny story. They have very much the same sense of humour and felt the same things were funny. They are extremely pleasant people. But there again, they are so mixed. It's a great pleasure to entertain them. It's an astonishing thing, I have never lived in a place where there is so little colour bar of any kind, and there is no feeling of rich and poor, absolutely none. I remember I went down to the local market in a colossal American car they'd provided for us, with our enormous Creole driver, and I went to buy something. As I was getting back into this monster car with Crowns back and front and all the rest of it, a market woman said, "Are you going up to the shop?" and I said, "Yes," and she said, "Good! Give me a lift." Now you wouldn't get that anywhere else in the world.'

Belize must be almost the only country in the world that isn't over-populated. Salvador and Jamaica, are so over-populated that, as Mary McEntee describes, 'It is almost like science fiction – they're so close together. Belize is the only bit of Central America that hasn't got people cheek by jowl.' There is one snag, though, and that is that it is on the route for the drug trade from Colombia to the States, and refuelling presents no problem since so much of the country is unpopulated and it is not possible to police the whole area.

'Everybody knows that it's going on and occasionally, if you happen to be flying about, you can see the empty petrol cans where they've landed and refuelled. Somebody has been paid to trundle out flares and this is awfully difficult to stop. There are quite enough strips in dry weather.'

There was one aspect of Belize which certainly hadn't changed since Joan Cheverton's day. Mary was talking about gardening.

'There are so many pests and the climate is peculiar. You've just got some plant growing and the heavens open and you don't see the sun for ten days. You may get twenty inches of rain. As for insects – and you know we've lived in quite a number of places in the world – I have never met insects like the ones in Belize; so many, so tiresome. We once had a visitor from the Foreign Office, and I was just getting up to go and have my bath before dinner. I said, "Oh, Peter, there's a tarantula on the wall, you know, but I'm going to have my bath." And this FO chap, Alan Payne, said afterwards, "Well, what happened actually is that the Governor took a magazine and went like that!" and he added, "It made my stay!" Personally, if I'd known there were tarantulas, I wouldn't have gone.'

Belize has the largest barrier reef in the world after Australia and it is almost untouched. It is quite magnificent, absolutely beautiful and, in spite of the increasing number of tourists, still barely damaged, even though fishing is such a large industry. It is impossible to swim off Belize City since the water is dirty and only about two to three feet deep, so one has to go about ten miles out to the reef by boat.

'There again, it's either a bit chilly or it's the hurricane season and one has to be a little careful. Like all the things in the tropics, there's always a snag.'

When Mary married Peter McEntee in 1945, he was still in the army. I wondered whether, when he changed his service, Mary knew what the future would be like?

'No amount of briefing was going to help, unless you broke up the marriage. Whether, if I'd been told that it was going to be thirty-five years of never staying in one place more than five minutes, I should have consented to it, I don't know. The army are much better looked after, and they usually retire earlier. The Colonial Service was marvellous for a man but very difficult for a wife. The grinding poverty and the entertainment you had to do out of your own miserable pocket, and every time you moved, it was either you bought some more Aladdin lamps or you had different kinds of electric plugs to buy. We were getting £550 in 1946, which even then wasn't very much.'

Speaking from my own experience, I could tell Mary that in Nigeria I had made five moves in a year. I did my own packing and in Eunugu, which was unspeakably hot and humid, I was packing china in wet newspaper, being watched by a very attractive Shell wife, who said languidly, 'But I've never had to do this in my life with Shell.' The army, of which I also had some experience, would not only have done the packing but taken it all away from your front door. But in the Colonial Service it was your job. As Mary said:

'You did the lot. We piled it on the lorry and it went chugging along with your dog on the top of it. I remember a cousin of mine once saying, "Well, of course, if you're poor, it's marvellous because you don't bother about money," and I said, "Well, anyone can see that you've always had plenty then, because the real thing about being poor is that you think of nothing else. It's grinding. You wake up in the middle of the night, you go to bed with it, you wake up with it, wondering how you can buy your child a pair of shoes, because we actually need a bottle of whisky to entertain with." It was literally like that. Fascinating as the life was, it didn't need to be like that. When we joined the FCO I got a dress allowance – of course, it was laughable – but I got a dress allowance of £25. I nearly died with shock when they actually admitted that I existed.'

But as we have all acknowledged in our time the life as a colonial officer's wife had something which was not offered to one in any other service. What was it? Something so intangible that it perhaps cannot be named. Perhaps it was simply a partnership with a husband. Mary summed it up:

'The number of people you've met is surely one of the charms of having lived this sort of life, much as one has moaned and groaned, saying "For heaven's sake, why can't I have a day off?" and so on, but what a lot other people miss who haven't had this.'

So you add and subtract the good and the bad, and come up with the good every time.

PART FOUR

The South Atlantic Islands

10

God Tempers the Wind

The Falkland Islands were first sighted by an Elizabethan navigator, John Davis, in 1592, and if Admiral Burney had had his way, they would have been named the Davis Southern Islands after him. However, it was the French who, in 1764, first settled there. Louis Antoine de Bougainville set out from St Malo with a carefully organized expedition. Not only did he take colonists from St Malo and three families of Acadians, but he also took seeds, plants, sheep, cattle and horses – the latter three all flourished on the tall, nutritious tussock grass which grew so abundantly there. He established his party on East Falkland at the head of Berkeley Sound, at a place which eventually became Fort St Louis; there the French prospered for three years, discreetly flourishing and hidden, in spite of the fact that British ships under Commodore Byron visited the islands. It was not until 1766 that Captain Macbride, who built similar fortifications at Port Egmont, and who circumnavigated the islands with extreme thoroughness, came upon the little Fort of St Louis. As he had been in the islands already a year, it must have been a dramatic moment.

After this the islands were caught up in international politics and Fort St Louis was amicably ceded by France to Spain in 1767, with the little band of colonists given the choice of remaining under Spanish rule or returning to France. The Spanish thought nothing of the French settlement, their fort, or their houses, but in spite of the fact that those forced to remain longed to get away, their kinsmen remained in this lonely outpost for the next forty years.

In 1833, they came under British rule. In 1841 Lord John Russell, then Colonial Secretary, was instrumental in the passing of an Act for the establishment of a government in the Falklands with legislative power, and it was after this date that sheep farming became the islands' chief industry.

The capital and harbour of Stanley is situated on East Falkland and when Dr Cheverton, the senior medical officer, arrived with his wife Joan in 1935, the main means of transport to the outlying settlements was on horseback.

Their living quarters were not luxurious: 'We lived in what had been the old officers' quarters in the Crimean War. There was a whole row of them. When the Crimean War ended, they didn't know what to do with them so they sent them down to the Falkland Islands. We had a two-storey block with a one-storey wing. The wind was sometimes so strong that upstairs in the bedroom, your bed swayed gently. Downstairs, in our study, we fitted linoleum with carpets on top; each door had a woollen-lined portière, the windows had woollen-lined curtains, and yet the turkish mats would gently ripple when you were sitting in front of the little peat fire. Everything was done on peat. Part of Rex's pay was so many loads of peat. Incidentally, it was government peat, and our loyal friends would come and look at the miserable fires we had in our rooms and say, "Anyone can see that you are a government servant, nobody else would burn peat of that low quality." The boy who used to bring our peat into the house was paid the magnificent sum of half a crown a week.'

As all colonial women know, a new station is a challenge. Sometimes the challenge seems almost too much to bear; at other times, with the help of good friends ready with advice, the difficulties and strangeness are soon overcome. Joan Cheverton was not one to worry about trivialities, though she had her moments of shock.

'I remember going into the kitchen the first morning and nearly having a fit. Half a sheep was lying on the kitchen table; I had never seen so much sheep all together in one. You couldn't buy less than half a sheep then. The cook thought I was terribly badly provided for because I didn't have a meat cleaver.

'It was terribly difficult to plan menus because food really was limited. The boats used to come in anything from four to eight weeks and we soon learned to find the dates, and if there was going to be an eight-week gap, we bought a lot of butter, and put it into a big petrol tin and salted it down. You became very inventive. The wind was such that I've seen cabbages blown out of the ground, so you lived very largely on tins. I remember sitting down and sending an order to Griffith MacAlister getting cases of tinned food, and spending something like £50 to £60 on groceries, which in 1935 bought you a lot, because I couldn't get the stuff, or the prices were so incredible. For instance, I imported a sack of oatmeal for porridge; by the time it had reached me my porridge worked out at 1¾*d*., while in Stanley they were selling it for 8*d*. or 9*d*. a pound. One would think one would get a lot of fish, but nobody went fishing – the weather was too rough, though one could sometimes get freshwater fish from the little rivers. In the two years we were there, I can virtually count the days on which we had beef; the rest of the time it was mutton. I do not mean lamb. You only had lamb at Christmas if you ordered it beforehand, from one farmer who supplied you at an enormous price. All the other farmers thought he was a damned fool. Fancy selling a lamb before the wool had been taken off! I kept a lot of ducks and a lot of hens, and had a big run, and went out and got the wild tussock grass and made clumps so that they were protected; I managed to vary our diet with a lot of egg dishes and poultry. Pork was virtually uneatable because it was raised on mutton. You threw your pigs the sheep's heads. When you smoked and salted your own piece of mutton it tasted like a nice piece of bacon, rather than the real piece of pork that had been mutton fed. It was a battle, trying to vary the monotony.

'We were very lucky because we had one of the old-established gardens which had hedges, but the wind was such that hedges just didn't grow. There was a dear old man who ran the Customs, and he told me, "Of course, the answer to that garden of yours is it needs night soil! That's what you want for good hedges."

'People used to take you, proudly, to see little clumps of parsley. One invited people in return and said, "come and look at my plants, I've got a new leaf". It was considered really worth seeing; we never aspired to a flower, just a new leaf! One longed for fresh vegetables. The patients in the hospital revolted because they said that Rex was starving them because they didn't have a mutton chop for breakfast every single morning . . . .

'Another great problem was keeping your house clean because of the peat. Everything was covered with a layer of peat dust. When you had a tea-party or anybody to any sort of meal, you had a little feather duster kept behind the sofa, and as they arrived at the front door you rushed around and did a sort of whisk, whisk, whisk, and cleaned a little bit of dust out of the way.'

To those not involved in the complexity of the pomp and ceremony of the government side of colonial life, the lengths to which officials went to keep up appearance must read like the plot of a Gilbert and Sullivan opera. Whether the Governor's lady is stepping with her shoe-bag and dress onto Turks Island and changing behind a bamboo screen, or eating asparagus with long gloves in Fiji, it seems wryly funny. In capitals such as Lagos, Nairobi or Delhi, it all appears perfectly right and proper. Nevertheless, however difficult it might be to arrive at some government house for an occasion effectively and tidily turned out, there is no denying the pleasure it brought, and the discipline it instilled to achieve a suitably chic appearance. The supreme, and often ridiculous, importance some people paid to an invitation to Government House will be told in another chapter. The colonial woman treated the whole affair with respect, but often with an almost tender sense of humour. Joan Cheverton certainly did.

'There were five cars in the whole place, and four miles of road which went very appropriately from the slaughter house to the cemetery, so when you got an invitation to Government House you rushed to the telephone to try and book the one and only taxi. If you didn't get the taxi because someone had got there first, you walked. You naturally wore long skirts, so every lady had a piece of elastic that went round her waist with a button and a clip to hitch up her skirt. You put on your wellingtons, mackintosh, sou'wester and put your shoes in one of those bags you used to have when you went to dancing classes. When you arrived, your hostess immediately led you into a room and you took off your outdoor clothes, put on your nice shoes and primped yourself up and went into dinner. The men were ushered into another room where some of them had to take off riding-breeches and put on evening trousers. It was a very formal life and we changed for dinner every single night, even at home. There was a wonderful town hall – I believe it was burnt down – built on a Swedish model, and we would have dances there. When they put up a notice saying "Lights on till 12", you knew you were going to town in no uncertain way. There was a platform where they sometimes gave concerts, but at the dances the stiffs sat on the platform – stiffs, because they wore stiff shirts. The Governor and his party would sit there, and everybody would hopefully get as near as they could, hoping they might look as if they were an overflow from the Governor's party. The men would sit one side of the hall and the women on the other, and the men would get up and walk half-way across the room – they never went right up to a girl – and one would nod his head at a girl and she would get up and they would dance, and then, at the end of the dance, they would part again and return to their side of the hall. It was all very respectable and very old-fashioned.'

As always in these far-flung colonies, it was the mail which depressed Joan. The post arrived at intervals of four weeks; sometimes it could be six weeks and sometimes as long as eight. Like others before her, she arranged the sack of letters and newspapers in chronological order and read them in orderly fashion. Nearly always the last letter was one of reproach for not answering the first. The letters might get to Montevideo and then would be held up for a boat to collect them to take them on to the Falklands. It was hard to convince impatient friends and relatives at home who were receiving news by a more regular post in three weeks.

The normal social life appears to have been Australian in flavour and this was not to Joan's liking.

'After dinner, the men went into one room, and the ladies into another, and you didn't meet. It wasn't a question of lingering over port and then not joining, they just *didn't* join. You just waited until it was time for them to go, and when they came and joined us, they all had a smoko before they left – great cups of tea and cocoa, exactly as if you had never had a large meal.'

Conscientiously, Rex Cheverton went through the medical records. The Falkland Islands had, up to then, been rated as a healthy station. Rex discovered that there were more nervous breakdowns and ailments of that kind than had been realized and so, from that time, it was classified unhealthy.

Soon after they arrived they paid a visit with the Governor to the West Falkland to see the doctor on duty. Joan tells a strange tale:

'The doctor was meeting his new Governor for the first time. He didn't get up when we came in, his hair was down to his shoulders; he had on a red tam o'shanter; his feet were up on the mantelpiece; he was smoking a pipe, and at intervals he spat into the peat fire. He was fed up! Nobody had told him that to visit patients he would have to ride. Nobody offered support, and on his first night they came and called him out to a case, and they tied him to a horse in the dark, and took him to see his first patient. He never wanted to see a horse again. He went away and the government sent out another doctor, and didn't tell *him* that he had to ride. By some mercy we had him to stay for ten days at the house, and we put him and his wife on our horses three times a day until at least they could sit on the darn things. They didn't have any riding things. A man could go down to the store and buy some old things, and I gave the girl a pair of my riding-breeches. But they didn't brief anyone in those days. For instance, they sent us to an hotel which had been burnt down nineteen years previously. There was only a little guest house, where we stayed for several weeks, because the Colonial Secretary didn't want to move out of our house because his crop – his vegetables – were ready and he didn't want to lose them.'

Again that old spectre, loneliness, materialized. Not for Joan, who had many interests and resources, but for other wives she met. She was amused to find that not only was a new face welcomed with delight, but, 'They would just literally say, "All of you come and stay," and you would be two or three in a bed. It was a new face, it was somebody to talk to! We found it fascinating but a lot of the wives found it very frustrating, very lonely. There was one girl there who was absolutely miserable, she didn't know how to settle in, how to adapt. She hadn't imagined anything so cut off, wild and lonely!'

The colonial woman appears to be always in the dilemma of either having too much to do, or, as in the Falklands, not enough.

In 1957 Sir Edwin Arrowsmith was Governor, and his wife, Clondagh, told me that the hospital in Stanley was then very good. Clondagh found a flourishing Girls' Brigade, and she was active in the Red Cross with a Falkland Islander, Mrs Eve Pitaluga. The old people were their special concern, and at Christmas the Red Cross committee gave those who were not fit enough to get out or had no one to look after them, Christmas dinners. They also collected for an ambulance.

Edwin Arrowsmith said that one of the most important people on the island was the ladies' hairdresser, as well she might be. As one who has been deprived of this aid for half of my life, I would think this is what I would take with me if I ever appeared on 'Desert Island Discs'. As Clondagh also said, 'That was the only place I have ever been where there was a hairdresser.'

As is usual within the colonies, trade had been the first consideration. In 1851, the Falkland Islands Company had been incorporated by charter as a trading company, and other than the Governor and the ladies' hairdresser, the most important person in the island was the head of this company. The company owned about half the farmland and the economy of the colony depended entirely on the export of wool to England. Shares were held mainly by people in England. As Edwin Arrowsmith said, 'The Falklanders always reckoned that they contributed more to this country than this country ever did to them. By and large, I think the company were good employers. Perhaps they weren't too keen on development of the pastures, but everything depended on the price of wool. For instance, when the Korean war was on, the market fairly boomed and everyone was happy. The major weakness was the one-crop economy. There was no airfield when we were there. All we had was the little ship – the *Darwin* – owned by the company, which came down every month or six weeks from Montevideo, and a wool ship which came out three or four times a year to take the wool back to England.'

It was good to learn that while the Arrowsmiths were there the Falkland Islanders tried to improve the pasturage. One farmer had planted Yorkshire fog which is considered a weed in England, but can grow without a fertilizer, a commodity which was too expensive to import to the islands in any quantity.

While Sir Edwin Arrowsmith was in his office, Clondagh

organized the house, sewed and knitted and often played bridge with friends in the afternoon. When they went round the camp on visits, they were always greeted by the farm manager, irrespective of the time of day, as to whether they would like 'hot or cold'? If you said 'hot' you got a cup of tea, but if 'cold' you got a gin and tonic, even at six o'clock in the morning.

Transport had changed from the days of the Chevertons. Now, despite the lack of road, there are more vehicles per head of population than anywhere else in the world. The Governor, whose lot usually merits an Austin Princess, had a London taxi which the Arrowsmiths had inherited from their predecessor. He found it more comfortable to sit in wearing his plumed hat. They also had two little float planes, Beavers, which often could not fly because of the wind which blew at twenty to twenty-five knots a day.

In what must have been comparable to a pleasant village life, except on official occasions, all kinds of games were played at Government House by way of diversion. They played poker, billiards, bridge, snooker and darts; they visited the Colony Club, a cinema once a week, and attended various dances.

The vegetables which Joan Cheverton craved, now proved no problem. The Arrowsmiths had a vegetable garden at the back of their house, well walled-in to stop the wind, and divided into small sections for extra protection.

'And everyone grew their own spuds!' said Clondagh. And than added, as did everyone I talked to, 'They were such nice people – so likeable.'

From 1964 to 1970, Sir Cosmo Haskard was Governor. His wife, Phillada, was keenly interested in the wild as well as the culti-vated plants of the islands. Great changes must have taken place since Joan Cheverton took people into her garden to show them a leaf. Phillada assisted in choosing the subjects and providing some of the slides from which the drawings were made for an issue of stamps depicting wild flowers and berries. There was sea cabbage, which grows on most beaches all over the world, scurvy grass, so named because the sailors used to suck the stems against scurvy when they lacked other green matter; diddle dee, which has a pungent quinine-tasting berry with which they could make extremely good jelly and jam; the tea berry, the pig vine, and many others.

By now, the macrocarpa hedges planted in the thirties must have grown very tall at Government House. Phillada describes how their gardeners were able to grow beautiful lupins, Iceland poppies and many other hardy flowers while all along the drive of Government House the daffodils were magnificent in the spring. All these flowers were also to be found in colourful gardens throughout the Falklands. Nevertheless, the wind is a factor, both in the Falklands and in the Antarctic.

'A calm day was very much appreciated and in the winter we did get those calm, beautiful days and you really felt like dropping everything and going outside. The temperatures might not range through a very wide scale. I suppose 18°F might be the coldest and anything over 50°F was a reasonably warm day. When we were there we had one day in six years when with the temperature at 72°F some Islanders were far too hot, and we all rushed and got our tropical cottons out and I have a photograph of myself in a cotton dress and my husband in shorts, which was certainly fairly unusual.

'If there is a wind, it immediately lowers the temperature and this was the thing that made the Falklands feel colder, but it was perfectly possible to walk outside with the temperature at 40°F in your shirt-sleeves provided there was no wind, but if there was, you automatically picked up an anorak because it kept the wind off.'

Peat was still the main source of warming the houses. Townspeople were allocated peat bogs on Stanley Common. At one time the Haskards had to cut some of their own peat. They competed with their open fires but not with their huge boiler which was eventually converted to oil.

'You go up to the peat bog and you have a peat-cutting spade with a hole in the centre of it, because otherwise your sod sticks to the spade. An expert cutter will lay the slabs of peat almost like a pack of cards on the bank. Throughout the Islands, peat was a very important thing, it was the only fuel until oil began to be imported. This oil was brought to the Islands by Royal Fleet Auxiliary ships.'

Though the standards were high from the point of view of 'showing the flag', Phillada did find that it was very much a do-it-yourself place. 'We used to have large parties; you might have 150 people for a dance and you had to lay on a supper. It meant several days in the kitchen for the cook and myself before-hand. We cooked the meat two days before, we made the puddings the day before and on the day we did the final touches to the puddings, made the salads and cut the meat. It would be a question of getting up at six in the morning. The Queen's birth-day was quite a strain, with the Parade which took up most of the morning and the preparations for the Ball in the evening. This took place in April on the Queen's actual birthday, because we couldn't do it in June because it would have been in midwinter.

'We only had one cook, a manservant who drove the car on the odd ceremonial occasion and was otherwise very much a houseman, and a maid. When, towards the end of our time, we wanted a maid, we had to bring one from Uruguay, though we would have much sooner had a Falkland Islander, but there really was a great shortage. We also had someone coming in to do the laundry, and when we had a party extra helpers would come in after their day's work. We also had an excellent Falkland Islands nanny for our small son and three very good men in the garden. But it was quite a strain when you were building up to a heavy period of entertaining. Over Christmas and New Year, for instance, one might expect to have something between three to four hundred people through the house in ten days.'

Phillada and her husband enjoyed travelling on horseback. Farmers, twelve years ago, used horses for sheep work and still do. Land Rovers, though, were increasingly in evidence, while many young men had their motorbikes, but, as Phillada said, there is no better way than on horseback to appreciate the camp.

'We had the most fascinating bird life. The number of species was small enough to get to know many of them and yet big enough to be of interest. The strong westerly winds would bring in stray birds from time to time which had blown off course, so you did sometimes get the most unlikely visitors. Among the birds of prey are the turkey vulture, the cavancho and the johnny rook. The Falklands is one of the few places where johnny rooks breed. Then the fascinating penguins, gentoo, rockhopper, jackass and a few macaroni and king penguin. We had the big black-browed albatross with a wing span of six feet. You could go up and photograph these beautiful birds, you could walk amongst them and they were utterly unconcerned. Albatross eggs are good to eat; they are not as fishy as penguin eggs and so they are occasionally stolen. Penguin eggs are only taken on licence. We had Upland geese in large numbers but they were shot for food so were less inclined to let one go too close. The steamer duck's call will always remind me of the Falklands – we had lovely roseate terns, and we had skuas, and if you were walking in skua country, you wanted to hold a stick above your head to stop them flying down and striking your head, they would strike the stick instead. They could really hurt though I was never struck by one . . .. We had kelp geese, oyster catchers, military starlings and tussac birds which used to eat the grubs off the elephant seals. It was quite fascinating to watch a group of elephant seals, who weren't particularly beautiful, and these delicate little birds coming out of the tussacs, alighting on them, rather like the birds which picked the tick off the African game. We had elephant seals, fur seals and sea lions. The fur seals were protected because they had been almost exterminated in sealing days, and a very flourishing population was building up on the Jason Islands and elsewhere.

'Then there is one wonderful island – Beauchêne Island. I think I'm probably the first woman to have gone onto that island. It is the most southerly island in the Falklands group, and it is estimated that there were probably between three to four million birds on it. We went there by helicopter, which in itself was quite hazardous because the birds could have got caught up in the rotors. I don't really know how a bird finds its own nest, it was just solid birds. They were mainly the black-browed albatross and the rockhopper penguin.'

Phillada went to South Georgia several times. There were women in there who she felt might like a visit. South Georgia is a dependency of the Falkland Islands and, as Phillada said, 'I would think it was the most remote place in which a colonial wife could ever expect to find herself. There was a government station with an administrative officer, who was a magistrate, and his duties were very largely concerned with the whaling stations which, at that time, still existed. The administrative headquarters were at a place called King Edward Point near Grytviken where in the southern summer the population grew quite large. I went down on different occasions in HMS

Protector, RMS *Darwin* and RRS *John Biscoe,* and I suppose there were about a dozen people in this small government community. There was the wife of the administrative officer and two other women, when I first went there. It was pretty lonely.

'The second woman who was permanently there was the wife of the constable–handyman. She had her children with her. She kept poultry which had to live inside during the winter. I remember them very vividly, looking out of a window at me. There was a fairly steep hill behind King Edward Point and in the winter it cast its shadow and I think for about three months of the year they didn't have any direct sun at all. So it was a pretty good effort for anyone to live down there and do tours of duty, in such isolation. Government staff were mainly people connected with meteorology and the whaling stations.

'When I first went to South Georgia, the Norwegians were handing over to the Japanese, who were handling things very differently because they were interested in whales for meat, so there was no waste and somehow one didn't feel so badly about it. The Norwegians were interested only in the oil. You would see half a dozen little Japanese on top of one of these huge whales with tremendous flensing-knives cutting the flesh away. Subsequently, the Japanese changed to a pelagic fleet and all the land bases were given up. In 1970 the Falkland Islands government handed over administration of the base at King Edward Point to the British Antarctic Survey, who acted as the agent of the Falkland Islands government. South Georgia remains a dependency of the Falkland Islands.'

It was part of Cosmo Haskard's job to visit the Antarctic as High Commissioner. As there were no women south of South Georgia, it was not necessary for Phillada to go with him. However, it was not in her nature to be so near a region of such fascination and not see it for herself. She managed to get permission from the Admiralty and travelled on a voyage which seldom, if ever, comes within the range of a colonial woman. The Haskards went south in HMS *Endurance* which, though not an ice-breaker, was ice-strengthened and was able to travel through ice. She was the Royal Navy's replacement for HMS *Protector.* There was a self-contained guest cabin, so Phillada did not feel that she was quite such an imposition as she might otherwise have been as probably the first women to take passage to the Antarctic in one of HM ships. These days there are of course package tours to the Antarctic, but to travel by courtesy of the Royal Navy is rather a different matter. One can only hope that there is no danger of the Antarctic ever becoming polluted by the incursion of too many tourists.

HMS *Endurance* carried a helicopter pad and on one occasion the Haskards went by helicopter to a British Antarctic Survey base where husky dogs were used for sledge work.

'The idea had been that we should go to Adelaide Island, but unfortunately, although we went down the coast of Graham Land, the sea was beginning to freeze. It was therefore not possible to go further than a short distance beyond the Antarctic Circle. The ice was still at the light, loose stage – it was rather exciting and something utterly beyond my imagination. To think of going through ice! When you think of the colonies, basically you think of the tropics. But here we were in the Antarctic, which was totally different. One day one had had forty-foot waves breaking over the ship and now there was calm. So it was not uncomfortable but fascinating though cold, and you certainly needed to be well wrapped up. On our return we saw Cape Horn and we went through the Beagle Channel, and I saw something of Patagonia . . . one just never imagined in the ordinary way of colonial life you would ever see or do such things, so it was an experience of a lifetime.'

As must be fairly clear by now, there were not many outlets or diversions for the Falkland Islanders. They had no television, the cinema once a week and, in Stanley, the famous 'box' with the rediffusion system over which music was relayed at certain hours, and some of the BBC programmes. Phillada devised a horticultural show and, later, a winter show. She wanted the people from the camp to join in, which was not so easy for the horticultural show because the exhibits were perishable. So for the winter show they had classes for homespun wool, knitting, crochet, and horse-gear making, the latter being something which she had learned to do herself and was very anxious should not die out. The older men could make splendid pieces of gear for their horses. The farmers and their families from the camp always came into Stanley every July or August for the Sheep Owners' Association meetings. The winter show was timed to coincide with this period. The winter show progressed famously to other interests, paintings, photography, and even toy-making.

There has long been a threat to the Falkland Islands from Argentina. In 1966, in the Haskards' time, the first serious incident took place. A plane which had been hijacked by nineteen young Argentines who expected to be hailed as the saviours of an oppressed people landed on Stanley racecourse. There was no airfield at that time. The population of Stanley went out to the racecourse to have a look, because they thought it was a plane which had flown off course. The Argentines discovered that they were not welcomed as liberators, which was hardly surprising as the islanders are as British as anyone in an English village. In due time the hijackers surrendered and were repatriated to Argentina.

The Haskards' son, Julian, started his schooling in Stanley, at around five years old. Some of the older children went to the British School in Montevideo, while some went to England. The Darwin boarding-school catered for children from the camp. Darwin was the largest settlement outside Stanley and the main headquarters of the company farms. To cope with younger children in camp travelling teachers went round the farms on all the islands, by sea, air or on horseback. They might teach for three weeks in a small settlement or in a shepherd's house and then set work for the children and carry on to the next place and return again later. These travelling teachers were either trained teaching staff or VSOs who were filling in their year before going on to university. Though this method was far from ideal, it did serve a purpose and bring some form of learning to remote areas. On a few farms a full-time teacher was employed.

When Julian went to prep school in England, he was eight and his parents were leaving the Falkland Islands. Phillada thinks that he could have gone on at the school in Stanley as far as 'O' levels if necessary but at that time very few children did so. For parents who sent their children to school in England, holidays were a problem. Parents naturally wanted to have their children out for the long English summer holidays, but that meant coming to the Falkland Islands in the winter. Communications also made it difficult in the Haskards' time when there were only twelve regular sailings for mail and passengers, with a six-week gap in the middle of the southern winter.

Teeth were still a problem possibly because of the soft water. It became usual for a dentist to travel round and set up at various settlements as required and passengers on the Beaver float planes were accustomed to the familiar sight of the dentist with his portable chair and paraphernalia occupying two seats in the aircraft.

People still wanted formality at Government House, though perhaps now they had dispensed with the elastic and the button for their long skirts. 'They were punctilious in arriving – and indeed departing – on time.'

Phillada has a last word for the Falkland Islands: 'I would like to mention the extreme kindness of the Islanders – I would stress the great welcome they gave. We made firm friends among them and that is something that I will always remember.'

11

Secreted Island

In 1506 the Portuguese navigator Tristan da Cunha, sighted the three islands – the largest was to be named after him, the others were Nightingale and Inaccessible – but he did not land. As with Ascension Island, the fate of Tristan da Cunha, a mere speck in the South Atlantic ocean, was changed when in 1815 Napoleon began his six years of captivity on St Helena, 12,000 miles away. Unoccupied until then, it was annexed by the British and a small garrison was placed there. When, a year later, the soldiers were withdrawn, a Scots corporal, William Glass, elected to remain with two companions, and so began the history of today's population of this minute island.

William Glass fortunately had his coloured wife and the first of his many children with him, and though other men tried to settle and came and went, only Glass and a few companions remained. By 1827, five coloured women were brought from St Helena as wives for other settlers, and the community life of the island began.

It was in 1961 that the world became acutely aware of the existence of this outpost of the Empire when a volcano erupted and the islanders were evacuated to England. As it happened, they were evacuated unnecessarily because the lava which looked as if it might overwhelm the settlement and cut off the water supply, only reached one house, and then turned off and flowed into the sea, over the landing-place. Within two years, the islanders chose to return to Tristan da Cunha. It is possible that the younger ones might have preferred to stay in England but felt compelled to return to look after their elders and only about half a dozen remained in the Western world.

The Tristan settlers were Italian, Dutch, American, Irish, Scottish and English, but curiously enough nothing has survived in the Tristan language but a kind of Scottish English. They will say things like, 'How you is?' or 'You is wery welcome.' Hugh Elliott, the first Administrator in 1950, described it as probably the same language talked by Wellington's troops before the battle of Waterloo – an old Sam Wellerish kind of English. There are in all about 264 islanders and seven family names – Glass, Green, Hagan, Repetto, Lavarello, Rogers and Swain.

Naturally, it would need a very special type of colonial wife to settle happily into this isolated and restricted life which might suit the islanders admirably, but is a far cry from our Western way of life, especially when cut off from nearly all communication with the outside world. When Hugh Elliott took up the post, Elizabeth, his wife, might have been hand-picked for this assignment. Not only was she a trained nurse and midwife, but she enjoyed the simplicity of the people and their way of life. There was one major snag and that was that she had to leave two children of school age in England, and only take her five-year-old son, Clive, with her.

Since Hugh Elliott was the first Administrator, there was no one to brief the little family, and though he went ahead of Elizabeth, he said, 'I couldn't pass any information on to Elizabeth or assess whether it was liveable in!' All Elizabeth could learn was that it was the place 'where people walk about on all-fours because the wind is so strong'.

The journey, if that was anything to go by, did not make a favourable impression.

'The journey was terrible – when I went, anyway. I went out in ordinary mail ship comfort to Cape Town with my young son. We then got onto a very small, 180-ton wooden boat that didn't take any passengers. I had to be signed on as crew at a shilling a day. We slept in fishermen's bunks that absolutely stank of fish and unwashed people. My son was five then – four when Hugh went – seven when we came back. We had seven and a half days on this very small boat in tremendously rough seas. We were even without wireless communication with anybody after about 100 miles out of Cape Town and 100 miles near Tristan – it is 1,500 miles from Cape Town.'

The island is forty-nine square miles, with a 6,760-feet peak. Seen from the air it looks like the spokes of a bicycle wheel, with a large number of volcanic gulches scattered around. The islanders live on a little shelf called Edinburgh, 100 feet above sea-level. Round one corner are the potato patches, the most important crop on the island since it is the staple diet, but the other side of the shelf is made inaccessible by a sheer 2,000-feet precipice. There were about fifty cottages on the shelf, and the Elliotts occupied one of the quarters of the Wartime Naval Station in a one-storeyed bungalow built of wood with a corrugated roof. Their furniture came from a Union Castle liner and was all curved to fit the cabins and saloons. Their oil-stove smoked abominably, and they had one bedroom for themselves with a small one leading off for their son, Clive. Apparently, they were considered extremely lucky for they had their own bathroom, a luxury the other expatriates had to share with other cottagers.

To begin with, Elizabeth found the island women extremely shy. They were not used to strangers, and though friendly and exceedingly pleasant, they were tongue-tied. Elizabeth somehow had to make a break-through.

'They would sit silently round the wall. I would have to make conversation and they were obviously quite embarrassed and would sit saying, "Yes, Mum. No, Mum," until I realized that they loved knitting. They got the wool from their sheep and they knitted the whole time, washing, carding and spinning it. In the old days, every garment they wore was knitted – jerseys, socks, underpants. One day I said, "Bring your knitting," and this was much better. They sat knitting and talked more easily. I had them in relays to my house, and then visited every house in the village. They had carding parties. As the men would help each other to build a house, so the women would help each other to card the wool. I started going to their carding parties. I would go up to a cottage which was full of women chattering away; as I came in there would be dead silence. They would go on carding, not saying a word. This was what it was like in the beginning. Eventually it got better and I would feel really pleased, when, after a while, I would go to a house where they were carding and I would say, "Hello, may I come in?" They would say, "Oh, it's only Mrs Helliot," and go on talking. They accepted you in the end. They were very good staunch friends, and very friendly. I don't remember having any enemies. We were very very fond of them.'

The medical side of life was fairly basic in those days, but fortunately the islanders, away from any form of pollution, enjoyed marvellously good health.

'When the Navy were there, the naval padre discovered there were very rich crayfish beds round the islands and he thought they should be exploited for the benefit of the islanders. After the war, a fishing company went out there – and the Colonial Office appointed an administrator – hence Hugh's job. The fishing company had to provide a doctor, a nurse, a school-teacher and an agriculturist in return for the right to fish there.'

With her nursing, her visits to the islanders, and joining in their recreations, Elizabeth was never lonely. It was unlike any other form of colonial life. There was no pomp or ceremony, no official entertaining, and yet one gets the feeling that the deprivations were met head-on with a spirit of goodwill.

'We were certainly never lonely, and certainly never short of something to do. There were 245 islanders and ten ex-patriate families. We weren't really short of people. Of course you were totally shut off. There wasn't a road, or a car, a telephone, postman or bus. There was nothing. No cinema, of course, but just surviving took you most of the time. You got used to a very simple way of life. I am no typist but can type and Hugh had no secretary, so I had to do his typing as well as my nursing job and looking after my son; and quite a bit of entertaining one way and another – having the island women to tea or going out to supper – cooking and the usual chores. One of the special women's trips was "picking penguins" (Pinnamins) and I went to the outer islands with the women. The penguins moult at a certain time of the year, and it's not as cruel as it might sound. You catch your penguin, the feathers are coming off anyway, and you pull the feathers off and put them in bags, and then they are used to fill mattresses and pillows. Otherwise the women really just stayed at home. They might go to the potato patch, but very few ever went to the peak – most of the women I knew had never been to the peak. They just sat outside and knitted on a nice day.'

Contact with their children at home was precarious. 'We only had letters four times a year; we did send signals – Hugh and I were allowed to send to each other 100 words twice a week; and when I joined him, we were allowed to send the children 100 words once a week.'

Clive must certainly have been a comfort to Elizabeth.

'Clive went to the village school, a church school with a schoolteacher, where he had one particular friend called Peter. He learned Tristan talk which is quite a different language. He used it as two separate languages. He would be with us, and then see a friend through the window and call something almost unintelligible to the normal outside world. He would go off with him and switch to the Tristan language.'

Elizabeth did all her own cooking, though, before she arrived, an island girl cooked for Hugh.

'Gladys came and cleaned and peeled potatoes. They didn't have much furniture in their houses so they were not much good at dusting, but they kept the floors beautifully. She was a real friend – I didn't treat her like a servant.'

Eventually Elizabeth joined in all the women's pursuits.

'The men would go off to the islands to collect guano, penguins' eggs and the carcases of petrels to be salted down for food, and the women would be left behind. The island women would also know when the wind was blowing in the right direction and that the men might come back. Somebody would be watching out on the cliff and the word would go round the island that they thought they were coming. You would have plenty of warning as they would be about five miles or more away, so you would rush off and make your pot of tea or coffee, put cosies over it, and then you'd go down with a kerchief round your head and a cake in your other hand. The moment a boat beached, we would tear down to greet the men and they would all have a cup of tea and something to eat before they went home.'

Only once did both the Elliotts climb to the top of the peak with an island couple. The worst part was climbing the 2,000-feet base, after which it was fairly gentle walking. There was green vegetation to hold onto round the base but otherwise it was sheer. Elizabeth kept her eyes fastened on the clouds scudding overhead. 'I felt quite green. The only thing to do was to hold on and look dead in front of me.'

When they reached the top, the weather closed in on them, and instead of the wonderful view, it was snowing and blowing a gale. There is a lovely crater lake at the top which they missed seeing. Coming down, Elizabeth's knees began folding, and by the time she got back she was having to be supported. It took her a day or two to recover.

Another single expedition was a visit to Gough Island. Elizabeth was the second woman ever to visit it, the first being the cook of the factory ship of the Russian whaling fleet who had carved her name on a rock in a cave. Gough was 250 miles from Tristan and the local boats, built largely of driftwood covered with oiled and painted canvas and without keels, were not considered safe so they travelled in a trawler.

'It was a terribly exciting place, full of sea elephants and seals – masses of them – totally untouched. When you see the sea elephants on the beach they are quite harmless because they can hardly move. If you go close to them they always face you and go backwards into the sea, looking at you. We used to see masses of whales in the distance.'

There were other recreations which they enjoyed.

'There weren't any games – you could walk or fish or swim. Well, you could swim, but being a volcanic island, the sand was dark grey and if you went off the edge of the beach, it went down – no gentle slope. Not good for children who bathed in rock pools. There were island dances which were fun. When a child was born, they had a private christening and when the child was a year old, they had a big celebration – presumably because it had got through the first year. Then the child had no more birthday celebrations until he or she was twenty-one. When you were twenty-one there was a big party. Then at thirty/forty/fifty/sixty and however long you lived, you had "big heaps" (a feast) on every decade. I had my fortieth which was "big heaps" in a big way. You would eat and then go to the village hall and dance – they all had heavy shoes and it was a thumping dance. At first, we danced to the fiddle and accordion which was nice. Many of the dances were distant folk memories of Strip the Willow, Gay Gordons and suchlike; one was called Tapioca's Big Toe. By the end, we and one island couple, were the only people who could dance it; they went over to what they called Foss Drops! The girls used to sit along one wall and when the music started the men just came up and grabbed you to dance. They never spoke while they were dancing, they were too busy concentrating on the steps. At the end the girls just returned to sit down again. This was the chief recreation. Going to church was another – if you call that recreation – everybody went. The Society of the Propagation of the Gospel was responsible for appointing the minister. It was rather High Church; Hugh used to read the lessons and we had the Administrator's pew in the front. In the church, the women sat on one side and the men on the other – we sat together but we were the exception. They were keen on their church and had a revealing simple faith. There was nothing much you could do if you wanted something badly but pray for it – which they did a great deal.'

Hugh was busy with conservation. He had two fears. One was that someone would accept potatoes from some ship's galley and introduce blight to the island, and the other that they would run out of water in spite of the springs. Now it is piped to all the cottages, but in the early fifties it had to be fetched from a stand pipe. The other serious problem was the rats. Two rats had come off a shipwreck years before and, of course, multiplied. There was an annual holiday, Rat Day, when all the men went into the potato patches with their dogs and slaughtered the rats. An interesting discovery was that the right whale, second largest species after the blue whale, visited the island seas for a few months every year to have their calves. When Hugh cabled the colonial office to ask if there was any method of scaring them to prevent them upsetting island fishing boats he was told that the southern right whale had long since been extinct. In fact a population of over one hundred had built up and he was able to prove this with a photograph.

Because the islanders usually ate the potatoes with their skins on, they were provided in this way with necessary vitamins, and consequently had the most wonderful teeth in the world. When a Surgeon Commander, a dental specialist, arrived to look at the islanders' teeth, he found that even the oldest inhabitant, aged eighty-seven, hadn't a trace of dental caries. Sadly this was not to last.

'When Hugh arrived, the fishing company had started its operations. Tristan had had an economy with no money at all – just barter. A ship would come in and they would give them water or a chicken, and the ship would exchange clothes, etc. The islanders had to be weaned onto earning wages from the fishing company, after which a shop was opened and the island-ers started eating sugar, biscuits and sweets. From then on people had as much trouble with their teeth as everyone else.'

When, in 1961, the Tristaners came to England, the Elliotts went to visit them in their camp near Reigate. It was November and very cold.

'They were very unhappy, and they weren't used to the cold. Quite a number got bronchitis and died – they weren't used to our germs.'

The day came in 1952 for the Elliotts to leave the island.

'I had handed over my nursing post to somebody else. On the day the Navy was coming to fetch us, the doctor suddenly came to me, saying a girl had appendicitis, and we had to operate, and that I had to give the anaesthetic. I was not an anaesthetist, so I was horrified, but he told me they would tell me what to do! It went on hour after hour and the doctor couldn't find the appendix. We radioed to the frigate which was on its way, asking if they had a surgeon on board to help us as we were not getting on very well! The reply was that they couldn't get there for several hours. In the event the doctor decided to sew her up again. He thought her chances of survival poor and he left me to look after her. She pulled through and as we set sail we heard she was getting better. When they came to England after the eruption, and we visited them, she was brought to me, and they said, "Here is Joan," – and there she was – very pregnant. Anyway, when the ship arrived, Hugh was piped aboard, and in turn the Captain made a formal visit in full uniform to our house. I was nearly in tears, I was so tired. I had had to put on my best dress and receive him. He brought the Bishop of Pretoria to the island with him, because there were a lot of islanders who were going to be confirmed.'

This all happened thirty years ago. The islanders are more sophisticated now, but according to an article by Hilary Jones, who went out there recently as a medical officer, they are still as warm-hearted as ever, the island is still as inaccessible, and it is still a pin-point on the map which is pink.

Elizabeth said, nostalgically, 'I think the women have quite an easy time now. They seem to have a lot of fun – more social events. However, we had children at home and were pleased to come back. But you can imagine that if you get used to a small community, you don't feel much like facing the big outside world.'

PART FIVE

Malaysia and Hong Kong

12

Lady Templer

The police in Malaya during the years 1946 and 1947 were aware that arms had been buried and hidden in the jungle by the Chinese who were working in Force 136, ostensibly for the British. They were also aware that they had returned to their former ambition to take over power in Malaya once the Japanese were defeated and the war ended. The Emergency when it came was triggered off by an Australian named Sharkey, a very senior communist, who went to an international top-level meeting of communists in Calcutta. There he decided that the time had come for direct action against the British Raj. He returned to Singapore where he attended another meeting of leading communists in Malaya, and then fortuitously departed for Australia leaving others to do the dirty work. The Emergency started within a week of his departure, in 1948.

The communists were thick on the ground in Malaya. Their first target was the rubber plantations. They suddenly emerged out of the dense jungle – generally about fifteen to twenty strong and visited twenty different plantations. Fifteen of the owners were away while the other five were shot in cold blood, and from then on these incidents spread all over Malaya. The police had to act quickly to form some kind of protection for the vulnerable planters. At this stage they could trust the Malays and began to train them as special constables in three weeks, after which they pushed a rifle in their hands and sent them to protect the estates. Help, in the form of army reinforcements, arrived from England. The army had been run down after the war and the police had to do most of the protecting and patrolling. There were atrocities all over the country, and ambushes on all the roads. There were few army vehicles and the situation was serious, with little equipment, and slow preparation. There were horrific cases of estates being overrun or police stations being taken with the weapons intact. There were no helicopters, no fuel, no armoured transport. It was grim and the whole country was seriously despondent. To add to the general scene of hope-lessness, Gent, the Governor, was killed on his way back to England, and the next Governor – Gurney – was ambushed and killed. And, as Jack Masefield, a police officer, said 'That was the low point – people were terribly depressed, and then the British Government sent us Sir Gerald Templer which was the turning point.'

In 1948 the situation in Malaya was serious. The communists, or communist terrorists, as they were known, were gradually get-ting the upper hand by intimidation. Hidden by the almost impenetrable jungle they would either cajole or threaten the villagers into acquiescence or cut their throats. Owing to Malay susceptibilities the Chinese were not citizens and could not hold land, and several hundred thousand Chinese 'squatters' had settled in isolated patches of state land bordering the jungle, where they grew crops of vegetables and subsistence cereals, providing the communists with part of the food they so desper-ately needed. It was to these vegetable-gardeners that Sir Henry Gurney, the High Commissioner, and Lieutenant-General Sir Harold Briggs, the Director of Operations, turned their atten-tion. Briggs had been appointed for a year but ultimately remained for eighteen months. He was to change the whole of the direction of the war in Malaya, for he realized that the enemy could never be flushed out of their jungle hide-outs by con-ventional tactics. After touring the country, he gave the responsibility for intelligence to Special Branch, and he hoped to harass the CTs with small patrols.

One brilliant scheme which he devised was a major factor

in bringing the Emergency (there had been no declaration of war) in Malaya to an end. He began to establish the 'squatters' whether they liked it or not, and a great many did not, in settlements known as 'new villages' away from the jungle perimeter. During the next two years, four hundred new villages were established, varying in size from a few hundred inhabitants to nine or ten thousand. They were given land, schools, health chiefs, water and electricity. To ensure their isolation from the communist threat, they were encircled by a high chainlink fence, and powerful perimeter lighting and guards. As time went on and the inhabitants settled, they formed their own Home Guard and helped to ensure their own security.

Sadly, in October 1951, Sir Henry Gurney was ambushed and murdered. His murder caused a mood of despair among the planters, the miners, the Chinese loyalists and the people as a whole. Mr Oliver Lyttelton, the newly appointed Conservative British Secretary of State for the Colonies, went to Malaya to see the situation for himself. He was besieged by angry planters, who, like the farmers in Kenya during Mau Mau, were indeed in the most vulnerable position and threatened to leave the country if some drastic action were not undertaken at once. The only action that Lyttelton found commendable was the Gurney and Briggs policy of resettling the squatters. When Lyttelton left Malaya, he assured all and sundry that he would suggest to Mr Winston Churchill, the Prime Minister, that the security forces, the civil administration, and the police should be directed by one man and reorganized.

But he did not say which man. This is what everyone wished to know. Surely it would have to be a man like Monty? Certainly no less! But was there such a man?

There are, mercifully for the born optimists, couples who so complement each other that you cannot think of one without the other. Whatever may be lacking in one is strong in the other, so that lack of tact is hidden by sublime tactfulness, talkativeness by silence, energy by sloth, artistry by practicality, and so on *ad infinitum*. This is, of course, leading to a couple who surpassed all these maxims because their relationship seemed so subtly perfect that it defies definition. Nor will I try to provide one.

General Sir Gerald Templer, General Officer, Commanding Eastern Command, was already an outstanding person as well as soldier. Once you had met him you were not likely, for better or for worse, to forget him. He was frightening to the weak, a challenge to the strong. He had an abrasive tongue and did not suffer fools gladly. But he knew a valuable person when he met one, as was the case with Freda Gwilliam, Adviser for Colonial Education.

For her part she thought him, 'absolutely first-class . . .. He was all you wanted to have in a first-class man in a first-class situation. When he was selected to go out to Malaya, we, in the Colonial Office, were very interested. I was going on my tour to the Pacific, Malaya, Singapore and back via Sri Lanka. The Colonial Office told me that I wouldn't be allowed to go to Malaya. Templer had said that nobody is going into Malaya, unless he sees them first. He doesn't want these Colonial Office types! So I said, "I'm going to Malaya!" So they said, "Well, you'd better go and see him!"

'I was told he would see me one day at exactly ten to two o'clock. So I went to his office and tapped on the door and went in, and he looked at me – the way he did! And somehow it sparked! He said, "What have you come for?" So I told him. He said, "All right, you can go!" I said, "Thank you very much," and out I went. I had the loveliest time in Malaya because these two are two of the people I'm most glad to have known all my life.'

This, then, was the man chosen by Churchill to carry on Gurney's work in Malaya. Peggie, his wife, witty, charming, and with a courage that equalled Gerald's, was to find in Malaya a role which ran exactly parallel to Gerald's, and to contribute, in her own way, to the ending of the Emergency.

It was in February 1952 that Peggie and her daughter, Jane, followed Gerald out to Malaya. In the aeroplane Peggie tried to reorientate herself to her new role, for she knew that to be a general's wife was one thing, but to be the wife of a Supremo was quite another matter.

It was Gerald's policy to make regular and systematic tours, covering eventually the whole country, and Peggie went with him whenever possible.

'Going round the villages with Gerald I really had the most immense acquaintance and not the sort of acquaintance one is expected to have because I knew all sorts of humble people really quite well. I used to go by myself. Gerald was escorted by the army. At first I had a detective all the time, but I thought this was too much because it would put everybody off – so I said that I didn't think he could protect me, so it was just as well not to have him, and the police agreed.

'I got to know a great many people by visiting even the smallest villages. I also got to know all kinds of simple everyday things, such as the water not coming through properly . . .. It was part of my job – to make people realize that we cared, which indeed we did, but I had to get it across.'

The day came when Gerald wrote Peggie a minute asking her if she could think of some way to raise the standard of living by giving the women some interest in the difficult circumstances. They had the Red Cross, the Girl Guides, and so Peggie had to think of something which would appeal to everybody of every race and creed, and to both the educated and uneducated. As she put it, 'I wanted something to bring people together, and yet let them enjoy themselves without being worried.' And she suddenly had the brilliant idea of the 'Women's Institute'. So she sat down and wrote to the Women's Institutes in London, which apparently amused them very much because she wrote, 'We have enough money to pay and will pay well. Will you send us your best instructor?' Which generously they did. They sent Margaret Herbertson who was excellent, and she and Peggie set out to start the WI in Malaya.

In the meantime Peggie went all round Malaya explaining her idea of having Women's Institutes in all the villages, but she insisted in her speech that they would have to form their own committees. She found that they were very knowledgeable about committee work and kept minutes, they knew exactly how one proposed, seconded and elected. Though Europeans were encouraged to join, they were not allowed to hold prominent positions on any of the committees. Before Margaret and Peggie arrived a notice was sent ahead to a village which simply said, 'A woman is coming to talk to women about something that might interest them.' The women turned up in their hundreds.

Naturally they were not allowed to mention race, religion or politics. In the Institutes at first they were up against the men who were furiously angry, and seemed to think of Peggie as some kind of suffragette, stirring the women up and, in the case of the

Muslim women, giving them ideas which were alien to them. However:

'It went with a bang from the beginning. I just used to go round the Women's Institutes and see. They simply loved it. And the good thing about it was that it got me into such remote places that I would never have gone to normally. We got to the stage when people used to come to me and say, "Who is your Women's Institute chairman at such and such a place?" They all learned to cook better, they all learned to knit – they adored knitting. After a while, the men came right round and used to make their wives join. That *was* interesting! They learned feather stitchwork knitting, patchwork, and many other things and we sent a list round of what there was on offer. There were many helpers of all races but we soon learned that the women were terribly clever with their fingers. You teach them smocking, and by the next week they do smocking far beyond the teacher's ability. I taught a lady who had no language in common with me to do feather-pattern knitting, because she was so adept at learning. I just seized her knitting needles and a ball of wool and after the first row she was a dab at it.'

They had to take an interpreter everywhere with them, though 'what they interpreted was nobody's business'. The expenses were the difficulty. There had to be books of instruction, and rules printed in several languages. For the first year they got a government grant, and each member was charged a very small subscription, 'if you don't, they suspect you – they think there's something in it, unless you ask them to pay'.

This occupation which took Peggie everywhere might easily have been used to get information for Gerald, but this she was never asked to do.

'It would have been fatal, for I had to be trusted. I would tell him – because after a bit you get the feel of a place – I think that's a bad village . . . I think there's something going on there. But I kept myself away from politics. I was always worried about Gerald, of course. The ADC and I, when he went out into a village and made a speech, we'd always try and stand in what we thought would be the line of fire. Because, apart from personal feelings, it would have been a terrible thing to have another High Commissioner killed. You can't really protect someone. A policeman came to see me once because there was a murder plot at some games we were going to the next day, and he said, "You do realize that if a man is prepared to be killed, the police can't stop him killing your husband!" Well, of course I knew it already, but it wasn't very funny going to the games and sitting down in a chair and thinking about it – wondering.'

They travelled everywhere in armoured cars or tanks which rattled and banged and were exhausting. Gerald used to stand up with his head above the turret since he could not tolerate the heat inside. Peggie commented that she 'supposed human heads were small' but, even so, he must have been lucky.

Peggie, herself, was ambushed once and treated it in a manner which might be expected, a mixture of disdain and humour. She was in the official car with Miss Herbertson and the ADC. She said, 'I thought it was a bit stupid, but they never did ask me, and it's pretty obvious that what goes up must come down, and so on the return journey they were ready for us.' She heard a lot of shooting, but she went on talking to the ADC and Miss Herbertson and didn't budge.

The ADC said, 'You know we're being ambushed, don't you?'

Peggie replied that 'No', she didn't.

The ADC asked if they would like to sit on the floor but 'the only conscious act I did was *not* to sit on the floor, because I thought I was just as likely to be shot on the floor and that would have been very undignified'.

To begin with the Chinese resented being put into the settlements. They hated leaving their vegetable gardens which they had tended for so long, and there were a great many sullen faces. Gerald got the pretty Red Cross nurses to go and work in the villages and this convinced the Chinese that the British were trying to help them. Nurses, at this time, were like gold in SE Asia and the Far East and could earn anything from £30 to £40 a week, but they worked in the settlements for only £4 a week and this did more to convince the Chinese than anything else, since by nature they are extremely pragmatic. They have a way of looking at a person and judging them by what they do and are seldom fooled. Certainly the Red Cross nurses made a deep impression on them. Before Gerald and Peggie had arrived in the country, the communists had said to the Red Cross that they must paint their crosses larger, because they didn't want to harm

147

or ambush them. If they helped a wounded communist they would never tell on him, and when Gerald arrived he never tried to make them, for this impartiality was the very essence of the Red Cross.

Though Peggie did not admit this to me I was told that she used to work at least twelve hours a day. This did not include the dinner parties they gave which did so much good in mixing the races together in a congenial atmosphere. In the kitchen and dining-room they had Chinese staff, the upstairs staff were Malayan who were enchanting. The gardeners were Indian, as were the messengers at the front door. Malays all lived in the village near by, but they didn't mix. Peggie used to visit them to see how their families were getting on. Jane, their daughter, was their housekeeper, and did this responsible task with great competence.

'I used to go round the staff village constantly and got to know the wives quite well. They wouldn't go to hospital if their babies were in trouble. Somebody's baby died and I didn't speak very good Malayan but I learned a speech by heart in Malayan explaining to them that they *must* go to hospital, and they said they hadn't understood a word I'd said, but they realized that I cared enough to learn this speech, and make it to them and so they would go to hospital.'

Something occurred which made Peggie wonder how much one should interfere with other people's lives – something which it is almost impossible to answer even in one's most secret heart. A Malay woman had had a baby and needed a blood transfusion, and her husband who was the head man of a village refused to let her have one because it was against their religion. Peggie was asked if she could persuade him, so she said to him, 'Will you come to hospital with me and watch her then?' When she asked the doctor he told her that the woman was dying. Peggie felt quite desperate. Then while they were all gathered round the woman, the husband said something which sounded like a conditional acceptance and the doctor said hastily, 'Take him out of the room,' and Peggie removed him, while they pumped a British soldier's blood into her.

Peggie involved the young army wives in their local WI, and they learned to love the villagers. It gave them a chance to get to know the people of the country.

'Normally,' they said, 'we just sit in the country and we don't know the people very well. Now it's such fun to drive along and look at a house and know exactly what's going on inside.' And so it became a benefit to everybody.

Prostitution was something that Peggie worried about. In a polygamous society cast-off wives added to the vast population of homeless women. They took to prostitution because there was no other means of livelihood. But what of the aged?

'This always worried me terribly because it wasn't a thing I could do anything about. Religion was not a matter I was allowed to discuss. I wasn't officially allowed to encourage birth control as the wife of a government official. Also the country women were against going to hospital, even when they knew that things were not right, and that they needed surgical assistance with the births.

'We did what we could to remove this fear, but families were ruled by the older women who were very conservative. The religious Muslim leaders were very enlightened in many ways, and helped us with this particular one. All I could say was, "I think it would be a good thing if you could have babies at two yearly intervals because they would be stronger," and I used to say to the men, "It's very wasteful having all those babies, and it's better having five alive." '

Literacy amongst both adults and children was another campaign. The children would learn at school, but once they returned home there was nothing for them to read. Peggie collected together a committee of schoolteachers, and then borrowed $10,000 from the Social Welfare Department, and a devoted committee of teachers wrote and distributed a magazine especially for children. The schoolteachers were splendid, and the children began to believe that perhaps there was pleasure in reading.

After the Japanese occupation there was serious malnutrition, and this situation was maintained to some extent by the communists during the Emergency, by making it dangerous for cultivators, and by their demands for food in unprotected areas.

Dried milk was available and safe, but was unpopular owing to the difficulty of mixing it, and of course what was left in the bottom of the tin could be dangerous. Peggie asked Horlicks to give them 1,000 milk mixers, which they did, but even so no one would use dried milk.

There was no doubt that the Women's Institutes could help gently but firmly to teach a new standard of living. The boredom of life for women out in the country during the Emergency was unparalleled and the WI brought a new dimension to their lives. The Chinese women in the towns were not so cooperative. They were (by origin) extremely family-minded and saw no reason to help other people outside this close-knit circle. But for the Malay and India villagers female emancipation was in the air:

'Once later on, we got to a very remote village. We came in by air and I saw a lot of women. This was a unique and almost incredible event as I had never seen such a thing before. A crowd of women at an airport for an official arrival! When I got out I went over to them and delighted said, "You're here!" "Yes," they said, "We're glad to see you, but it is not you we've come to see! We've come to see the High Commissioner as Representative of the Women's Institute!" And then I knew we had won, because for women to come and meet Gerald officially was unprecedented. To feel that they as Women's Institutes represented something important enough to come and meet him – it did show we'd achieved something.'

Peggie picked up the Malay language as she went along, but as there were so many dialects she sometimes had a Chinese interpreter with her. This young man who was about twenty-six had quite a time repeating some of the conversations.

Two radical changes had taken place in Malaya. The women had found a new freedom, with their Women's Institutes, their committees, which had also won their husbands' approval. As for the men in their new settlements, they were beginning to appreciate freedom from fear. Peggie and Gerald's work, though incomparably different was running smoothly and parallel. After two years Gerald decided that it was time for him to go.

Let Freda Gwilliam have the last word.

'I was having my session with him, and going through the things I'd brought to ask him about. And his PA tapped and came round the door, "Very sorry, but Lady Templer says the Chief, and the WI women of such and such a village have come in, and they want to have a photo with you and Lady Templer." Now that was more important than anything else! Out he went just like a lamb. "Oh there you are darling," she said. "Come along. Here's the Chief, and here's the President of the WI." And he shook hands with them all and had his photograph taken. Now, that did more good than anything else, and it was that quality about them that people don't understand.

'And of course her courage! When she would go off into a kampong, and refused the escort, saying, "Who's going to trust me?" And she took her life, and the lives of our WI people, into her hands. Marvellous!'

13

Spreading Goodwill

One of Peggie Templer's most ardent helpers was Mary Marshall Smith. But to read the list of her activities from 1948 until 1962, is to realize that here was a person who threw herself into the life of Malaya with all the vigour and eagerness that her enforced absence during the war had deprived her of using.

Mary was engaged to Frank Smith before war broke out, and was to follow him out to Malaya and marry him once he was confirmed in the Colonial Service. Frank had just got to that stage and Mary, having left her job, was saying goodbye to her parents prior to sailing to Singapore, where they hoped to marry when the Japanese got there first. Frank was taken prisoner, sent to Thailand on the infamous 'railway of death' and, as Mary said, 'They had a bad time, as many books have testified. We got very little news during that time – only a few postcards were allowed (twenty-five words only) but it's quite a long story. I feel Malaya has been in my thoughts much longer than I was there – I had heard so much from Frank – long descriptive letters.'

Late in 1945 Frank returned and they were married but did not return to Malaya for health reasons until 1947. They were sent to Kedah in the extreme north of Malaya though they had no idea where they were to be stationed.

'The policy was, I think, to move them so that they got to know the work from different angles. Kedah was an interesting place, quite strange to me at first. We arrived at Penang and thought we would be sent to Singapore. At that time they had a very clever method of not telling the men where they were going until they actually reached the port of disembarkation. We used to say, perhaps you wouldn't go if you knew where you were going to be stationed! Going to Kedah was like jumping in at the deep end – very exciting.'

But Mary appears to have embraced the life and all its aspects. One of her first priorities was to learn the language, which she eventually spoke fluently. It was just as well that she had already started speaking Malay before arrival.

'In Kedah, a very formidable lady who was medical officer descended on me one day in a hospital where we were preparing children's food – things were very short then – and asked me without any form of introduction, "Do you know anything about Girl Guides?" Foolishly, I said I had been one before I realized I was being coerced into running a Guide company in Alor Star, in the Malay language! It was in the arts and crafts school/technical college. It was fun – a form of introduction in a way. I decided to take the government exams as a stimulus, and Frank was very pleased, and I had far more opportunity of getting to know the people.'

In spite of her enthusiasm, her hard work, and her happiness with Frank, that old enemy, loneliness, sought her out.

'I suppose loneliness was the problem initially and a feeling of isolation. When one goes from home, one looks to people from one's own background. Until one realized that people basically are quite similar and, at any rate, though we had so much in common, one does have that feeling of loneliness.

'There were, of course, practical problems – a lot of them. Mosquitoes, insects, snakes, leeches and not many amenities. I remember meeting the lady medical officer again and she noticed I had red scars all over my legs from mosquitoes. At first they tended to go rather septic. She said, "Don't you know that Kedah is famous for its insects?" Almost as if I might wish to be an entomologist.

'There were some outstanding women, and she was one of them, but there was also a great shortage of women as leaders, trained women of either British or local background. I think that that was one of the needs which even we, in our humble capacity, and other people such as Lady Templer, realized. I think that's what led Lady Templer to her inspired work when she founded the Women's Institutes. She saw that the women, especially in the country places, needed some outlet that wasn't just political or religious. She had this idea, and didn't waste any time once she had it in implementing it. When we were even further north than Kedah, in Perlis, she used to come up for meetings – very often at quite short notice, which was a very good idea, I thought, to see how things really were. Although she had very few words in common with anyone there bar about three of us, somehow her genuine goodness, charm and interest came across, and it was very interesting indeed to see how she impressed the people, not just because of who she was. I think the Malay people have a good way of summing people up – they are not obsequious and they are not patronizing either – they seemed able to judge.'

One of the charms for Mary in Malaya, was the lack of any colour barrier. She doubted whether she would have enjoyed India in the days of the Raj, and disliked some of the remarks made by certain women, 'I winced sometimes when I heard some of these remarks, it seems as if they *ipso facto,* regarded themselves as superior to the people of the country. I think the men on the whole in the MCS were well chosen – they had a real concern for the people, and a sense of fraternity and service. It made it worth while – otherwise I don't know how one could consider going at all.'

Mary was often 'commanded' to go down and talk to the sister of the Sultan of Johore, who was a widow and recounted many interesting reminiscences. She liked to practise her Malay though it was so hot that the strain of speaking made 'the perspiration run down the backs of my knees while I was battling with words'. The climate was extremely tiring for white women but nevertheless the Women's Institutes meetings and many others had to be held in the middle of the day when the women were not working, or fetching their children from school. On those days there was no question of a restful siesta.

'We used to go out maybe three or four times a week, to a different village, to a different branch of the WI. The best thing to do, I found, was to have a glass of water with some salt in it – even though it might be a teaspoon of salt, you didn't taste it at all – you were already dehydrated. Sometimes Lady Templer would come up . . . Sir Gerald saw the need for greater medical services in these very outlying places and he started a scheme whereby a member of the Red Cross would be seconded from home – the UK – and a social worker of some kind came with her, so we often had two women working together. Of course, they wouldn't know any Eastern language because they were only there for about two years, and the greatest need was in the most outlying places, so we might go by jeep or car and then walk, sometimes up river, carrying all these drugs and pills. That was really a very useful part of the work – spreading goodwill and actual practical health education. Sometimes I went with them acting as liaison, interpreting, or even dishing out pills. We would set up a little camp under a tree or maybe in the local school.'

One of the problems for someone who got so preoccupied with local community life was the constant moving. The Smiths were rarely in the same house for more than two years, so Mary had to face creating a new home, garden and, possibly most difficult of all, new friends, and finding something useful to do. She moved from Perlis, Kedah, Trengganu, Kuala Lumpur, Alor Star, State of Johore, Selangor and wherever she was, she was involved in welfare, Women's Institutes (linked with Associated Country Women of the World), Girl Guides, as well as teaching, and holding increasingly responsible ranks. Like Peggie Templer, she believed in the local people taking over responsibility as quickly as possible, and she did not share the widely held view that the Colonial Service had made no effort to train people for Independence.

'The family system in Malaysia impressed me,' she said. 'No one ever seemed to be left out of things. There didn't seem to be the same number of lonely people there are here. That is interesting. There are lots of people who live alone, widows – nice interesting people – who spend a great deal of time alone – why is it? In Malaysia they do seem to make more effort to include women in their circle – the older people particularly. They certainly feel a strong bond.'

Being involved with the local people a great deal, Mary used the Malay language more than she used her own during the last five to ten years. She was a founder member of the Women's Institutes, and in Perlis working with the Women's Service League, she used to have sewing meetings in her house every Monday at one time. Her husband would count the shoes outside the door to see how many women were inside working away and there were seldom less than forty to fifty.

She also had a short turn as headmistress of a school before going on leave.

'I remember that it came to the time when the entries for the new year were coming in and a mother passing me something across the desk. It was a local gold brooch. I had to tell her that I was not allowed to take any presents though it was very nice of her – as tactfully as possible. Things like that you had to be very careful of.'

Rosemary Peel went out to Brunei where her husband John was British Resident in 1946 with her two elder children. She was pregnant at the time and expecting her third child in October. The Residency was not all it might have been, for the British Military Administration had taken all the decent furniture; John had managed to get some hospital beds, and there was a certain amount of black PWD furniture. Slowly but surely Rosemary added cushions and soft furnishings – but she made one grave mistake. She filled the cushions with kapoc without removing the seeds, and the flying foxes arrived in the night and ripped open the cushions in search of the seeds.

Since a Resident's wife is expected to do quite a bit of entertaining and three children need a great deal of attention, Rosemary had engaged a PNEU governess while in England. No sooner had she arrived when she began to feel ill. She was sent down to Sarawak for tests and they discovered that she had a tendency to diabetes which had been aggravated by the tropical climate. When she had to go home, Rosemary tried teaching the children herself, until they finally found another governess who had come out to Singapore with the ATS, had done a Diploma in Education and been to Bristol University.

At this time John was getting quite a few messages in code and had to send to North Borneo for the code books to get them deciphered. The messages were mainly about Peter Brooke (Bertram Vyner Brooke's son, cousin to Sir Charles Vyner Brooke, Rajah of Sarawak) who was trying to get back to Sarawak. He could easily have gone to Brunei, where John was godfather to one of his children, and then just gone across the river. They were warned not to let their governess see anything confidential because she had belonged to the Communist Party at Bristol University before 1938, which they only discovered after they had demobbed her.

Rosemary thinks this warning was unnecessary.

'She was just interested in seeing the country and getting a bit of a job which would take her round – after all, we had various nice people to stay – the rest house wasn't in being in those days so everyone came to us. She travelled home with us, but made off as quickly as she could – I was having another child and I think she thought she would be trapped.'

But poor Rosemary wasn't feeling up to the birth of another child. There had been food shortages in Brunei at this time, and she was not strong. However, a wise doctor advised her to take iron, and 'Quentin was quite a bouncing boy – I was so afraid I'd have a pygmy.'

There was only one thing to do about the deficiencies in Brunei in the forties – grin and bear it. There were no amenities or comforts, an odd punka, the odd fan, and Flit against the mosquitoes and flies. A very different picture from the booming oil city of 1982. In those days the Sultan was living in comparative poverty. He had married a local girl of no particular family, and they were living in a river village. Some time later, when the oil money had begun to flow, and with it the Sultan's life-style, John got a message from Grosvenor House that the Sultan wished for an audience. The Sultan asked John whether the Queen had to take the advice of her ministers. So John replied that of course she did, for it would be a major dilemma if she were not to do so. A minister who was with the Sultan saw John to the door and remarked, 'I think the Sultan's ministers will be very grateful to you for what you've explained.' Soon afterwards, the Sultan abdicated in favour of his son who had finished at Sandhurst, as he said he wanted more time for poetry and meditation. The point of the Grosvenor House meeting became apparent when he made himself chief minister.

Though the present Sultan can afford to play polo and meet people, he would not have done when Brunei was impoverished. Rosemary and John went back in 1971 and were struck by the changes – the good hospitals, the schools, the mosque with a golden dome.

'It was nice to see how well people looked. When we were there just after the war they weren't looking well. The driver we had we were told had TB, he was always going sick – well, he's running the school bus service now.'

It was difficult for Rosemary to communicate with the women

because 'their Malay and mine were not quite the same, because they talk Brunei–Malay. But we did try to get things for them to restart their crafts. Our Sultan had a wife from Malaya, and she was quite a nice little downtrodden thing, sort of rather sad; she had to do all his cooking because he was afraid of being poisoned. She wasn't really very good at arts and crafts, but she bought us local things to give us as presents, the silverware was one of the things they did. We managed to get one of the firm's silver, and we would try to get them gold thread to go back to their weaving, which is rather special. The basketry went on during the war, because that was something they just picked and dried, but it was very very good. We tried to encourage them, we used to buy the baskets, and told them not to use too clashing colours. One of the things we tried to do was encourage the girls to go to school, because so few of them were sent to school, and they wore long sarongs and couldn't run in them, and we thought if they saw our children running about it would make them dress more suitably. I'm afraid now they've gone back to the girls being in purdah. We tried to do local things and encourage local things. Our third daughter, our Brunei daughter, is a craft teacher now, with special distinction in basketry.

'Well, she's done things I wanted to do and didn't achieve!'

How many of us can think and say those very words?

14

Fragrant Harbour

Richard Hughes writes in his book *Hong Kong – Borrowed Place, Borrowed Time* that, as he arrives by ship: 'I have shared with fellow passengers immediate identification of a faint smell of flowers on the wings of the wind from Hong Kong.' I have also entered Hong Kong twice by ship but remember quite different smells which will always be identified with journeys to Canton by river and sea, as well as to Hong Kong itself. It is the smell of thick, brown, oily water, of washed linen, of not unpleasant drains, of charcoal and half-cooked or rotting vegetables. Those are the smells I remember, not, alas, flowers.

My first visit to Hong Kong was in 1948. The harbour was then a miracle of beauty as we threaded our way through the sugar-loaf islands. I thought it the most beautiful harbour in the world, apart from Rio de Janeiro. The main island was mountainous in the hinterland, covered with green shrubs and as we circled the island on an excellent road, round every bend there were views of the silken sea, of white sandy bays, with a few scattered expensive-looking houses lived in by the Chinese. The town of Hong Kong was a fascinating dream dominated by the grey Government House, and the Peak where those lucky managers of Jardine Matheson, Shell, or other industries had their luxurious homes. It was a time when days were spent leisurely at the Chinese theatre, where you could stay all day if you had the stamina, or meeting people like Santha Rama Rau at the Hong Kong Hotel, dining on board naval ships, eating food so superb that one repudiated one's previous preference for French cuisine.

A year or two ago I returned to Hong Kong. To my utter bewilderment I looked down from my window in the Mandarin

Hotel. Where was Government House? Surely not that small insignificant grey building with a drooping flag clenched between a positive web of roads which appeared to rise behind and around it like a game of spillikins? The roads, the high-rise flats, the traffic, the people, had multiplied a hundredfold. I asked to be driven to the Repulse Bay Hotel where I had spent my honeymoon.

'Well?' I said, when my taxi stopped.

'You are here,' the driver said. I looked at the building straight off the road. Where was the long drive, the bougain-villaeas, the tall trees which flanked the long approach?

'It is to be demolished,' the taxi driver told me.

Hong Kong was ceded to Britain in 1841, at the very height of the opium trade. William Jardine and James Matheson were at that time running a highly successful trade between British India and China. In England, both the Whigs and the Tories turned a blind eye to this pernicious drug, except for the young Gladstone who spoke vehemently against it. In 1837 the amount of opium reaching China was worth well over £4m. It was then that Governor-General Lin Tse-hsu of Hu-Kuang decided to stop this abominable habit and went to war against the British. The British residents were forcibly evacuated from Macao and found themselves at anchor off a strange island called Hong Kong. When in 1841 the British won the opium war Hong Kong, which at that time no one particularly wanted, became another British colony. By 1845, India's revenue from opium was more than one-fifth its total income, and Hong Kong became the most convenient harbour to handle this trade. Hong Kong, so recently empty and scorned, began a period of smuggling, war, enemy occupation, fire, typhoons, and – at Yalta – a threat of a return to China. It has survived and until 1997 (when the treaties expire under which the New Territories and Kowloon north of Boundary Street were leased from China) it will probably continue to give the appearance of a well-organized ant hill, where every individual ant knows exactly where it is going.

Hilary Clark went out to Hong Kong in 1961 as a physiotherapy tutor in anatomy and physiology. She had originally gone on a three-year tour, but she met and married Trevor Clark and remained for eleven years. She discovered that there were some problems to her job in the School for Physiotherapy:

'In 1960 all the staff was British or ex-patriates of one sort or another, but by the time I left it was largely Chinese. In the early days we made mistakes because the Chinese have a thing against touching people who are not in your family circle. They were very good at theory, but when it came to actually treating patients, and having to touch people many of them would resign. So after two or three years we became far more particular when we enrolled them so that they knew exactly what would be asked of them. They are very concerned with their large family circle. If any of those people get hurt or are ill, they will do anything to look after them. But if it is outside their circle, they are not interested. Indeed, it is not correct to be curious about people outside one's family. In England, if a girl is in training, the first thing she finds out is where the patient lives, what the patient does, whether he has a family and so on. The Chinese girl will not ask any of these personal questions; she will only be able to tell you exactly what is wrong with the patients.'

Not without cause, massage has come into disrepute and prostitution is one of the most flourishing trades in Hong Kong. It seemed to respectable girls hoping to take up a career that they were being asked to act like the girls of 'ill repute':

'It was very difficult when they knew there was massage included in the course to enrol girls or boys – because they felt it wasn't quite the thing to lay hands on other people. So we had to play down the massage part. We had to stress the point that it was physical rehabilitation by exercise and that sort of thing. Then, having explained it, we introduced it very slowly.'

Another problem Hilary discovered in her work was the prevalence of drugs, especially heroin.

'I used to organize outside lectures and tours for my students, and we used to go to the drug addicts' island where they were treated. We also went to the special part of the police headquarters that dealt with drug addiction; they had a kind of small museum, showing how drugs were being smuggled into Hong Kong. A lot of our patients had histories of drug addiction. Heroin, of course, was the killer, and those were probably the ones one came across as patients. Opium isn't nearly such a harmful drug; after all, the last Chinese Empress smoked throughout her whole life, and didn't come to any harm. I think it was a pity that it was made illegal so that heroin took its place, which was much easier to administer. I never had any trouble with it among my students. The addicts were either drop-outs or people living in those huge housing estates. The living conditions were terrible. For instance, the whole population of a place the size of Stirling would be crammed into high-rise flats with very few facilities. They were built mainly through the Hong Kong Housing Authority or by the government. The Kadoorie brothers were more imaginative and had farming complexes in the New Territories where they taught people to farm.'

One familiar problem in the Colonial Service – money – did not arise since they were comparatively well paid by the Hong Kong government. It was much easier to save and create a pleasant home:

'You could buy all sorts of things for far less than in England. I remember that as a young physiotherapist I'd never been so well off. I could save enough every month to buy something nice like a radio or something for the flat which I needed, as well as saving.'

Nevertheless, when the time came Hilary was glad that Trevor had been posted to the Solomons. As he rose in rank, so their commitments became more arduous, and the pressure of life, both working and in official entertaining, and the noise of the island had begun to pall. The scale was certainly tipped in favour of the Solomons when they looked back on the Cultural Revolution which broke out in 1967:

'They started rioting in Hong Kong and it went on for about nine months. The students that I taught in those days were very, very uncomfortable. In spite of the trouble in the town they all went to work in the morning. You got to work, but at the same time you listened to the radio to find out the trouble spots so that you could avoid them when going home. You could hear the helicopters droning backwards and forwards looking for riots. The Chinese suddenly became withdrawn because they were waiting to see what would happen; even if they had wanted to, they couldn't escape from Hong Kong.'

Once they had a bird's-eye view of a riot when lunching with the editor of the *South China Morning Post* whose house was half-way up the famous Peak.

'We had a view right down the main Garden Road which took you down to the Star ferry. The rioters were trying to get up to Government House and the riot police were all out and we could see them all lined up with their riot shields and batons, and the rioters throwing stones and trying to push the police back. And I remember Alec, the editor, turning to Trevor and saying, "Trevor, do you think this is the end of Hong Kong as we know it?" And there we were with our glasses of gin in our hands. You were almost part of it but you weren't. It was all, in a way, unreal. You were there watching.'

In Macao it was no better. Everywhere there were notices saying, 'Down with Imperialists', 'Hang David Trench' (the Governor), or 'The British are Running Dogs'. Hilary went there once and, putting it mildly, she said: 'It was an uncomfortable time, then.'

A few years later, the Solomons beckoned.

PART SIX

The Mediterranean

15

The Divided Isle

Cyprus is a most beautiful island, and wherever you go there are traces of past conquests. It is both an historian's and an archaeologist's dream.

Dr Rex Cheverton went to Cyprus in 1942 having already been there in 1928. On his first visit he appears to have concentrated mainly on surgery, but in 1942 he went to eradicate malaria. Joan was not allowed to go with him from British Honduras:

'They were evacuating women and children to South Africa but it was too far to evacuate me, and they wouldn't let me go to England because I had two small babies. I had to evacuate the house the day after Rex left because it belonged to the doctor who succeeded him. By a miracle, the British Minister of Guatemala said that he would give me a job, so every three months I had to go to the Foreign Office and get a permit. Rex wasn't allowed to send me enough money to live on, so I taught, I coached people, and I worked in the press office. Then I wrote a report for the Foreign Office and the British Council. They decided to open the British Council in Central America as a result of my report. When it was safe to travel, I got ready to go to Cyprus, then, suddenly, ten days before we sailed, they transferred us to West Africa, where they said no children were allowed.'

Rex Cheverton had taken over a major project in Cyprus to rid it of the mosquitoes and when he was told to go to West Africa he said, 'Look, I want to finish this job,' to which the Colonial Service replied, 'Sorry, you either stay there for the rest of your life, or you do as you are told.' So Development Funds handed over the £300,000 which was the cost of the project and the doctor who followed Rex Cheverton finished his work of eradicating the mosquito.

Sir Hugh Foot, now Lord Caradon, was first in Cyprus from 1943 to 1947 as Colonial Secretary, and Acting Governor in 1944. It was a very different Cyprus from the one he returned to in 1957. As Hugh's wife, Sylvia, said, 1945 was a good year 'when the lion lay down with the lamb' – for the Turks and the Greeks were amicable. 'There weren't many Turkish families that played bridge or tennis but those that were educated enough certainly played games with the Greeks, and their coffee shops were side by side.'

That was how we had found it in 1954 and why I found it so difficult to understand what the men working in BEMO were talking about on our picnics. It appeared to me as if the Turks had nothing to do but to sit in the sun drinking their coffee without an evil thought in their heads.

When Hugh was not Acting Governor in the forties, the Caradons lived in a lovely Colonial Secretary's house which no longer exists, and, as with almost every colony in the world, the garden was run with prison labour. Sylvia had her two small children with her for whom she engaged an Armenian nanny. Miraculously when she went back seventeen years later, the nanny, Alexei, turned up and became her maid. Eventually she happily married an English corporal.

With their usual warmth and generosity, Sylvia and Hugh had made many Cypriot friends, and undoubtedly Sylvia, who had never lost touch with them, had been looking forward to seeing them again. One can imagine the shock Sylvia felt when she was told that if she met any of her old friends in Ledra Street or anywhere else, 'Turn your face the other way, for their sake.' Her first thought would naturally have been to run towards them and embrace them, but she was absolutely forbidden to.

The first thing that shook her on arrival was the fact that the front door was locked:

'We drove up and the front door had been locked for so long that nobody had thought of opening it, so that was the first symbolic thing! It was locked for several weeks until I asked about it. I found it was opened only to colonels and higher ranks so I said, "Well, let's have it closed if it's like that, either everybody or nobody." '

While Denis and I were there the Field Marshal had had a bomb put under his bed, and it was a miracle that it did not go off. It was because of this that so many precautions, which shocked Sylvia, had to be taken. It was not easy for the Foots, a peace-loving couple if ever there was one, to replace a soldier of such distinction and fortitude. Even in my small way, when I approached George on behalf of my Greek friends, I noticed the difference between a soldier on active duty and the man I had first met in the drawing-rooms of Risalpur, India. Sylvia put their position in a nutshell when she said: 'It was immediately clear who were those who would give us a chance and those who were so prejudiced in their own minds, not knowing, of course, that we were deeply attached to the Field Marshal.'

Though, to begin with, Makarios was the enemy, Sylvia was eventually able to get to know him and to feel a great affection for him. I had interviewed him once for an article and I said to Sylvia that I thought he had a magnetic personality and she said:

'Well, he had a lonely personality also – he was a very touching man. I feel that the Colonels in Greece menaced and threatened the Archbishop, saying, "Unless you treat the minority fairly tough, we will see to it that you go." And in the end they did see to it. I was really fond of the Archbishop, later I became very fond of him. You see, I had that marvellous job of handing over the garden, the grounds, the house, the silver, and the pictures to him. He came every day, and we had two hours every afternoon. One day he came and we were to sort the silver, because it was all Cyprus silver. I kept him waiting and I apologized, I said, "I'm so sorry, but my son has a bad throat," and he said, "Your son has a bad throat and you think I'm going to count silver. I'm going to see your son. Remember, I am a priest. If there is a sick person in this house, I must assist first and foremost." He went upstairs and sat by that boy the whole afternoon.

'He also told me that every year he sent £50 at Christmas to the head of police in the Seychelles. He said, "He was very kind to me and he taught me English with great care, so every year I send him £50 for the poor of the Seychelles."

'The last great "do" we had with him was thrown by him in the Ledra Palace. It was one of those days when the air-conditioning breaks down, and the heat was 120°F or thereabout. I was sitting next to the Archbishop, and I had a favour to ask him, and I said, "Archbishop, I shall not see you again." He was always very cagey about people asking favours, so he turned to me and said, "A favour, lady? What sort of favour?" I said, "I want you to look after my cat." Because I knew like all Greek Orthodox priests, he would treat the cat as something sacred. He said, "And this cat, is she a lady?" She was a neutered cat and I hadn't a clue how the Greek Orthodox Church looks upon fixed cats. So I said, "She is a lady, and she has had children, and they were all run over in front of the house, so she will have to be kept. She has no children." There was a long pause and he turned and said, "And this lady cat, she is alone?" and I said, "When I go she will be," and there was another long pause, and a smile in his eye – I shall never forget it – I said, "Like you, Archbishop." He knew the day we went he would be overcome by all those ambitious people who wanted to become ministers – and then he would be the loneliest man on earth!' Certainly the Archbishop had no illusions about people, or those around him who were jockeying for position.

It was time to go. Hugh Foot had completed his job, and Sylvia could once more embrace her Cypriot friends. The practising of stand-tos in Government House which had taken so much getting used to, were a thing of the past. They had prayed that it would mend and it did mend. But Hugh was under no illusions. They left on a destroyer, and standing on deck they watched the Greek air force and the Turkish air force escorting them.

Sylvia said to Hugh: 'You've done it!'

To which he replied: 'Just wait another ten years.'

16

The Boadicea of Malta

On 26 August 1890 Gerald Strickland, 6th Count Della Catena of Malta, and later created GCMG 1st (and last) Baron Strickland of Sizergh Castel, Westmorland, married the Lady Edeline Sackville, eldest daughter of Reginald Sackville, 7th Earl De La Warr, Viscount Cantelupe, Baron Buckhurst and Baron De La Warr and West. Lady Edeline was born at Knole, Kent, on 10 September 1870. Sadly their only two sons died at three months and ten months in 1893 and 1902. These tragic but not uncommon deaths in the years when child mortality was high and birth control practically unknown deprived the Stricklands of their only sons. Six girls followed in fairly quick succession – Mary in 1896, Cecilia Victoria in 1897, Mabel Edeline in 1899, Margaret Angela (born in 1900 but only surviving until 1901), Henrietta May Caribbea in 1903, and the youngest, Constance Teresa, in 1912. This was a modestly numbered family judging by many others in Victorian days, but it by no means lessens the strain on the mother, who in this case spent sixteen years in pregnancy and giving birth.

One has the impression that from childhood Mabel replaced the sons in all but physical form. She is like the island of her choice, strong, indomitable, and though exceedingly shy, undefeated. She has dedicated her life to Malta, but it would appear to have deserted her, though her loyalties remain firm. Nevertheless, at eighty-four she is returning in spirit to the land of her childhood, Australia. When I asked her where she had been happiest, she began to sing, 'Waltzing Matilda'.

Her first childhood memories are of Antigua when her father was Governor of the Leeward Islands.

'I can recall long white sandy beaches, picking shells . . . my mother in a pony cart, the monsoon, pineapples and bananas growing, and red hibiscus.'

Then, in 1904, she was off to Australia, first of all in Tasmania and later in Western Australia, spending her formative years there, from 1904 to 1917. Australia is God's own country. As she points out, it has welcomed thousands of Maltese settlers who have made good 'down under' while with the second generation there are more Maltese in Australia, mainly in the Eastern States, than in Malta.

In 1917 the Strickland family were to return to England, but, instead, Mabel was to come into her own dominion.

They were to travel on board the P & O ship, the *Kaiser-i-Hind*, and just before sailing the Reverend Mother of the Blue Sisters near Sydney, told Mabel that as there would be no doctor on board, she must make it her duty to look after her mother. Mary was looking after Contie who was still very young, whilst Cecilia 'did little other than brush mother's hair which I was not allowed to do. I was probably better at milking than brushing hair.'

Passing through the Suez Canal, Lady Edeline was taken very ill. She apparently had no desire to return to Sizergh and longed to go to Malta where she had spent her happy honeymoon and given birth to six of her children. Perhaps she knew that she was dying, and wanted to embrace this transitory happiness for the time left to her. Lord Strickland was not the man to deny his sick wife such a request and the family transhipped to the cruiser, HMS *Newcastle*. After a hazardous journey during which they were fired at by an enemy submarine, they arrived in Malta on 8 June 1917. Strange as it may seem, Mabel remembers nothing of this part of the voyage from Port Said to Malta. One can only surmise that the strain of her mother's illness had had an adverse effect upon her. The responsibility of caring for her must have been a strain on so young a girl, and perhaps she, too, guessed her mother was dying. Since Mary was seventeen she had been acting as hostess to her father, Cecilia appears to have chosen the more glamorous tasks, so, as Mabel admits, 'I was always with my mother, as none of my older sisters were.'

Their villa, Villa Bologna, was in the hands of some nuns who had to be accommodated elsewhere, so in the meantime they lived with their Uncle Charlie. Villa Bologna had been built in 1745 by Fabruzzio Greck, legal adviser to the Grand Master, as a dowry for his daughter, Maria Theresa, on the occasion of her marriage to Nicholas Perdicomati, whose father was created Count Delicatania by Grand Master Pinto in 1745. The second Count had no sons so the title passed through his two daughters and Sir Nicholas Scaberras Bologna became 5th Count. As he did not marry, the title passed through his sister who married Peter Paul Bonici, and their daughter, Louisa, married Walter Strickland, with their eldest son, Mabel's father, Gerald Strickland, inheriting the title when he was fourteen. The villa is impressive and beautiful. The architecture is Italianate with a marble staircase leading up to the ballroom, and superlative stonework on the façade, worked in the honey-coloured stone of Malta. Gerald Strickland's second wife was Margaret Hulton, the daughter of the newspaper magnate and therefore exceedingly rich in her own right, and in her time she improved the villa with a great many modern amenities.

Mary now joined the Women's Royal Naval Service, and Mabel, who had done ciphering for her father in Australia, became a cipher officer. She had brought a crate of white leghorns with her from Australia but decided that rearing chickens was not enough contribution to the war effort.

She comments rather wryly: 'Everyone was in uniform except cipher officer Strickland, as you had to be twenty-five to do ciphers and wear uniform. My mother got slightly better, I used to see her in the garden in a wheel-chair and then she had a relapse. I was very slow doing my ciphering. Alison Thorburn could do 600 words an hour, but cipher officer Strickland, 200. It was agony! Alison was wonderful, and would help me and I got up to about 450. Then my mother got worse, and one day she sent me to work while she got some sleep. I knew that she would be gone by the time I came home, and I also knew that if I went to work I would probably route a ship over a minefield, so I had my hair washed instead. And I was right. She slipped away in my absence. This did not make me any better. I continued to be tall, weedy, and morose!'

Mabel then demobbed herself on Armistice Day. Everyone in uniform received a medal. 'This was a chip on the shoulder for a youngster, and I had to wait until 1944 for Lord Gort and Oliver

Stanley to get an india rubber and scrub out my misty past and give me an OBE.'

From now on Mabel transferred her tremendous fund of admiration and affection to her father. Had she been a son I would hazard a guess that she would have patterned her life on his, and that even as a woman, he was the one great influence on her life and her career.

She is a big woman, tall, with what can only be described as a 'presence'. Photographs of her as a young woman appear all eyes. She has large magnificent eyes, and though she has described herself as 'morose' there is nothing morose in her expression. She has a humorous face, a deep voice, a mannish walk. She has the courage of a lion, and I would pity the person who crossed her. Her interests have never been intellectual. She is essentially a farmer, a journalist and a politician. Her garden at Villa Parisio was magnificent. She introduced the avocado pear, and possessed a fund of knowledge on citrus fruits. Though she went to the opera in Valetta possibly three times a week, it was to meet young men in the intervals rather than love of music which persuaded her to go. She has never spoken much Maltese and had to have an interpreter beside her during political meetings, though she says she can understand the gist of what is being said. In 1922 her father offered to send her to Cambridge but she refused.

Once a High Commissioner described her as being a mixed-up kid. She thinks that that would be the result of being brought up in different countries but wearing the United Kingdom insignia. 'I was entitled to be slightly mixed up with a rotten memory, but basically Malta has always held me.'

Certainly she has given her all to Malta. As an employer she offered her employees security of employment and is a very kind-hearted and generous woman. As someone who knows her well, said, 'Of course she has her defects, as all of us do; she is rather dictatorial in temperament, but then, how could she be otherwise – to be who she is, to have got where she has. "Miss Mabel", as she is called everywhere, is known throughout the world, her prestige is enormous and she has been a forceful figure on the Maltese political scene.'

In May 1919, Sir Gerald Strickland brought his daughters

back to England, rented a house at 24 Eaton Place and opened up Sizergh Castle. It was all splendid for his motherless children but Mabel alone did not fit in. She says of herself, 'I was tall and morose and was always suffering from backache. I did not fit into the London season, though my mother's relations (the De La Warrs from Knole) were very kind to Edeline's children. Grandfather De La Warr had four girls but I discovered that I was very Australian and very foreign, and it was their very kindness that drove me back to Malta.'

But it was not only her shyness at the great balls which drove her from the English social scene, and since she sometimes came 'home with the milk at 3.00 a.m.' she cannot have been wholly unpopular. She recalls with gratitude the kindnesses bestowed on her, and one can only deduce that in spite of all the efforts made on her behalf she continued to suffer painfully from an inferiority complex.

'What I cared for was riding, and there came a time after my sister's marriage when the proper thing to do was to hunt, so I hired a horse and all I knew about hunting was that one should keep up with the hounds and huntsmen. Well, the hunt met, and we started off. Then to my great surprise, instead of jumping the fences, they started opening the gates and riding through. This did not fit in with my Australian upbringing. Anyway, I kept up with the hounds and the huntsmen and there were only about three of us left, and the fox went over Falton Knot and so did I. Jake Wakefield, when he came up to the huntsman said, "It is a clear conscience that rides Falton Knot." They had all gone round up the road! That settled me! I knew that I didn't fit in.'

In spite of her strictures of life in England, one person made a deep impression of a romantic nature. This person was Mervyn Clive who was brought over to Sizergh one day and fell in love. During the forties she wrote of him, 'Later Clive came to Malta during the Church crisis of 1930, although I told him not to. It was, however, very gallant of him, but his effort ended in failure. I remember him saying that the last time that any of his family had anything to do with the Roman Church it had ended with the massacre of St Bartholomew. Later Mervyn was killed in the war.'

In 1982 I asked Mabel who had been the greatest influence in her life after her father and she immediately said, 'Mervyn

Clive', and that she had been engaged to him, but didn't marry him because he was not a Roman Catholic. Perhaps family pressure proved too much for her, but over the span of sixty years he remains fixed in her mind as the one great romance of her life.

When Mabel returned to Malta she became an integral part of the island. In 1921 her father was made a Member of the Legislative Assembly, became Leader of the Opposition, and his political followers were known as the Constitutional Party, while Mabel became his Assistant Secretary. From now on she was deeply involved in Maltese politics. When her father married Margaret, the fourth daughter of Edward Hulton in 1926, it was, perhaps, a factor in guiding Mabel to her great work in the newspaper field.

'My father was always writing in the early days in the *Malta Herald* and my stepmother was a Hulton and so I was very much in the newspaper world, and round about 1935 I said to my father, "Why don't we have a daily paper?" and he said, "Who is going to edit one?" and I said that I would.'

And so Mabel became the editor of the *Times of Malta,* and the *Sunday Times of Malta.* From now on she was to spend thirty years devoted to journalism and farming. When her elder sisters had married there had been, as was the custom in those days, marriage settlements. Mabel had told her father not to worry about her and that she would be content with Maltese property, and he let her have the orange gardens at Siggiewi, and other land. Later she was to create a house and garden of great beauty and hospitality at Villa Parisio, at Lija. It became the centre of social life both for the navy and visiting politicians. Though she never married, she was always surrounded by men, of whom many were close and trusted friends.

While Mabel was editor of the newspapers they were exceedingly well run. Nothing got past her. Expense accounts of the correspondents going abroad were rigidly checked. If some special news was missing in the morning paper she would want to know why. She was a hard but fair task-master. When she took to politics she retired from the editorship and became the Chairman of Allied Malta Newspapers from 1950 to 1955, and in 1966, Director of Progress Press Company Limited.

She was vigilant, energetic and single-minded. When her father was going to England with his second wife, she reproved him when he asked her to accompany them. 'I do not believe in absentee landlords!' she said, and though she was to visit England herself two or three times a year, it was always on essential business such as a newspaper conference.

Everyone, however humble, has some moment, or some period in life which stands above all the rest. For Mabel, her greatest moment, her finest hour, was the war of 1940 and the siege of Malta. She will be remembered, when all else fades, as the editor who never failed to produce her daily paper throughout the war under the most appalling conditions. Though the edges might be singed, the print blurred, there it was on every subscriber's mat without fail each morning. She will be remembered for her indomitable courage, and the spirit of service she instilled into her staff, never for one moment expecting them to do more than she was prepared to do herself. She never doubted the outcome of the war and she never failed.

She took her colours from her father. Every year he would make a speech that Malta could and would be defended. Under the offices of his newspapers there were five wells. He had the wells pumped out to show that they could be turned into shelters in case of war. Then he had staircases built which Mabel thought at the time was to give the stonemason, Barbara, some work, but, in fact, it meant that if one staircase was blocked, there was another to use. While he was Prime Minister, he had brought in two edicts on languages. Knowing that Mussolini had his eye on Malta, he stopped Italian being taught in the schools, and insisted that Maltese should be the language of the courts because he considered it a scandal that people should be tried in a language they did not understand. He died in 1940 and so missed the siege and ultimately the fruits of his labours.

Mabel had also been airing her views and attacking fascism in articles in the press in no uncertain terms. The fascists paid her the compliment of nicknaming her 'She Devil' which undoubtedly delighted her.

As it became increasingly apparent that war could not be avoided, Lord Strickland said to Mabel, 'If it is war, we must not sleep in the same house again.' And then added, 'Where will you sleep tonight?' Mabel said, 'In the office, sir,' for she always called her father 'sir' when he asked those sort of questions. She tells of that last peaceful night:

'We had a wonderful night in the office, everyone telephoning to each other. The morning came and nothing happened. At six o'clock I thought it might be a good idea to go home. Just as I was getting to Porte des Bombes, I saw a flight up in the sky. So I said to myself, "Sammy Maynard has manned his Gladiators." ' Strange though it may seem, the only air defence for Malta were three out-of-date training biplanes, Gloucester Gladiators, named by the Maltese Faith, Hope and Charity. 'Then the beastly things started dropping eggs, and I did not think much of that! Anyhow I got home safely. I remember one of the pilots named George Burgess coming to Villa Bologna one day and my Dad took off his hat to him when he met him at the gate, and said, "I salute you." '

It was not until shortly before the fall of France that these hardy and overworked pilots were reinforced by five Hurricanes. When the Germans occupied Sicily, the Hurricanes were outmatched and Spitfires began to reach Malta, but alas, as Stewart Perowne records in his book *The Siege Within the Walls*, 'The first consignment of fifteen arrived, flown in from the veteran *Eagle* which had set out from Gibraltar on the 7th March. Sixteen more followed on the 21st and the 29th March. Forty-six more were flown in from the United States carrier *Wasp* on the 20th May; yet so utterly inadequate was the aircraft housing in Malta, that within three days the German "Fliegerkorpe II" had destroyed or damaged almost all of them on the ground, and only six fighters remained serviceable.' It had been a sadly blind spot in the defence of Malta that no underground tunnels had been dug to house aircraft. As Mabel said, 'It was the most appalling disaster. Then Menzies, on a telephone call to Churchill, agreed to release the Spitfires that were due for Australia, and they were serviced within three minutes of their landing.' This is, of course, later on in the war, and in the meantime Mabel had other problems.

'It was on the third day of the war that Paul Bonello came to my office and told me that I was too English to be of any use to them, so I tore strips off him – I was so angry! Then he said, "If you want us to follow you, we want to know the truth and only the truth, because in peace we don't mind what women do, but in war we are realists. So it has to be the truth and nothing but the truth." I agreed with him, and this is really how I became a good editor.'

One of her duties was to go to Government House and edit the Governor's broadcasts. He told her that whenever he spoke in public he must always mention God (he was a member of the Plymouth Brethren). Mabel, no doubt with a flicker of humour, said, 'Yes, sir. Where will we put God in?' He would re-read the broadcasts and usually decide to put the Almighty in towards the end. 'So that was that! It was very impressive in a Catholic country that a Governor sent out by a non-Catholic country before the Ecumenical days wanted to mention the Almighty, although basically it was not a Catholic practice.'

There is no doubt that Mabel found Dobbie's religion a sore trial. It was all very well for Churchill to describe him as 'a soldier who in fighting leadership and religious zeal recalled memories of General Gordon, and looking further back, of the Ironsides and Covenanters of the past', because he did not have to suffer this 'zeal' day by day. Mabel had no time for the evening duty of going to Government House at seven o'clock, when Dobbie would stand against the mantelpiece and pray aloud. 'It was all very reverent.' He would ask the Almighty to bless the convoy, and then pray for the people who were prisoners in Singapore, but he never prayed that the bombing might stop, 'because that was God's will'. In the same way he told Mabel that it was God's will if he was killed when watching the air-raids from the roof of St Anton Palace. Though he infuriated her, she had to admire his immense sincerity and the strength of his prayer.

By 1941 Mabel needed all the decisiveness and courage imaginable. Malta was in a desperate situation over food. Mabel, who had been fifteen stone at the outbreak of war, now weighed eight and a half – very little for her big frame. Victory food kitchens were organized, handing out one meagre meal a day. Seed potatoes had to be imported and the first consignment from Northern Ireland failed to arrive. The state of the children was pitiful, while by the time the animals were slaughtered for food they were more than likely skin and bone. The vital convoys bringing essential food, petrol and oil, were not getting through.

The following anecdote demonstrates Mabel's extraordinary

resilience in times of stress. Her father had died but she still had her step-mother to care for in Villa Bologna. She recalls: 'I came back from the office after a pretty tough day. I was lying down on the floor of the Villa when a battle opened and stupidly I dived under the bed which annoyed me very much. I said to myself, "Get out of it, you coward." So I got to my feet and the water from Ta'Qali reservoir came flooding in through a breach in the wall of Villa Bologna, and flooded into the shelters. So I rushed down to the shelters and made the refugees come up to the high land of the villa. I made Lady Strickland come up to the top of the villa upstairs, then I splashed through the water – it was about three and a half feet high, shouting for everyone to get out of the shelters all round. Our own shelters were stuck up on high ground. The water turned down Long Street towards Carinthia Palace which helped to lower them. The cellar at Villa Bologna was full and the furniture kept knocking against the marble floor. I thought if there was a bomb everybody on the top storey would come splashing into twenty feet of water! So I took them all out to the high land and I asked Lady Strickland to come with me. The old lady said, "You've brought me up here, and I'm not coming down – I cannot have you change your mind like this, and I'll not come down tonight!"

'I realized I had no alternative so I got the butler, Joseph, and said, "You must persuade Lady Strickland to come down and we will put her in the Rolls-Royce up in the high land in the garden." Finally Joseph persuaded Lady Strickland to get into the Rolls-Royce and she was taken to the high land together with the refugees. It made sense at the time.

'So I went on splashing about through the night. At 2 a.m. old Dobbie, who was still up, telephoned me and said, "You must bring Lady Strickland here at once." So I thanked him heartily. He knew that I was in strong opposition to his policy but he was tremendously generous. So I splashed back to Lady Strickland and asked the old lady to come with me to St Anton. She said, "You got me up here in the Rolls-Royce and I'm staying here tonight!" Once again, Joseph had to be recruited to persuade her that she had to go to St Anton. We got the old lady out with the car splashing through the water. The old lady complained bitterly that at two o'clock in the morning nobody had given her any food.

'We were at St Anton for about ten days, thanks to Dobbie's courtesy.'

Life in Malta was grim indeed. The people were living the lives of moles in their rock shelters, while the victory kitchens were probably supplying the only meal they had a day. The surrounding sea had been mined, the German air-raids from Sicily were constant, the strain almost unendurable. Churchill while in Washington had received the fatal news that Tobruk had fallen to the 'desert fox' Rommel. Malta's future looked desperate.

On 10 May 1942 Churchill telegraphed Auchinleck in the Western Desert: 'We are determined that Malta shall not be allowed to fall without battle being fought by your whole army for its retention. The surrender of this fortress would involve over 30,000 men, army and air force, together with several hundred guns. Its possession would give the enemy clear and sure bridge to Africa, with all the consequences flowing from that.' Tobruk had been taken, the attack on Malta was due to begin. It might be small but it was vital.

Earlier in April Churchill had learnt that his 'General Gordon' of Malta – General Dobbie – was at the end of his tether, and that he could no longer rely on his judgement. It was Mabel and Audrey Jackson – the wife of the Lieutenant Governor – mere women, who had known this only too clearly, and for some time.

Audrey Jackson appealed to Mabel to break censorship. 'Everybody knows that you know how to do it. If you don't we will all be prisoners of war within six days – he's preparing to surrender.' 'He' was the exhausted and God-fearing Governor. Mabel takes up the story:

'I produced one telegram after another – dozens of drafts. Audrey said that none of them would do. It was all very awkward. I said that I must have a little more time, and so we left it at that. And then, as if by some miracle, and I don't know to this day who sent them, two young airmen came into my office, and said to me, "We know you want to break censorship. We will be in England the day after tomorrow." I asked them to come and see me the next day.

'Nevertheless, I did not know quite what to say or how to handle this business. Lord Mountbatten had been very pro-Dobbie when he had been Captain of the *Kelly* and had disagreed with me completely. But before it was too late he came striding into my office and said, "*Now* I know what Dobbie feels, and that he will surrender the island! And *now* I know why you will not put up with him."

'Rather startled, I said, "What's happened to you, Dickie?"'

'He replied, "He sent for me, and announced that I, the King's cousin, had said at a dinner party that I was in favour of a negotiated peace. How could he repeat what I said at dinner parties!"'

'I said, "This is outrageous."'

'Dickie said, "Now I know why you oppose that . . .. Well, I've asked him to lunch tomorrow on board the *Kelly* and, what's more, I've told him that you are coming, too, and we're having it out."'

'I said wryly, "That's a nice invitation."'

'The next morning my heart was in my boots. But at 7.30 a.m. a rating came and asked for Lord Mountbatten's suitcase, because Dickie always said that if he was torpedoed he had to have some clothes to wear, as he could not just put on anything, and I had Dickie's suitcase. I asked the rating what had happened, and breaking censorship, he told me that the *Kelly* was ordered to Crete, so His Lordship wanted the suitcase, and that the ship would sail in three hours. I handed over the suitcase and the *Kelly* sailed for Crete. Forty-eight hours later the *Kelly* was torpedoed and Lord Mountbatten was swimming in the sea. His life was saved by a Maltese rating.

'So I went on producing a variety of draft telegrams, but none was passed by Audrey Jackson. I decided to send a telegram to Dickie Mountbatten which read, "What I then said is now vital." The telegram passed the censor because nobody knew what I meant. Major Bertram Ede let the telegram through and twenty-four hours later Dickie made the tremendous mistake of replying, "What you want will happen." Bertram handed the telegram to Dobbie. Later I asked Bertram why he had done so and he said that he did not know himself, or it was the mere thought that he had broken his oath of office. So he went to the Governor and told him, "These telegrams which I do not understand have been through and I thought that you ought to know because of the people involved."

'Dobbie sent for me and asked, "What do you mean by

sending ambiguous telegrams? There are only three people – the person who received it, yourself and myself, who can understand the telegram you sent. In your opinion, there ought to be another Governor of Malta?"

'I took a long breath and said, "Yes, sir."

'General Dobbie said, "I'll make every one of you pay for it."

'I was petrified. Then he said, with sudden kindness, "Well, perhaps you are right. Perhaps you are right!" And I retreated.

'That morning I went out with Major-General Beckett round the guns in an air-raid. He said it was good for the gunners to be inspected while the attacks were on! However, the editor of the *Times of Malta* was hardly in a fit condition to benefit from this experience!

'Years later, after the war, I met General Dobbie on top of a bus in London. It was the most extraordinary meeting. We shook hands and he was very friendly, but I did not say to him, which I would like to have done, "Perhaps we were both right." He was very generous to me!'

In the meantime Mabel had written three letters for the air-men to deliver. One was to Dame Irene Ward, MP, one to her sister, Mary Hornyold, and one to Max Horton, all stressing the fact that Dobbie must go.

Mabel comments on Dame Irene's sterling work for Malta. 'Dame Irene Ward put a question in the House of Commons which I have as to whether it was Churchill's intention to hold Malta or not and would he please make a statement. She did not get a satisfactory answer and Dame Irene threatened to move the adjournment of the House so that the subject could be debated. This was effective. They could not stifle her and so she saved Malta.

'I also got a telegram from Dickie Mountbatten, saying, "What you want will happen." He got into trouble over that but Dobbie was recalled. We waited ten awful days to know who would succeed him. The telephone rang about ten o'clock one night with an official message that at midnight that night General Sir William Dobbie would be relieved and His Excellency, the Viscount Gort, VC would assume the government of Malta. I could hardly believe it. General Gort came out with surrender terms. He told me that he would never use them because he was not having another Dunkirk. He had it on his mind that he had been sent out for that purpose. It was never off his mind. Later, as the siege lightened, Lord Gort took the island ten to fifteen days beyond starvation point because there was no such thing as surrender for him. He told me later at Claridges, that if there had been a forced surrender, he would himself have got into a boat for Syracuse and he had made up his mind to fight it out there. We only had four days' rations left when the August convoy came in. Lord Gort told me that his only worry was that he could not do anything about me. Captain Clark, his naval liaison officer, later confirmed that Gort wanted me to go with him, but he could not see how to achieve it.'

Mabel's admiration for Lord Gort ran contrary to her feelings for Dobbie, but nevertheless Lord Gort was not at all sanguine about the situation. Much against Churchill's approval and own personal habit he rationed himself severely, bicycled in the boiling heat, and since he was doing more physical and mental work than anyone on the island it was surprising that he survived.

Mabel has written her version of the Santa Marija Convoy, 15 August 1942: 'An attempt to raise the siege of Malta by the most costly naval and mercantile fleet of World War II was the running of the August convoy.

'Fourteen merchant ships sailed from Liverpool with a strong naval escort, and fourteen merchant ships made it past the Straits of Gibraltar. Three and a half reached their destination. I recall three and a half, because the *Ohio* limped into the Malta harbour with a British destroyer lashed either side to keep her afloat. She carried vital cargo of oil and food. Her arrival was the turning-point in the survival of the island. I did not see her coming in and I greatly regret it. I knew she was expected and prayed that she would make it, for without coal or oil, there was no energy, and everything would come to a grinding halt. The old-fashioned windmills that had previously provided energy for raising water and grinding corn were extinct, and, for that matter, so were the ox and donkey that we used to thrash corn with in my younger days. Not that there was any corn to thrash, but energy meant electricity, and the ability to pump water.'

The ships that came in were the *Melbourne Star*, the *Rochester Castle, Port Chalmers* and *Brisbane Star*; the latter was carrying flour, and when she was torpedoed, the bags of flour helped to seal the hole. One by one, they limped into the harbour. The *Ohio* was the last to come in. I can still remember the refrain of the school children singing, "Ohio, we love you! Oh, Ohio, we love you so!" "Mussolini, are you blind or can't you see the navy – the navy?"

'It flashed round the world that the siege of Malta was raised, but this was far from the truth. It only meant that the island had not fallen. The siege was not raised until 19 November.'

There is no doubt that when a great strain is shared by a man and woman as it was by Mabel and General Gort, a deep sympathy and affection is formed. Mabel, in spite of her protestations about her early love for Mervyn Clive, was as susceptible as most women to attractive men.

In 1946 Jack Gort returned to Malta and this is the sad little piece that Mabel has recorded:

'Jack Gort came back invalided from Palestine. I had done my best to dissuade him from going. In fact, he asked me to go to Palestine with him. He lay at St Anton, where General Shreiber was Governor. I asked to see Lord Gort and got a "No" from General Shreiber and I was livid. I got a message from Gort which he sent via Muscat the gardener, saying that he would never walk round the garden again. That was the end for him. He had asked to see me, and I do not think it would have hurt Shreiber to let me see him.

'Then I got this ghastly news that Gort had died. Jack had died. I did something which I never do in my office – I sent for a double whisky and drank it, and as I was a working editor, I had to correct the "leaders". I waited until I got home and then I cried. I was cross because Max Horton was right when he used to say that I cared for Jack Gort. I was angry because I did not want Max to be right.'

One does wonder why General Shreiber did not allow Mabel to see Gort at this last moment.

In 1947 Mabel had another distraction. Lord Louis Mountbatten thought that he was going to get a seagoing flag appointment in the Mediterranean and had asked Mabel to buy him a house in Malta. However, Lord Mountbatten was made Viceroy of India, and the house Mabel had bought for him was redundant. It is now the Xara Palace Hotel on the Mdina ramparts. Mabel had paid £12,000 for the house and Lord Louis had told her that he could not afford to repay her, and to re-sell it. When she found this difficult, she turned it into the hotel which it is today, and became its chairman in 1966. It is in one of the most beautiful positions in Malta and has the most delicious and charming Victorian atmosphere, with few of the modern trappings which the everyday tourist seeks in the new hotels which are growing like mushrooms all round the coast of Malta.

It does seem extraordinary that the little girl who was dominated by her 'elders and betters' is by 1943 the source of great strength to her family. From her letters it would appear that she is very close to her sister Mary. She supports Cecilia who loses her child John at seven months at Villa Bologna; she cares for her widowed step-mother, and she continues to work at her office fifteen hours a day. She also has something pertinent to say about the colonial system when one Mr Cohen, OBE is moved from Malta to take up an appointment as Assistant Secretary in the Colonial Office in London.

'It is the weakness of the whole colonial system, this constant reposting of officials; one gets a good man in the place and a strong one, and then he is replaced, possibly by a fool. Real progress and understanding of a complex island like Malta are made quite impossible.'

In August 1950 Mabel began her political career with Lord Strickland's policies very much to the forefront. As the *Times of Malta* said in its leader on 19 August:

> Despite her shrewd political acumen, there are points on which Miss Strickland knows no compromise. They are the principles of honesty, loyalty and justice for which Lord Strickland and the Constitutional Party have always stood and when any of these principles are at stake as they are today, there is no rest in the large single-storey villa at Lija, which is her home.

Mabel's opponent then as now was Dom Mintoff. Mabel did not pull her punches in the long battle against Mintoff – one which she was ultimately to lose:

'The items of Mr Mintoff's Labour Party programme which raised constitutional matters are mischievous, destructive to the island's good relations with Britain, and to Malta's value as a link in the chain of the British Commonwealth's defence and to the island's own safety.'

That year she was elected Vice Chairman of the Reconstitutional Party and to the Legislative Assembly. She left the latter a year later and was unseated in 1953 when she formed her own Progressive Constitutional Party, unsuccessfully contesting the 1953 and 1955 elections. In the 1955 election her sister, Cecilia de Trafford, stood for Labour and polled about 360 votes. As Mabel wrote to Mary: 'The point is not what she polled but what it meant to the people who would not vote because they could not understand why she took one line and I took another. The abstention was high and I don't blame them. It was Mintoff's cleverness.' It is easy to imagine the use Mintoff made of the sisters' opposing political views.

It was possibly some compensation to Mabel that she was now leading a highly entertaining social life. 'Yesterday I lunched on the Royal yacht with Prince Philip and his staff and no one else . . . he is a very wise young man and I'm not worried about him or his ability to appreciate and weigh up positions.' Stewart Perowne, who has known Mabel for a great many years, told me that at Christmas her drawing-room was and still is, festooned with Christmas cards. There was always one from the Queen, every known Admiral, the whole lot on strings – simply packed, hundreds! Mabel also sends a crate of oranges to the Queen every year from her famous orange trees.

In the early sixties Mabel was fighting against the British government, led by Macmillan, for Malta's survival. Malta needed money, while the Maltese needed reassurance against 'the drip, drip of sedition in the local socialist press and by the slogan "Britain's word is dirt" painted on selective walls where service personnel picnic or foregather'.

The navy was being reduced to one frigate and one submarine employing 500 men, and in the event of redundancy in the docks, there was only a totally inadequate provision for unemployment benefit. Mabel feared riots, and an undermining of local confidence in Britain's intentions with regard to the future of the island. The position which had been outlined to the House of Commons in 1958 when the Colonial Development

Corporation had promised to invest one million pounds, had changed. Mabel's bone of contention was the British government's responsibility for the Admiralty leasing the naval dockyard in Malta to a company which was only a subsidiary of C.H. Bailey, Wales, and therefore the Colonial Office could not interfere in the affairs of a private firm. She writes stringent letters to Mr MacLeod, Colonial Secretary, whose policy of handing the Empire over lock, stock and barrel, she so strongly opposed. She was fighting a battle for her beloved island, and so she continued fighting.

She sums up the crux of the political problem: 'the real political problem apart from the economic one, is the imbalance of those men and women who spent their adolescent years from eleven to fourteen in the shelters between 1940 and 1944. Many are consequently illiterate and thousands are emotional.'

In 1962 her party won a few seats at the election. Mabel did not believe unequivocally in independence for Malta because of the economic effects it would have brought about. Eventually independence came in 1964 when it was accompanied by a defence arrangement with Great Britain and a Financial Treaty with the continual employment of about 11,000 people in the British Military Base.

She was the victim of violence during more than one campaign, when she was hit by stones from a wild mob, undoubtedly aroused by Mintoff and his henchmen; this was especially so during the referendum campaign in 1956. One who knows her well explained her courage and determination:

'When the Mintoff government resigned in 1958, it showed Miss Strickland at her finest mettle. Miss Strickland's press was under a constant state of siege. They had barbed-wire surrounding the press at all times, and a very stringent police check, and it demanded real courage to come out with her views in the newspaper at the time . . . all the workers at Allied Newspapers share this pride as the papers, ever since their foundation, have never missed an issue, not even at the height of the war. An echo of that came on 16 October 1979 when the press was set on fire by a mob and it made publication virtually impossible the next day. But the spirit that Miss Strickland bequeathed to her staff prompted them to move to another printing press and the paper came out the next day, just the same. This was again in the tradition of courage and determination that Miss Strickland showed ever since she came on the political scene.'

One of the tragedies of this last event was that all the records were burnt which will make the history of the Allied Newspapers and Mabel's own story hard to piece together.

In 1968 Malta was at the height of its clash with Britain over defence cuts. Though Mabel was now sixty-eight, she made frequent visits to London during this year to fight for the island's future. Her Progressive Constitutional Party was small and unrepresented in the House but she fought on with her influence and her wide acquaintance. She knew that the two governments had valid problems to solve. The British government, the defence of the pound sterling, the Maltese government, the change in the island's economy from being geared to Britain's defence services to one of industry, tourism and development of Malta's dry docks. Aggravating each other's problems would solve nothing. The Maltese government would have to take the country into its confidence and announce constructive plans. She was saddened by what she considered Britain's betrayal when she moved her troops and air force from the island: 'No amount of airborne power available in the United Kingdom can produce the same result as a well-equipped force on the spot in a strategic position.'

When I went to see Mabel in Malta in 1981 she was being cared for by a stalwart and faithful Connie Bolchino. Connie protects her from importunate intruders. I noticed how her expression changed when she looked at Mabel – it softened miraculously. The power to claim love and affection is still there. When Connie left the room, Mabel looked at me and said: 'Don't you want to know how she came to me?'

I agreed that I did.

'She came to me when she was thirteen, and she was crying – she has been with me ever since.' And I knew from her expression that the affection was returned. At eighty-four the politics, the newspapers, the hotels, and the constant battles were put aside, but for Mabel – Connie remains.

PART SEVEN

The Pacific Islands

17

Sa Mbula Vinaka – Live Well

Tonga and the Fiji Islands were discovered by Tasman, the Dutch navigator in 1643. In 1773 Tonga was visited by Cook who found the 'hospitality was overwhelming'. There was brisk trading from dawn to dusk, and far from the natives being hard bargainers, Cook found them 'more desirous to give than receive'. When the ships finally sailed on 8 October their decks were laden with coconuts, bananas and yams, and between them they carried 150 live pigs and 300 fowls. Because of the affability of the natives he called them the Friendly Islands, though Sparrman, who saw many war clubs, concluded that the islanders did not always live so amicably together. Today the islands are better known as the islands of Tonga. In 1777 Cook was back in Tonga where, 'Fraternization reached such a point that some Tongan girls virtually lived aboard the ships and moved with them from island to island.' Cook had learned that two extensive groups of islands lay within a few days' easy sail: Fiji to the north-west, a high rich country peopled by numerous 'cannibals, brave, savage and cruel'; and Samoa, whose people had much in common with the Tongans, in the north-east.

Decades later, in 1949, John Peel (later knighted), who was in Singapore at the time, was offered the post of Resident Commissioner in the Gilbert and Ellice Islands. Rosemary, his wife, had given birth to a baby boy and was in England:

'We decided we would go straight there. I telephoned Sir Arthur Grimble, and asked him what I thought were quite sensible questions, but I don't think he did! I wanted to know about taking out a nurse, because if you are going abroad like that to an unusual place you can most probably get one for export. But I don't think he was interested in that sort of thing, it was remote as far as he was concerned – a woman on the telephone wondering about taking a nurse out to the Gilberts! We went out in March, and Nurse had her twenty-first birthday on the way out.

'It was not easy there because it was very bush, and there were lots of rats – and cats to keep the rats down. The cats were always having kittens in one's wardrobes, and the rats ran through the house through the hollow tubes which were used instead of beams – they lashed them together with coconut string! John put a trench coat over the end of one to hang it up, and the next morning there was a hole right through the lining. Those sort of things were tiresome, and, of course, the local domestic help was less sophisticated. But we had our own Chinese boy and his wife both in Brunei and in the Gilberts – they got themselves there via Australia – I still marvel at their resourcefulness. It was very helpful because their standard of cleanliness was high. We hadn't received any of the government china or glass and so on to begin with – only what I'd taken out. After we'd been there six weeks, the High Commissioner of the Western Pacific, who was in Fiji, cabled John to say he would like him to go to the Solomons. We had hardly unpacked, and John just said he wouldn't think it was on, that our nurse had a contract for the Gilberts, not for the Solomons!'

One can imagine Sir Arthur Grimble's comments on the importance of nurses! Only a mother with four children can appreciate Rosemary's dilemma. Then a relationship evolved which I fear was only too common in colonial and service life, especially in small stations where jealousies and pettiness are blown up out of all proportion to their importance:

'Our nurse fitted in very well with everyone – except one. In a way, one woman can spoil a posting. Looking back, I think I was pretty naïve really in spite of having four children. This particular woman wanted all the young men to revolve round her in spite of being married with two children, and she said in other people's hearing, which was reported to us, "Do we have to entertain the nurse?" So poor Nurse got left out of things, and after all, she was one of the few unmarried girls from a nice home. There was one other unmarried girl, but quite often they weren't asked to the parties, though all the young men were! I was fighting on their side, so it made for an unhappy situation. I had this woman round to the Residency and told her that I thought she had the wrong attitude, and I said, "When your daughter grows up, and perhaps is a secretary or something, would you like it if people said 'Do we have to entertain the secretary?' " But it didn't make any difference. There was constant chat about who was in her house when her husband was away! John had to move one young man, and everybody was up in arms about it, and said it was a terrible thing to do. However, this young man married a nice American girl he met on his new posting.'

One has to imagine the smallness of the Gilberts, Rosemary's position there, her newness to Tarawa, her isolation with a busy husband and a young nurse whom she probably did not wish to bother with her problems, to sympathize with her battling against the jealousies and the insensitivities of those women already established there.

'They did other things which made life difficult for us. We inherited a visitor's book. We hadn't quite got the courage to throw it away. After all, John's father had been a Governor so he knew a good deal about signing books! If people signed the book, then one entertained them, but if they didn't bother, then it wasn't necessary. There were only forty Europeans – some of them very rough Australians – and they certainly weren't going to sign the Resident Commissioner's book! When it came to the New Year, we thought perhaps we would give a party. I think we made a mistake because we gave them wine which they didn't like. And this same woman came and said very loudly, "Where's the whisky?" and so our boy had to produce it. Later she said for all to hear, "Come on, chums! Come round to us and have a beer." Really, she quite spoilt what could have been a happy posting. Also the tradition there, which wasn't so in Malaya, was that you didn't entertain the Resident Commissioner, but that he entertained people but was never asked back. Well, that made it rather lonely in a way. There they all were exchanging dinner parties whilst we stayed at home. They'd raided the Residency and taken all the Muscovy ducks which had been left by the previous RC people and they had divided up other spoils before we got there. They said, "This person's coming from Malaya, and we don't know anything about him." So we had our difficulties.' That was putting it mildly!

Freda Gwilliam would have been a sympathetic listener to Rosemary's problems, for this is what she had to say about the Gilbert and Ellice Islands:

'They were not connected by air with the rest of the world until about the early sixties, and the administration was carried out by Her Majesty's Overseas Service, and they could only get to the islands by sea. They had copra and trading ships on very infrequent and wholly unreliable service, and the isolation there was absolutely incredible. I mean, Arthur Grimble gave a lovely concept of them, but what he couldn't give was the feeling of utter isolation, of people who had had to send their children away, and who couldn't get a weekly or fortnightly or monthly letter – because there was no regular post, so that only in an emergency, or a *cri-de-coeur,* could one send a cable. That was the isolation! Also the fact that your basic supplies were not necessarily there: I mean, if you broke your last needle, you could not sew. There was nothing in the store, and there was no way of knowing when the next ship was coming – and if the ship did come, you didn't know what particular supplies were on the ship. That kind of deprivation, of which those of us who live comfortably have no conception, were part and parcel of life.'

On reading this, one feels that Rosemary made almost light of her not inconsiderable troubles.

Patricia Maddocks went out as a Field Officer, after her first husband had died, first to Mauritius and then to the Pacific where she lived in Honiara, the capital of the Solomons, and where her territory included the New Hebrides and the Gilbert and Ellice Islands 'and that is thousands of miles'.

'To get in a circle, I used to go to Fiji, and I would have to stay there for a few days, and then on to Tonga. I would go to Tonga for two weeks and get them sorted out, and I was also asked to Brunei which was rather nice. But transport there was by Air Intergroup and sometimes by Air Inter-island, but they didn't all have air strips, so if they didn't, you had to go by boat and that would be a tiny little cargo ship with one cabin at the back which you shared with whoever had a ticket. They were nearly always men, occasionally they were nuns, and if I wasn't there, the nun would be sharing it with men, without turning a hair.

'In the Gilberts they were open-handed charming people, but they had scarcely any land. They were great big people, short but big. I found transport very difficult there, because there were long distances between the islands so you couldn't go by canoe. I *have* been nine hours in a canoe, that is the longest. It was murder!

'The Gilberts had these tiny narrow atolls. In the capital, one end was horseshoe shape, and one was eleven miles long. I walked through that, through the villages there and slept the night in the villages with a horde of Red Cross helpers, which was their idea of how to do Red Cross work. They were all locals. They put one girl among them, to make it respectable I suppose, and all the rest were men from other islands. I was trying to train people to be Field Officers – it didn't work out. I had one man who I thought was very good, but the Europeans didn't go for him at all and so it was no good in the end. But he had such good ideas for doing things which no European would have known about, because we didn't know the things he knew. He knew that if a nurse or partly trained nurse, retired and went back to live in her village, that village would be allowed to have a medical cupboard as long as they built one that would lock up, and then she could administer the contents to the village. Well, that would be a great help! They wouldn't have to trek into the capital every time and sometimes they were out on other islands where there was no medical help. And this chap got all his leaders and chiefs to build medical cupboards where there was a nurse. Another thing was that when sick people were brought into the hospital on Tarawa, they were always accompanied by at least one or two relatives and while they were in hospital the relatives had no means of support, so these chaps went singing to earn money to feed the relatives of sick people. But I don't think that would ever have struck the Europeans because we would never have known about it. So when they do get a few of their own officers it will be very much better.'

Time schedules were unknown, especially in the Gilberts:

'Once I remember I was booked onto a plane and the engineer went out to service the plane. There were only three taxis on the island, and two were not there, I don't know where they were, and the driver of the third was dead drunk. So the engineer pushed the driver across the seat and drove the taxi himself out to the airport, and swished up to his aircraft at right-angles, jammed on the brakes, and they didn't work. He went straight into the aircraft, so we couldn't take off for ten days because there wasn't another plane.'

It seems strange to think of the only two bits of transport in the whole island colliding!

How did they communicate in this handful of islands with eighty or more dialects? How did they amuse themselves when the Noël Coward records had palled, the once-a-week cinema was anticipated, or it was too hot to hold the bridge cards, and only the silent boys refilling the glasses of gin in their flowered lava-lavas seemed important?

'Well, they first of all use pidgin, but the pidgin was different in the New Hebrides to what it was in the Solomons, and there again, I couldn't start. I knew a bit of Nigerian pidgin. As for the latter, I played golf. In the Gilberts there was the funniest golf course in the world. I went with a woman to the club, and I said, looking around, "Come on, now, where's this course? Let's get started." And she said, "Well, it's here! We're on it!" "Oh!" I said. "Are we?" We appeared to be on the beach as far as I could see, so I said, "Where's the first tee?" and she said again, "Here, we're on it!" There was a little red post on every tee and when you got to the green, so to speak, you took a piece of wood and you swept the sand up to the hole so that your ball had a passage. It was an incredible place. All sorts of thorns and scrub between you and your destination, your objective.'

Thinking of Stevenson's descriptions, and Grimble's turquoise shimmering blue seas; surely the bathing off the coral must reveal untold treasures, of fish clad in every rainbow hue?

'No! You see in the Gilberts they had lavatories that stuck out into the water on posts. You walked along a log if you were clever enough not to fall in and at the end of the log you would find a little hut, which probably didn't have a door, and it stood up on legs in the sea – so you didn't really want to swim in the Gilberts! Government House had proper ones, but I always remember the taps in the bath were marked Hot Well and Cold Well.'

We were talking about the colonies and how and when they got their independence, the moments of emotion, of gladness, of regret, and sometimes, looking into that crystal ball, a very real feeling of fear.

'Take Fiji,' said Freda Gwilliam. 'I love Fiji. Just when Independence was coming up, the first High Commissioner for Fiji in this country was someone who'd been a very good teacher in primary school in Fiji. I liked him particularly because we had a very difficult English Director of Education out there, and he was one of the people who could really do harm by attitudes. A brilliant educationalist, but the wrong attitudes. But Joe had stood up to him, and that made me very pro-Joe. And I said to him, "What flag are you going to have?" So he produced the new flag, and there was a Union Jack in the corner. "Oh," I said. "*It's* there!" And he said, "*You're* always welcome." When the people for whom we're working or have been working, see that we can also work with them, that tie is very strong. But the women can cut it by their attitudes. The women can do more harm than good, because we're never neutral. My great theme is – no woman is neutral – she's for or against. And so she can never be ignored.'

On these formal occasions it was immaterial whether it was 120°F in the shade or not. The women prayed that their make-up would not run, that their one and only hat would hide their faces sufficiently if it did. Even crouching to climb into the car would make one pour with perspiration, as one's feet swell in the unaccustomed shoes, the clinging stockings. On other occasions it was entirely up to the Governor and his wife to judge how far they wished to torture their lower ranks. The colonial women had slavishly to follow the Governor's wife. Hats, gloves, stockings, were noted and either thankfully put into a bottom drawer or pulled out and dusted, or, as in Jill Weston's case, written home for.

'I went out to Fiji with Hugh in 1948. He had already been there for eight years. The Governor and his wife when we first arrived there were very delightful, relaxed people; we made friends and used to play bridge with them. Then they were succeeded by another Governor whose wife was a tremendous stickler for etiquette, and we were all very worried because we'd heard we had to wear long white gloves if we went to dinner in Government House, and we were unable to buy white gloves in Fiji – very few of us came from circles that would normally use white gloves. So when we acquired our long gloves, we didn't know how to use them, whether to take them off for dinner, whether to tuck them in, and some of us got the wrong sort – and I wrote to my mother telling her that she had taught me most things but not how to eat asparagus in long white gloves. We were all very much disturbed and worried by this tremendous increase in etiquette. However, it soon settled down, and the edict to wear gloves was withdrawn.'

The Westons' relationship with the Fijians was an extremely happy one, and still is. They would have stayed longer had it not been for their children:

'When we were there the Indians were just about to overtake the Fijians in numbers, and were by no means as happy with the colonial set-up as the Fijians were. The Fijians, if they were asked if they wanted us to stay on would say "Yes, certainly!" because we protected them against the Indians. They were always very loyal to us, and, of course, immensely loyal to the Queen. Her visit in 1953 was a tremendous occasion, with a great deal of jealousy about who was invited to the functions. There was a big ball at the Central Pacific Hotel, and functions of various sorts for the Fijians and the Europeans. I believe when the Queen first arrived she was really quite upset because she was greeted with total silence by the Fijians because that is their way of showing respect, which she hadn't expected.

'As for our own lives, we had a wonderful life for young married couples, apart from the humidity, the complaints the children had, and lack of energy. We had a very pleasant social life, with delightful girls to help in the house. For young children before they had to go away to boarding-school it was almost ideal. But, of course, when they had to go away to school there were worries, difficulties, and it was quite a debate in our day as to whether a woman's place was mainly with her husband or her children. I remember we all had ideas! There were some marriages on the rocks – I don't know what the right answer was! There was no answer!

'In our case, we sent our eldest son home to prep school when he was about nine. He was desperately homesick and in the end we decided to leave Fiji because we couldn't bear this situation. It was made easier for us to leave because at that time Fiji was just coming up to Independence, and Colonial Officers were being offered early retirement – at forty-five I think.'

There was one aspect of life in Fiji which Jill found delightful, though fortunately it was not practised against the Europeans. It was similar to the extended family in Africa, and was a form of communal living where everything was shared. It was, however, sometimes unfortunate for the more intelligent man who wished to improve the lot of his immediate family:

'You would find the other Fijians expected him to share. If they wanted anything they must have it. Anyone could come into your house and say, "I want a chicken, or a bullock, or whatever," and it wasn't done to refuse. They would sometimes come to one's house and say "That's nice" and expect it, but it wasn't normally practised against Europeans. Many Fijians who had a good salary, and had collected a good amount of stock, were in great danger of the other Fijians coming along and acquiring their possessions, and reducing them to the ranks again.'

Today one has the impression of a cheerful and extremely friendly people, given to dancing and singing. Their musicality is famous. They sing everywhere, in church, on social occasions, even on buses. It is as natural as breathing. Though the Fijians are on the best of terms with the Europeans, one has only to dip into history to find extremes of cruelty on both sides. The first Europeans to land, after Captain Bligh had anchored beyond the reef in front of Suva, brought cholera to the Fijians, killing thousands. They quarrelled among themselves and killed each other. Sandalwood brought many a white adventurer who then sold it to China, and reading of their villainous behaviour, one finds one's sympathies lying with the cannibalism of the islanders rather than with the whites whose mercenary behaviour changed cannibalism, which had once been the ceremonial right of the chieftain, to a practice among the common people.

In 1835 missionaries arrived at Lakemba in the form of Mr Cross and Mr Cargill. Mr Hunt and Mr Lyth followed with their wives. It must have been a terrifying time for women, especially when there were cannibal feasts in progress which made the Fijians wildly exultant and uncontrolled, not unlike the behaviour of some Europeans after too much whisky.

In time all the different denominations poured into the islands to save the so-called sinners' souls with their own particular brand of Christianity. Jehovah's Witnesses, Methodists, Catholics, Seventh Day Adventists, Mormons and many others, and I suspect, knowing the Fijians' susceptibility to music, that the one which sang the gayest hymns probably had most appeal.

However, Rosemary Greenwood, whose husband was Attorney-General, found there were more Methodists than any other denomination. Despite this, 'marriage wasn't considered a very binding or important thing, but it worked very well, and the mother and the grandmother were important and everybody looked after everyone else in the village. There was a good family feeling. I suffered from this habit of borrowing because one maid I had used to borrow my dresses. I discovered this because on one occasion she tore my dress. On the whole they were pretty honest, there was very little crime there.'

The medical scene had made progress since Patricia Maddocks's days in Fiji.

'They had a medical school that trained assistant medical officers. I think they did three or four years. Anybody from any Pacific island could come and train there; they weren't actually doctors, but they could dispense, and they had dispensaries with an AMO dotted round all the islands of any size, and probably a trained nurse or two. They could deal with all the ordinary ills perfectly well, as well as minor surgery. There were quite a number of qualified Indian doctors but there was only one Fijian doctor the whole time I was there. There were various GPs in the towns. Mostly Australians or New Zealanders, some English and a few Irish. But there was nothing lethal like malarial mosquitoes, no wild animals, no poisonous insects, no parasites, no tropical diseases – only white ants which eat the wooden houses!'

Life was pleasant in this Garden of Eden. The Greenwoods explored and everywhere they went the Fijians welcomed them with their traditional dish of *kava* – the root of a bush ground up and mixed with water and then squeezed out through a leafy fibre. It tastes like peppery mud, but you develop a taste for it, and it's mildly stimulating; it leaves a very clean taste in the mouth and is wonderful if you have a hangover.

Patricia Maddocks worried about the people of the islands being cut off from medical help. She was convinced that deformed children were quietly put away, and she gives this as her reason:

'It was never proved but there were very very few deformed children, and there were a few that I did find who, I think, were thalidomide children, but I couldn't prove it. Had I been able to prove it, they would have been able to get help through this fund that has been set up for them, and the Chief Justice, who had just left, told me that if he could find proof he would get it seen to, but I couldn't find proof. They had never had thalidomides in the country officially, but they may have had samples. I think that must have been it because all the mothers with the afflicted children were nurses, so it was probably available to them. I got one of those children into a home in Fiji where there was a wonderful man doing work with handicapped people of all kinds, and this child was without legs at all, and her arms finished in a point at the elbow. She was about ten, I suppose. And when I went to see her later on they had taught her to read and write, and she wrote with the points of her elbows, and she wrote beautifully, as well as any other child of her age. She was a bright intelligent child, and they put her body into a basin with loose legs and if she swung her body from side to side the legs moved and she could walk on a flat surface, and she was so happy. He was a wonderful man.'

Though Patricia Maddocks had no medical training except for first aid during the war, she seems to have achieved a great deal in helping the people in the Pacific.

'There were a lot of deaf children and I was making a card index of all those I found; I think it was due to swimming in coral waters. They got coral ear and their ears would run and the mothers wouldn't do anything about it. I didn't do much for them in the way of medical help except try and take them to the doctor and teach them how to cope with a drowned man – artificial respiration. I had one of those lovely rubber bodies, they enjoyed that! I also taught them what to do if a man fell out of a palm tree and broke his back. I taught a group of women one day how to do this, to immobilize somebody completely, so that they could lift him, and so it involved tying up the ankles, the knees and so on, all the way up the body, and I did it to one woman, and when I untied her, I said, "Now I want one of you to do it to another person." Well, no one would volunteer to be the body, so in the end I volunteered. They tied me up most effectively and then they stood back and laughed! I think they found this funny because they'd been cannibals until quite recently!'

Hilary Trevor, whose husband was Chief Secretary, felt that Western civilization was not a good influence on the whole, even though it might have tried to instil some sensitivity towards animals.

'You couldn't stop Western civilization, even if *we* hadn't been there; people would have come in and once they had seen civilization in the form of beer cans or transistors, or watches, they wouldn't want to go back. We did find that. Very often they'd come to Honiara and take a job. We had garden-boys and people who worked in the government. They'd suddenly get into a mood when they'd had enough and they'd suddenly, without telling you, go back to their villages. Particularly the garden-boys. They seemed only to come to earn enough money to buy a sack of rice, shorts and a shirt perhaps, and then they'd pack up and go to their village, where they would lie under a palm tree and fish. Their needs were very few.'

As in Hong Kong, Hilary worked in the Solomons as a physiotherapist:

'There was one physiotherapist for the whole Protectorate, as it was then, and she was an American nun – very dedicated, but that was all they could afford, just one for the whole place. She was persuaded to take leave when I was there, because I said I would like to do it, so I did it for six months. After Hong Kong, life seemed rather difficult, there were always unexpected things happening. A boat had to come in from Australia each month with supplies, and sometimes Australian dockers would be on strike and the ship would be late and you would get short of various things in the shops. You'd be short of drugs and things like flour. There was local meat. Once we bought a whole cow from the local mission, and of course we had to cut it up. It had to be done in the cool of the evening, so it was strung up on a tree in the garden, and we asked a Solomon Island friend to come; he was a great, tough chap, Dominic, a young Administrative Officer, and he got an axe and divided it into two, and then about six of us – husbands as well – set about cutting up the meat. We cut it into joints, and two of us wives had the bags and labels all ready to put it into the deep freeze. Then Dominic and the people who had helped would get the less good bits of meat which they were delighted to have.'

'While we were there, or perhaps it happened just before we went there, they started to introduce rice-growing in Guadalcanal where Honiara is. Up till then they had been buying imported rice from Australia, and when they grew their own rice and it was cheaper, they wouldn't buy it – they didn't think it could be so good. And my own boy, Ben, he wouldn't eat cheap rice until one Christmas I gave him a sack of rice, local rice, and I think he felt he couldn't turn it down. And once he tried it of course he realized it was just as good, if not better, than the imported rice.

'We did a lot of entertaining and they were very big eaters. Trevor used to entertain the House Assembly once each session, and that would be a sort of buffet and then we used to have huge great sandwiches and sausages, and food in bulk – I was always afraid of not having enough.'

Hilary had been glad to leave Hong Kong for the Solomons. She found that the pressure of working, entertaining, and the noise of the city had become a strain. Also the Cultural Revolution in 1967–8 had been an extremely unpleasant experience. Like most people's conception of the South Sea Isles, however, Hilary was disappointed by her first glimpse of Honiara. There is always, one suspects, the preconceived idea that any island in the South Seas is going to be like the romantically portrayed Tahiti, a Loti or Gauguin paradise. But Honiara was like a shanty town:

'Tin roofs and shacky shops, and not at all like the South Pacific somehow. In the villages you got those lovely leafy houses, but the town was really very disappointing. So I think a lot of wives never travelled, because it was difficult, and I think they were very discontented, those of them who didn't go out.'

In the late seventies, a great many of the young men were out on contracts and possibly on one tour, so their wives did not get involved with the local good works, unlike Hilary who sought out the local women, gave them first-aid lectures and taught them to sew.

PART EIGHT

Aden

18

Gateway to India

In 1957 a friend said to me, 'What a romantic life you lead!' her voice inferring – 'Poor dear! You always choose the trouble spots! How tiresome!' Driven out of China by the Communists, two years of troubles in Cyprus, and now – Aden. My husband and I were beginning to wonder whether, indeed, we were Jonahs, and even in strike-bound but peaceful England people were already saying to me in curious voices, 'How long, darling, did you say you were staying here?' as if I might stir up trouble in Kensington or the green Dorset hills!

Of course, then the popular concept of Aden was of a thin bone-dry coastline back-clothed by a range of pitted volcanic mountains lying like a leviathan against a heat-hazed sky: the dazzle of chrome-coloured oil tanks, the taste of oil lying thickly on one's tongue, and a slight sense of relief that one is under no obligation to land. The more romantically inclined will perhaps see it as the gateway to India, or, going the other way, the Suez Canal or even, as the once ancient and flourishing main port for the trade route of frankincense and spice from the Hadhramaut and Dhurfar; a city visited by Rimbaud and Gide; and a land where, not so long ago, men of initiative and adventure could trade and then, provided with the correct amount of unscrupulousness, rise up and become millionaires.

However, in the year 1957, I noticed that the face of Aden was changing:

With the ever-increasing importance of oil, the restlessness of history and geographical placement, it is losing its colourful oriental squalor for occidental uniformity. Thus beside poverty and mouldering houses, great square blocks of honeycombed flats are growing like mushrooms, huge areas of rubble land are portioned off to build the new civil hospital; roads skimming the harbour are being subjected to dual carriageways, and the airport spreads like a slow rising tide beside the salt marshes with their webbed windmills which retracts as its importance diminishes.

I certainly did not have my crystal ball before me when I wrote those words twenty-five years ago, though I did find it surprising that we arrived by *Britannia* and did not land in a Sputnik on this lunar landscape.

Joan Thorne moved from Arusha to Aden and I thought it might have been a shock to her after Africa:

'It wasn't, really, because it was so entirely different. Though it was rather a shock when we arrived. Having had rather a nice house in Africa we were put into a new block of flats in the Ma'alla stretch looking over the cemetery. I thought it was really awful.'

I knew the flats well having lived in them myself, and I remember the cemetery and the view of the long wall where the Arabs defecated, while from another window a low wall protected them in their prayers, long rows of white humble rumps. The flats were very small, and Joan thought them:

'Absolutely minute and hot. Some trouble had just started and Robin was doing part of the sort of security team so he was away the whole time. In fact, the moment we arrived he went off and didn't come back for three days. We didn't know a soul, and my son was then about eight or nine, so he and I had to do all the unpacking. Oh, those horrid little flats! I thought, "We must be able to improve on this" so we started moving the furniture around, and about an hour later Matthew said, "Well, we're back where we started" and we were. There was nothing you could do. Then, partly because of the troubles, or perhaps it was just going to the equivalent of a town, no one took very much notice of us so we were a bit lonely for about six weeks, and then suddenly the Commissioner of Police with whom Robin was working, invited us to a few parties and from then on it became an absolute whirl of parties – two cocktail parties a night and five dinners a week. The services were something new to us – in Africa it was always government officials or business people – so in Aden there were really far more nice people than one had ever had a chance to meet before.'

Those days when the merry British danced until dawn on the roof of the Crescent Hotel – the very heart of Aden – when there was an avaricious gleam in the eyes of the shopkeepers at Steamer Point as the tourists poured out, identically dressed, to buy the duty-free goods; when you still signed the book at Government House and pulled on your long white gloves to dine there – those days were Aden's 'Last Post' for the British. Adenization was slowly but surely taking place. The Arabs were on the Legislative Council, and were government officials in most departments. In spite of border trouble there was little, in Aden itself, to tell the visitor of the unrest barely seventeen miles away. The Arabs in Aden were friendly but lethargic, unwilling to work hard, while starvation and near tragedy could be lightly dismissed as the Will of Allah. But, as in Cyprus before the bombs began to fall, there were the signs if you looked for them, and the give-away murmur of husbands' secrets.

June Knox-Mawer in radiant youth and burning enthusiasm was a correspondent for the *Daily Express*. Her husband, Ronald, was Chief Magistrate and between them they grew closer to the Arabs than a great many of the British. Their special friends were Sultan Saleh bin Hussein of Audhali, Sultan Ali of Lahej, and their unofficial PA or ADC – the middle-aged Farid. June and Ronald were enviably allocated No.1 Downing Street, a large airy house in the suburbia of the Khormaksar isthmus, which may have initially helped the good impression Aden obviously made on June. One reads her book *The Sultans Came to Tea* and wonders. 'Where was *that* Aden? Was it really like that? Did I miss it?' The answer probably rests in the affirmative. It was like that but one did not have June's energy in seeking it. One makes excuses: the heat, the horrid little flat, the children's health, one's own flagging energies – but they are only excuses and it is a pity:

By the time Joan Thorne was in Aden, Sultan Ali had gone.

'He'd rather disgraced himself by going to Cairo, and his

successor was a rather elderly, well-behaved one. We went to Perim which had been a coaling station with one house on it and the water was just the sea-water boiled up. But the most marvellous fishing, and lobsters! We went with one of the princes from Lahej who was very dashing, incredibly handsome, who spoke no English at all, and none of us spoke Arabic. He was an excellent driver and we went in two Land Rovers, and he drove much better than either of our drivers.'

Joan Thorne felt the magic of the Hadhramaut:

'We flew from Mukalla and had about a week there. Absolutely glorious architecture. The buildings are beautiful and dazzling white. And the blue of the water and the sky, and the blue paint work. Do you remember the houses had all the windows and the lattice work in that rather lovely sort of Prussian blue? We were also very lucky because we had one trip through the Aden Protectorate, but we had to have an armed guard there, followed by a Land Rover bristling with guns. To begin with, Robin was working closely with the police, then latterly he became an Administrator of the colony. It was that rather odd set-up with the protectorate and the colony, the Governor, the Chief Secretary and the Financial Secretary who was supposed to be impartial. Robin was eventually in charge of the colony under the Arab Chief Minister. An extremely nice person whom he liked very much, but it was always this awful problem of getting together the protectorate and the colony. The colony tended to think of the protectorate as wild men and the protectorate people despised the colony people as shopkeepers and artisans.'

Joan did a weekly shop in the famous Crater which was at first quite safe but was eventually banned. This is an extinct crater surrounded by frozen lava and in its claustrophobic heat there was a town of flat-roofed houses, of narrow streets, a pulsing stream of humanity, of goats whipping up in their hungry jaws anything from brown cardboard to torn cloth, and the object of Joan's visits, to those who had the eye to see, the *suk*. Crater was a complete world of tiny scenarios. Here was an old man cooking some spicy fritters on a small charcoal burner; Indian women threaded their way in and out of the crowds, their legs clearly visible through their bright saris; tall Somalis stalked by, carrying their canes, and their *lungies* reaching down to their ankles made them appear even taller than they were in fact; Yemenis chewing *qat* with fanatical and dreamy expressions in their eyes; children with velvet eyes and long hair; proud straight boys leading blind beggars as gently and as carefully as if they were balancing precious china in their hands; and over all the strong mingling smell of urine and spices which both repulsed and allured.

During the winter months, the climate is pleasant and cool, but never cold. During those last few precarious normal years, life, which had ebbed slowly to a standstill in the summer, began to grind gradually to a quickened tempo; the air became full of fierce bargaining, the mail got answered at last, the newspapers read and digested, and an interest in things beyond the confines of a simple battle against the heat quickened; ships seemed to stream in and out more purposefully; buildings grew nearer the sky; agencies vied with each other for trade; life took on English norms; prices soared as the canal grew busier, and everyone was happy. But for the English there was one desperate longing! It was for green grass, for any form of vegetation, which was entirely lacking except for the sprinkled lawns of Government House, the privileged officials, the small millionaire minority. There were the Sheikh Othman Gardens in the border town of that name, and sometimes the colonial women took their children there to sniff the unscented flowers, to touch the green leaves. When we came back my young son of five picked a flower every day and put it carefully on a chair by his bed as something rare and precious.

Joan Thorne could not, and did not, live without her greenery:

'I put a sweet potato in a pot and it sent out a glorious shower of greenery. At last, we moved from our horrid little flat to one in the Cable and Wireless building. It was the top one and you could practically goggle from the window; you looked straight down into the deep water. The road was between the flats and the sea but after that it dropped sheer, so from the top of this very high building you could look down and see shark and other fish like sting rays – you could just see them floating about.'

Every day the wives would take their children to Goldmohur (named after the trees which grow there) where a bathing area was netted against the sharks. There was sand and a stall selling Coca Cola, and thatched shelters against the sun. Sometimes the bathing resembled swimming in fish soup when small fish, like whitebait, came in their shoals. These were collected to make fertilizer, and as they were piled and died on the beach the smell was unbelievable. Joan remembered: 'The curious thing was that in the middle of the hottest of the hot weather, which I think was probably September – May and September were the hottest months – suddenly the water went icy cold. By icy cold, I suppose it went down to about 70°F or something, overnight, while it was boiling hot outside. Caused by some odd current from the Indian Ocean.'

The British passion for Federation, was, as always, the bone of contention in the Colony of Aden and the Protectorates. Nasser in Egypt was vehemently against this British government's ideal. Nor did every colonial official believe in it. Robin Thorne was one. Joan said: 'I don't think he ever thought that a Federation would work. I think perhaps some of the Protectorate Arabs were more war-like than the Yemenis. This was, perhaps, one of the problems in that the Yemenis came down in their hordes and provided all the labour.'

Barbara Cannon was the headmistress of a girls' secondary school in Zanzibar. When the changes came in the early sixties, in Tanganyika, Uganda, Kenya and Zanzibar, she was on leave in India. She had planned to return to Zanzibar via Mombasa, but when she arrived in the port she heard that the revolutionaries had taken over Zanzibar. She did her best, but it was quite obvious that by her standards she couldn't continue, so she came back to London to see what other jobs there were.

At that time, 1964, there was a comparatively new and promising girls' secondary school in Aden, and this seemed a perfect place for her to go with her experience of Islam. So off she went to Aden. There, this school was very much in purdah – it had high walls all round, and it had a guard at the gate, and all the girls used to arrive in buses, taxis, cars, looking just like little black beetles, except they wore beautiful shoes which peeped out from under their robes. An old guardian counted them all in and then shut the gates behind them. They would then throw off their black garments and come out in really very fetching school uniforms – purely traditional western. And they did very well. As the revolutionary changes came, so the young people were caught up in the freedom of their country, and they began to change even their appearance. And from these black enveloping garments they developed beautifully well-tailored coats, waisted, with elegant little veils over their heads which were far more seductive than anything else.

Then, of course, as politics became all-important they and their brothers were caught up in them, and the girls, as well as the boys, took to the streets, even turning on their school staff. Poor Barbara! From her hopes of a peaceful job, she found herself barricaded from the outside, and locked into her head-mistress's room. Her staff were also locked in.

Alas! We withdrew so she came back to England. But Barbara is one of the people who should be remembered because she is the epitome of a person who saw a job to do and did it with courage – perhaps too brave a courage, but it didn't matter, the standard was there. I think the Arabs thought she stood for all that was rigid in British colonialism. But she didn't. She was the agent of change.

As with so many places on the map, trade governed destiny. Aden, so strategically placed, had run through the usual gamut. Stormed by the Portuguese in 1513, and before that by the various peoples who tried to corner this rich port of transhipment; the Egyptians in the fifth dynasty; the surrounding tribes of Ma'an, Saba, Qataba, Ausan, Himyar and the Hadhramaut as far back as 1000 BC. The chieftains of these tribes took advantage of the great demand for incense and spices from Rome and heavily taxed the caravans which had to pass through their territory, so that the rest of the population which derived no benefit from this source concentrated on the production of food, and built dams and deflectors, some of which can still be seen, particularly the Sheba tanks which were built in steps up the side of the mountain to hold vast quantities of water.

When the European powers became interested in the Red Sea trade, the Portuguese, the Dutch, and English, the French and finally the Turks, conquered Aden, and by the sixteenth century the area was divided in two main parts, the Yemen and the Hadhramaut. In 1839, England occupied the town and made a treaty with the ruler of Lahej, whose descendant was an interesting friend to June Knox-Mawer, and who was eventually removed by the British for his pro-Arab inclinations and his friendship with Nasser.

In 1872, the Turks re-occupied the Yemen, and in 1914 an agreement was reached on the boundaries established by the Anglo–Turkish Commission between Yemen and what was, in 1967, the Western Protectorate. The Eastern Protectorate which bordered the Yemen was then the bone of contention between the Imam of the Yemen and the British. Until 1927 the whole Protectorate, Eastern and Western, came under the government of India, after which the Colonial Office took over, though it still remained the charge of the government of India until 1937.

The Thornes, who had been there nearly nine years, went through the various innovations: the stepping up of military forces; the building of the township of Al-Ittihad between Little Aden and Aden; the change of Governors from Sir William Luce, to Johnston, to Sir Richard Turnbull. Until Robin Thorne was forced to leave by events beyond his control, they lived a life bounded by strict security.

'We went out to dinner at our own risk, and eventually were warned not to go at all. There was that terrible case, a girl whom we knew very well, quite a young bride, and they had a dinner in Ma'ala and their servant had put a bomb in the bookcase. She was killed instantly and several others were terribly badly wounded. After that we were more restricted. We could go swimming but we had to be escorted. We were lucky because we were near all the top brass and Government House, so we were in an area that was particularly well guarded. Of course, Goldmohur, the bathing beach, was beyond, so that came into the security area, but we weren't encouraged to go to Khormaksar, or even to Ma'alla. They suggested we kept numbers down to six so that no one knew there was going to be a big party. And then the daughter of the Chief of the Air Force was killed at a children's party.

'We used to do all our own marketing and I probably went on a bit longer than some of the people because we didn't have NAAFI facilities, so if you wanted vegetables and so on, you had to get them. At that stage we only had one servant. You know how difficult it was with servants in Aden because there was so much competition from BP and Shell. Also, in the services a captain was entitled to one free one, a major to two, and a colonel to three. So we had one little boy, a very nice little Yemeni, and I used to do the marketing while he got on with the flat, but it was pretty unpleasant the last few weeks when I went to market in Steamer Point. We weren't escorted and I felt very unsafe – I suppose it was the atmosphere, and I don't think it was really fair on the people in the market, because they might have been discriminated against. When at last I told someone that it was becoming a rather unpleasant experience, they said, "You shouldn't go. We have been sending our servant – the people in the market don't mind that, but they don't like being seen fraternizing with or even serving Europeans – but if you send your servant, he might be just a chap shopping for himself." So after that, he went, but, of course, it took much longer because he had to catch a rare bus, or even walk, whereas we used to take the car in.'

There had been the good memories, the happier times:

'We went to a lot of Arab weddings and, funnily enough, they didn't mind European men at all. One great Arab woman friend of mine said she didn't mind how many European men there were because they just treated her as a friend, whereas these Arab men stared at you! The weddings were the occasions for these marvellous Paris creations to come out, beautiful clothes, enormously expensive, a lot of them from Harrods, and a lot of them were literally Paris ones covered with sequins – very elegant with a glorious dress sense. We would feel very shabby! It was very difficult to keep cool in Aden. You would make up in the air-conditioning and then you would go out and begin to absolutely pour, which the Arab women didn't do.

'We were very friendly with a big Aden family – the Aukmans – and also the Garnhams. Garnham was Director of Education and the Aukman father ran the local paper, and all the rest of the families had endless degrees – they had more degrees than jobs. They were educated in England, America and France. I remember going to one wedding and Mrs Aukman's son was marrying a girl and I asked, "Do you like her?" "Oh, yes," Mrs Aukman said. "She is a nice enough girl, but she is very very black," but, in fact, she was only very slightly a darker shade of coffee than her mother-in-law.'

As the trouble in the colony increased, so the parties at

Government House decreased. Joan Thorne took on the job of housekeeper at Government House when her son came home to England:

'First it was for Lady Luce and then, Natasha Johnston – that was very fascinating because she was Russian and a cousin of Princess Marina, so we had all these rather fascinating people staying – the Duke of Edinburgh's sister, to whom I forgot to curtsey, and she nearly killed me with an icy glare – it was terrible. Once, before the real troubles began – the last two and a half years were really bad – we had Princess Alexandra out and we had a ball for her at Government House. Natasha helped me with the decorations and we got pineapples over from Mombasa – ones that were rotten and they were going to throw out from the factory – and we sprayed them with gold paint, and there was a marvellous smell of pineapple everywhere, and pineapples in the middle of the tables with gold tablecloths. Of course, things were very formal then, except when the Luces were there and he used to play bicycle polo. Lady Luce was awfully good at being a Governor's wife and I thought she did terribly well.'

The real trouble started when Sir Charles Johnston allowed himself to be persuaded that Federation would work. Joan is probably correct when she comments:

'I think the Foreign Office have a completely different training from the Colonial Service – they never take a decision; they always say, "Well, this is one view, and this is the other view." They see both sides, and I think Sir Charles Johnston found it terribly difficult to take vital decisions. I think in the end he did. I think he allowed himself to be persuaded that Federation would work. The first bomb at the airport was just after Federation.'

The Thornes were directly affected by the Aden troubles. The British way of life was folding, soon there would be nothing to stay for, and even the big businesses felt their days numbered. But Robin Thorne had a near miss to his life:

'My husband was blown up by one of those letter bombs. They had just made three new appointments. I think they called them Assistant High Commissioners and my husband was one of them, and so they decided to send three letter bombs to these three Assistant High Commissioners and my husband opened his and it went off. He was incredibly lucky because he was sitting at quite a heavy desk so below he was protected by this desk, and also I think he must have pushed it away from him automatically because his chest was covered with scratches and scars. He lost most of his fingers on both hands but otherwise nothing much – though his face was terribly scarred. His poor little secretary who was in the room with him was literally blown to the other side of the room but was quite untouched. They didn't know at first whether Robin had any internal injuries but fortunately he hadn't and everything else was superficial. It was just his hands. He was taken to the RAF hospital where they had a marvellous plastic surgeon, and he really did a magnificent job on his hands. He was wonderfully encouraging from the moment he had done it all; he told Robin there was absolutely no reason why he shouldn't drive again, do almost anything with his hands, which was very encouraging for us both – he said he would be able to write.'

They were home for six months while Robin had physiotherapy at Roehampton and then returned. They had done nine years, and though Joan thought it 'was an incredibly healthy place – no mosquitoes, no bugs, nothing could live except human beings', I feel that this must have been in comparison with some of their posts in Africa. Personally, I did not find the lack of mosquitoes a compensation for the extreme heat.

But there were other trials for Joan:

'I was very nervous, especially after Robin was blown up. I used to come down from the flat and find MLF scribbled on the back of the car in the dust and wonder if there was a bomb in the car, but I didn't want to make a fuss by ringing up.' In any event, Dick Turnbull decided they had had enough, 'so Robin came back just about a month before "Mad Mitch" '. That, in itself, is another story!

Farewell the Ladies

School children today may have to read colonial history as part of their school curriculum. However graphic the books it will be difficult, if not impossible, for them to capture the real flavour, the genuine experience. They may think of the ex-colonial women charitably as fuddy-duddies, darling old things with their memories and *folie de grandeur*. They may even believe that the only heritage the British left was the long motorcades, the screaming sirens, the over-dressed uniforms. But the ex-colonial wife or servant will know that they left much more than that. She will remember the separations from her children or her husband, she will pray that it was all worth while, but it may be difficult for her not to weep.

There will still be the exchanged Christmas cards and presents, the money sent hopefully to the 'boys' though their addresses have become hazy, and the likelihood of arrival uncertain. It is, after all, not only the red on the map which has disappeared but the very shape of the countries themselves. Frontiers change with new leaders, military governments give way to civilian and vice versa. The man who led the dance with visiting royalty with such genuine good-will is in all probability dead or has disappeared without a trace. Did the colonial wife as she bade farewell to her household in her colonial home foresee this? Did she predict the necessity of locking her doors and windows, of walking the streets in fear? Did she perhaps realize that her servants might soon be matching her nostalgia, and talking of the 'good old days'? They would remember the good times, the gifts, the gaiety and, more than anything, the security.

There is still a faint whiff of nostalgia for the slow journey, the excitement of arrival, a beloved face on the quayside. There is nothing to replace the thrill of reunion which blotted out the first sight of the shabby government furniture, or the taste of the poorly cooked dinner by the new cook – so soon to be sacked – the garden parched to a cinder, the brown trickle of water from the tap, the warm drink served on the veranda. Jetting around to distant lands it is hard to visualize the changes which have taken place in the last twenty years. One has to hunt for old plaques, monuments, the outward and visible signs of past glories. Women no longer have to dine in mosquito boots, rise at dawn to catch the only cool moments, or follow an anxious African through the bush to try and save the life of his sick baby, because the nearest doctor is a hundred miles away. It is no longer their responsibility to share a husband's lonely life.

The pleasant contacts with the past linger on, and as the ex-colonial woman readjusts herself, to what may possibly be an even lonelier existence in her own land, there is nothing better than picking up the telephone and hearing that familiar voice from Accra or Timbuctoo saying with a great bellow of laughter, 'Is that you? I've just arrived – when can we meet?' And it is a relief to meet on an equal footing at last. In a world where class distinctions are fast disappearing it seems only right that racial distinctions should also be defunct.

The growing generation should seek out those colonial men and women who have a tale to tell. They deserve their place in history because, whether they were willing or not, they followed the flag and by their own lights they did their duty.

And now, 'Farewell the ladies! God bless you!'

BIBLIOGRAPHY

James Morris, *Heavens Command* (Faber & Faber, 1973)
James Morris, *Pax Britannica* (Faber & Faber, 1968)
James Morris, *Farewell the Trumpets* (Faber & Faber, 1978)
Sir Drummond Shiels, *The British Commonwealth* (Odhams, 1952)
Stanislav Andreski, *The African Predicament* (Michael Joseph, 1968)
Margery Perham & Mary Bull (eds), *The Diaries of Lord Lugard* (4 vols. Faber & Faber, 1959–63)
E. Moberley-Bell, *Flora Shaw* (Constable, 1947)
W.D. McIntyre, *Colonies into Commonwealth* (Blandford, 1966)
Africa
Robin Short, *African Sunset* (Johnson, 1973)
Joy Packer, *Apes and Ivory* (Eyre & Spottiswood, 1953)
Boyd Alexander, *From the Niger to the Nile* (Vols I & II, Arnold, 1907)
Herbert Alexander, *Boyd Alexander's Last Journey* (Arnold, 1912)
Olive MacLeod, *Chiefs and Cities of Central Africa* (Blackwood, 1912)
Margaret Lane, *Life with Ionides* (Hamish Hamilton, 1963)
Margery Perham, *East African Journey* (Faber & Faber, 1976)
Patrick Marnham, *Fantastic Invasion* (Jonathan Cape, 1980)
Shiva Naipaul, *North to South* (Andre Deutsch, 1978)
Charles Douglas-Home, *Evelyn Baring: the Last Proconsul* (Collins, 1978)
Elspeth Huxley, *Four Guineas* (Chatto & Windus, 1954)
Oliver Ransford, *Livingstone's Lake* (John Murray, 1966)
M. Aline Buxton, *Kenya Days* (Arnold, 1927)
Malaya
Noel Barber, *The War of the Running Dogs* (Collins, 1971)
S.S. Chapman, *The Jungle Is Neutral* (Chatto & Windus, 1949)
Harry Miller, *Jungle War in Malaya* (Arthur Barker, 1972)
Vernon Bartlett, *Report from Malaya* (Verschoyle, 1954)
Pamela Gouldsbury, *Jungle Nurse* (Jarrolds, 1960)

Bibliography

South Seas

June Knox-Mawer, *A Gift of Islands* (John Murray, 1965)

June Knox-Mawer, *A South Sea Spell* (John Murray, 1975)

Caroline Mytinger, *Head Hunting in the Solomon Islands* (Macmillan, 1943)

Rex & Thea Ricnits, *The Voyages of Captain Cook* (Hamlyn, 1968)

Tony Cross, *St Helena* (David & Charles, 1980)

Ian Strange, *The Bird Man* (Gordon Cremonesi, 1976)

V.F. Boyson, *The Falkland Islands* (Oxford, 1924)

The Mediterranean

Lawrence Durrell, *Bitter Lemons* (Faber & Faber, 1956)

Stewart Perowne, *The Siege within the Walls* (Hodder & Stoughton, 1970)

Sylvia Foot, *Emergency Exit* (Chatto & Windus, 1960)

Hugh Foot, *A Start in Freedom* (Hodder & Stoughton, 1964)

Bradford Earle, *The Siege of Malta* (Hodder & Stoughton, 1961)

Aden

June Knox Mawer, *The Sultans Came to Tea* (John Murray, 1961)

Harold Ingrams, *Arabia and the Isles* (John Murray, 1942)

D. Van Der Meulen, *Faces in Shem* (John Murray, 1961)

Miscellaneous

Flora Shaw, *A Tropical Dependency* (An account of the ancient history of western Sudan with an account of the modern settlement of northern Nigeria) (1905)

Frederick Lugard, *The Dual Mandate* (Blackwood, 1922)

Mary Kingsley, *Travels in West Africa* (Folio Society, 1976)

Alain Gerbault, *In Quest of the Sun* (Hodder & Stoughton, 1929)

Rupert Gunnis, *Historic Cyprus* (Methuen, 1936)

Basil Davidson, *Africa in Modern History*, (Allen Lane, 1978)

Harrison Smith, *Britain in Malta* (Progress Press, 1953)

INDEX

219